PROFESSOR NORRIE'S COMMENTARIES ON FAMILY LAW

By

Kenneth McK Norrie

Professor of Law

at the University of Strathclyde

Published in Great Britain in 2011 by
Dundee University Press
University of Dundee
Dundee DD1 4HN

www.dundee.ac.uk/dup

ISBN 978–1–84586–119–3

No natural forests were destroyed to make this product; only farmed timber was used and replanted

British Library Cataloguing-in-Publication data
A catalogue for this book is available on request from the British Library.

Typeset by Fakenham Prepress Solutions, Norfolk
Printed by MPG Books Ltd, Bodmin

Preface

In 1999, in a vain attempt to increase the circulation of the *Scottish Law and Practice Quarterly*, the Editorial Board (of which I was then a member) decided to introduce a new section to that journal, giving short updates in various aspects of Scots law which it was hoped would prove of sufficient interest to practitioners (and perhaps others) that they would subscribe in greater numbers than they had been doing hitherto. My contributions were in Family Law. For the following five years the SLPQ struggled on but as a journal it never caught the public imagination and subscribers slowly evaporated away until continued publication became unfeasible. The journal ceased publication with its last issue in January 2004, a mere nine years after it had first metaphorically hit the bookstands. But during these five years I had become accustomed to sitting down each quarter and writing a short piece on such aspect of family law as had caught my interest. So when SLPQ folded, I offered my continuing services to the *Journal of the Law Society of Scotland*, a far longer-established publication with a much greater readership and one which had, especially since Mr Peter Nicholson had taken over the editorship, once again begun to take articles discussing the substantive law: the *Journal* under his editorship has greater aspirations than being a mere in-house magazine for the Law Society of Scotland. Peter Nicholson was happy to accept my offer and since April 2004 he has accepted, with no editorial interference and minimal editorial amendment, 1500 words each quarter on whatever topic within family law I happened to want to write about.

I have always found writing these quarterly updating columns to be an invaluable discipline, ensuring that I keep myself up to date not only with the academic literature (limiting one's reading to that is always a risk in the universities) but also with the real issues affecting family law practice today. New cases, new statutes, new official reports were the obvious source materials, but so too were my research trips abroad and I have tried to bring home lessons from other countries which face the same family problems as we do but which often tackle them differently. These columns are now offered here as a collection of Commentaries. Of course, my own predilections affected which issues I would find interesting and want to write about. Some topics recur within the Commentaries: the children's hearing system, the Hague Child Abduction Convention, same-sex relationships, and cohabitation appear more often than other centrally important aspects of family law. But this is not a textbook designed to give a broad overview of the legal regulation of families in modern society. It is, very much, a collection of short articles on topics whose only common feature is that they interest me and contain enough to interest others too. Nevertheless, given that I wrote them each at a time when the topic was new or fresh, republishing them here as a collection provides what I hope readers will find a fascinating chronological history of a dozen years of developing law. And these years have been truly revolutionary, though they seldom felt it at the time. For what strikes me now, rereading particularly the earlier Commentaries, is how fundamentally family law has changed since 1999. The implementation of the Human Rights Act 1998 and the Scotland Act 1998 is not the only explanation for the changes that have occurred. Attitudes have changed too to the role that family law is perceived to play in society. More and more is Scots law regulating family life as it is lived today and more and more is it eschewing any role in giving guidance as to how family life ought to be led.

The Commentaries were not designed as individual chapters in a book and I don't expect many readers to start at page one and work their way to the end (though doing so will bring its own rewards). Rather, this is a book which I hope readers will dip into to provide them with understandings of law reform as it was happening, and in this way to gain a better understanding of the law as it presently is. To the Commentaries as they are reprinted here, I have added sometimes new titles, rubrics, and updates, in an attempt to make them usable in a book format, and to ensure that developments subsequent to the original date of the Commentary's publication are brought to the attention of the reader. I hope that most readers will find at least something of interest in this diverse collection of my disparate thoughts, and will better understand Scottish family law as it is today.

I should like to thank Carole Dalgleish of Dundee University Press for encouraging the idea of turning my quarterly columns into a unified collection. Valuable research assistance was given to me by Emma Morrison, a student at Strathclyde University School of Law, for which I am grateful. I am also very grateful to Peter Nicholson, the editor of the *Journal of the Law Society of Scotland*; the Law Society of Scotland itself, which holds the copyright on articles appearing in their *Journal*, were gracious and generous in permitting me to reprint the articles here – most remain (without, of course, any update) easily accessible via the *Journal*'s rather splendid website.

Kenneth McK Norrie
School of Law
International Technological University of Strathclyde
February 2011

Contents

2011

Table of Cases

Table of Statutes

Table of Statutory Instruments

Table of European and International Provisions

PART ONE

COMMENTARIES PUBLISHED IN THE *SCOTTISH LAW AND PRACTICE QUARTERLY*

Commentary No 1: April 1999

Three Adoption Cases

Since the launch of the Court of Session into cyberspace (www.scotcourts.gov.uk) in February 1999 (which is, incidentally, one of the most user-friendly court-based websites currently on line), it has been possible to access court judgments within hours of their being delivered. The Scottish Parliament will be, we are promised, fully accessible electronically. The ease with which information can now be retrieved makes it a good time to instigate this column where, on a quarterly basis, I will write about such aspects of Scottish family law as deserve some comment in the light of new decisions, new legislation, new proposals or new developments. Topics will be chosen mainly because they interest me. But the hope and intention is that the comments will interest others as well. The beauty of communication within the age of electronic information retrieval is illustrated by the fact that I am writing this first column in downtown Boston, Mass, having just a few moments ago logged off from the Scottish Courts website.

This quarter's column concerns adoption law. I have chosen this because of a recent clutch of decisions which are neither factually unusual nor legally groundbreaking but each of which raises curious questions which might require fuller consideration later. All were decided in the first quarter of 1999, two from the Court of Session and one from the House of Lords.

The case of the disappearing parent

S v *M* 1999 SC 388 was decided by an Extra Division composed of Lords Prosser, Caplan and Allanbridge, Lord Prosser giving the unanimous opinion of the court. An adoption order had been made by the sheriff at Airdrie, he having first dispensed with the mother's agreement on the grounds (i) that she could not be found and (ii) that she had persistently failed without reasonable excuse to fulfil the parental responsibility of maintaining personal relations and direct contact with the child on a regular basis. The sheriff's decision was overruled. It is unusual for a parent's agreement to be dispensed with on the ground that he or she cannot be found and for that reason, if no other, the discussion by the Inner House of the circumstances in which this ground may be relied upon is to be welcomed. However, there are other aspects of the decision that are worth noting. The mother had reappeared shortly after the adoption order was made and an appeal out of time was permitted, to allow her to argue that the adoption agency had not done enough to try to find her (and, therefore, that the sheriff was wrong in holding that she "cannot be found"). Interestingly, though the case was remitted back to the sheriff for reconsideration, the Inner House acknowleged that it would be impossible for him subsequently to hold, in the presence of the appellant, that she cannot be found. This suggests that the facts founding a decision to dispense with parental agreement to adoption can be reappraised after a decision based on these facts has been successfully challenged on appeal. Yet normally a sheriff could not be criticised, and certainly not overruled, for holding that a parent cannot be found when that state of affairs is true when he is called upon to make the decision but his finding subsequently loses its basis with the re-appearance of the parent. It is not a ground of appeal against such a decision that the parent is later found, even within the appeal time-limits. A sheriff's decision is not wrong just because it subsequently becomes wrong. Rather, in this case, it was the fact that there was an independent ground of appeal (that the adoption agency had not done all they could to trace the parent) that allowed the matter to be examined again, and at that re-examination facts subsequent to the original decision would be relevant and could prove decisive. It is unclear whether the same result could follow with the other grounds for dispensing with parental agreement. A person who "is incapable of giving agreement" might later become capable and so, if an appeal on an independent basis is successful and the matter remitted to the court of first instance for reconsideration, that ground could no longer be used. But a subsequent re-acquisition of capacity after a finding of incapacity would not in itself give a ground of appeal. The same might be said for a parent who "is not known" at the date of the original decision but whose identity subsequently becomes known. Likewise, circumstances may change such that while it was unreasonable for a parent to withhold agreement at the original hearing, it is no longer unreasonable at the rehearing after an appeal. A finding of serious ill-treatment is not susceptible to re-appraisal through subsequent developments, but the final ground for dispensing with agreement is serious ill-treatment *and* the unlikelihood of re-integration of the child into the parent's household, and that likelihood may well vary with time. It seems, therefore, that the only ground which cannot be re-appraised after an appeal is failure to fulfil parental responsibilities, for that is the only ground that unequivocally refers to past events rather than present circumstances.

It is curious, therefore, that in the present case the sheriff's additional dispensation of agreement on this ground was also remitted for reconsideration. But this was not because of a change in circumstances. The sheriff had found that the mother had persistently failed without reasonable cause to fulfil the parental responsibility of maintaining contact with her child. Since it was a matter of undisputed fact that the mother had not kept contact, the crucial element was "reasonable cause". Essentially, the sheriff's decision was overruled on the basis of natural justice. Because the mother was not present at the hearing of the adoption application (since she had not been found) she was unable to put her own side of the story and the sheriff was unable, therefore, properly to assess whether there was reasonable cause. Consequently, this ground too required re-examination. This line of argument applies, however, only when there has been a breach of natural justice which denies the parent the opportunity to speak – it could not, for example, be said that the sheriff could not assess reasonable cause when a parent simply refuses to explain his or her failure to maintain contact, or does not attend court after receiving intimation.

The case of the child with two fathers

The case of *J* v *Aberdeen City Council* 1999 SC 405 (composed of the Lord Justice-Clerk, Lord McCluskey and Lord Cameron of Lochbroom) raises a quite different issue. An order declaring a child free for adoption had been made by the sheriff at Aberdeen and the decision was upheld by the sheriff principal (Risk), but they were overruled by the Court of Session. The appeal was actually on the narrow point of whether the sheriff had been right in refusing to grant an adjournment sought by the appellant, but the real interest in the case lies in the question of the appellant's locus. The mother of the child was at all material times married to the appellant's brother and, though the appellant was not registered as the father, he and the mother claimed that he was the father and he was indeed treated as such by the adoption agency. A few days after the freeing order was made, the appellant and the mother "entered into what purported to be a parental rights agreement" under s 4 of the Children (Scotland) Act 1995. The sheriff expressed doubt about the validity of the parental responsibilities agreement, but in order to avoid making a decision on the issue he dispensed with the appellant's agreement in any case (on the grounds of unreasonableness and persistent failure to maintain contact). The sheriff principal upheld the freeing order but held that the appellant had no locus at all (on the basis that the parental responsibilities agreement was of no effect since the law presumed the appellant's brother and not the appellant – the party to the agreement – to be the father). The Court of Session, on the other hand, held that the fact that the mother had entered into a parental responsibilities agreement "provided substantial support for the displacement of the presumption" that the mother's husband was the father, and that "in the circumstances adherence to the presumption without regard to the whole circumstances appears to us to be unrealistic". The circumstance which seems to have weighed most heavily with the court was the fact that the adoption agency had consistently treated the appellant as the father. As such, they held that the appellant had locus to appear (and, allowing the actual appeal, that the failure of the sheriff to grant an adjournment had denied the appellant the opportunity to be heard). The court was, however, careful not to hold that the appellant was the father, nor that his agreement to the freeing order was necessary or required to be dispensed with. At most, he was a person "claiming to be father", who required to be considered under the terms of s 18(7) of the Adoption (Scotland) Act 1978.

The facts of this case raise in stark form the problem of the relationship between the presumptions of paternity contained in s 5 of the Law Reform (Parent and Child) (Scotland) Act 1986 and the acquisition of parental responsibilities and parental rights by means of an agreement under s 4 of the Children (Scotland) Act 1995, which itself brings the male party to the agreement within the definition of "parent" for the purposes of the Adoption (Scotland) Act 1978. The problem stems from the fact that s 4 of the 1995 Act allows agreement to be made only between the mother and the "father" but does not define who the father is for these purposes. Section 15 of the 1995 Act defines "parent" to mean the child's genetic father or mother, so "father" presumably is genetic father. But is a s 4 agreement any indication of genetic paternity? The Court of Session seems to have thought so. Yet there are severe problems with this and it is respectfully suggested that the approach of the sheriff principal is much to be preferred. Section 4 agreements are registered in the Books of Council and Session without any verification of the facts – in particular the fact of paternity. The Keeper will accept and will register any agreement submitted, except those that are extrinsically invalid (eg if both parties are female, or if in the place for the father's name is written something like "J Smith, Grandfather"). But if the fact is false (ie the man named as father is not so) then registration does nothing to protect the validity of the agreement. Yet since it will appear to be valid and will appear to have state sanction, it may in practice be given effect to. The assumption of the Court of Session that entering into the agreement is evidence of paternity may well be justified if there is no evidence or a presumption pointing elsewhere and in these circumstances the agreement should receive effect, at least for the purposes of parental responsibilities and parental rights. However, because the agreement does not create a presumption, in other questions, such as succession, it can be no more than evidence of paternity, perhaps even strong evidence. The difference between strong evidence and a presumption is that the latter but not the former can be given effect to in the absence of court decree. But in the present case the court went significantly (and dangerously) further and assumed the facts alleged in the agreement to be true even in the face of a statutory presumption that they were not. A presumption that person A is father is to all intents and purposes a presumption that persons B, C, D etc are not father. If this is so, then an agreement between the mother and B or C or D should be presumed to be of no effect and therefore to be no indication of where parental responsibilities and parental rights lie. A statutory presumption cannot be overturned on the unverified word of the mother and the person claiming to be father: it can only be overturned by a declarator of paternity under s 7 of the Law Reform (Parent and Child) (Scotland) Act 1986, in which action the agreement might well constitute strong evidence. The flaw in s 4 (apart from its very existence) is that with registration in the Books of Council and Session, not otherwise a place where registration creates rights, the Keeper is obliged to accept the facts as stated, and these stated facts, whether true or not, have legal consequences. It ought not to be possible to register an agreement with a man when another man is presumed to be father. The law ought to be amended so that the Keeper is prohibited from registering agreements where the female party is married or was married between conception and birth of the child who is the subject of the agreement, or where someone other than the male party to the agreement is registered in the Register of Births as the father. This would, of course, change the nature of registration, by imposing an investigative role on the Keeper, and perhaps even make the Books of Council and Session the inappropriate place for registration, but such a change is the only way to avoid the confusion such as was caused in the present case. In addition, it should be made a criminal offence to give false information on the face of the agreement (as under s 53 of the

Registration of Births, Deaths and Marriages (Scotland) Act 1965). At present, however, the Court of Session, by indicating that the agreement can displace a presumption, are accepting that a statutory presumption can be overturned merely on the word of the parties, that word not even being given under oath. Does this mean that in an action for declarator of paternity, the word of the parties is sufficient proof in the absence of any other evidence? I always suspected that the ill-conceived provision in s 4 of the 1995 Act would cause more trouble than it was worth, and this case illustrates some of the difficulties.

The case of the nearly adult adoption

On March 11, 1999, the House of Lords handed down a fairly short judgment in the case of *Re B (A Minor) (Adoption Order: Nationality)* [1999] 2 AC 136. Lord Hoffmann gave the only reasoned speech and the other four judges (including Lord Hope of Craighead) concurred. The question before the court was whether an adoption order could be made in circumstances in which the only benefits would be those flowing from the acquisition of British nationality that would be a consequence of the making of the adoption order. The child had come to Britain with her mother when she was 14 and had been enrolled in school here. When their period of residence expired, the mother returned home but the child remained in the care of her grandparents (and remained in attendance at the English school). The Home Office threatened to deport the child and so, in order to ensure that the child could remain in England in order to complete her education, the grandparents (with the mother's support) sought to adopt her. The judge at first instance granted the adoption order but the Court of Appeal recalled the order, on the ground that in making its welfare judgment the court should ignore benefits that result solely from a change in immigration status. The House of Lords found this approach to be contrary to the express terms of s 6 of the Adoption Act 1976, which required the court to have regard to all the circumstances and to give first consideration to the child's welfare throughout his or her childhood. The adoption order was restored because of the significant benefits which would accrue to the child (in terms of education) during the remainder of her childhood.

The Adoption (Scotland) Act 1978, since its amendment by the Children (Scotland) Act 1995, has promoted welfare from first consideration to paramount consideration, and has extended the time-scale of the welfare assessment from childhood to life. So if anything the Scottish legislation gives even stronger endorsement to the approach of the House of Lords than Lord Hoffmann found in the English legislation. But the jurisdictions might well come to different conclusions in cases presenting slightly different facts. Lord Hoffmann accepted two propositions which the Home Office had made in the case: that adoption should not be made when the adopters do not intend to exercise parental responsibility, and that the court will "rarely" make an adoption order when it would confer no benefits during childhood but a right of abode for the rest of the adopted person's life. The second proposition does not now reflect Scots law and benefits after majority are expressly part of the welfare assessment, and may indeed justify the adoption even when there are no other benefits. This, in fact, sits rather uneasily with the prohibition on applying for an adoption order after the child's 18th birthday, but it does clearly permit an adoption before then when the only benefit accrues after then. If the child is living with persons who are not his or her parents and there is no possibility of that settled arrangement being challenged (eg grandparents looking after the child after the deaths of the parents, or persons looking after the child under the terms of a residence order) the only extra benefit that adoption will give is a right of succession, which may not crystallise until many years after the child reaches adulthood. In Scotland there is now no difficulty in making an adoption order solely in order to confer upon the child that benefit; but in England the lack of benefit during the child's childhood may prove an insuperable difficulty. The first of Lord Hoffmann's propositions is equally applicable in Scotland, and would prevent adoption being used to give a right of succession from the estate of a person who never acts in real terms as the child's parent.

Update

The adoption legislation in both Scotland and England has been re-enacted since 1999 but none of the issues discussed here has been significantly affected by the Adoption and Children Act 2002 or the Adoption and Children (Scotland) Act 2007. Welfare, in both Acts, is now to be assessed throughout the child's life (2002 Act, s 1(2); 2007 Act, s 14(3)).

Section 4 agreements under the Children (Scotland) Act 1995 remain unamended, and they have now been joined by s 4A agreements between the mother and the other (female) parent who becomes parent by the terms of the Human Fertilisation and Embryology Act 2008, discussed at Commentary No 39 below.

Commentary No 2: July 1999

Lesbian Cohabitants in Canada

The most important development this quarter has been the publication by the Scottish Office of its Consultation Paper, "Improving Scottish Family Law", which I had intended to make the basis of this month's column. However, my response to the Consultation Paper is published in full elsewhere in this issue ((1999) 4 SLPQ 157), and so instead this column concerns an important decision of the Supreme Court of Canada, which was handed down on May 20, 1999, and which deals with an issue that the Consultation Paper does not but which, as I point out in my response, it should have dealt with.

All lawyers in a jurisdiction as small as Scotland need to be, at heart, comparatists. This will become all the more important as we find our feet in dealing with the new challenges of human rights law, for many legal systems in the world have been dealing with questions of human rights for a long number of years. Valuable lessons can be learnt from the experience of others. The Canadian Charter of Rights and Freedoms, for example, fundamentally altered judicial methodology, not least in family law. The courts in Canada have the power to strike down legislation which is found to infringe the rights guaranteed in that Charter, and the reasoning they adopt might well become a fertile source of guidance to Scottish courts faced with challenges to legislation of the Scottish Parliament. A decision that is likely to be as generally educative as it is fundamental in its own area is that of *M* v *H* (1999) 2 SCR 3.

Discriminating against gay and lesbian people

This case involved a lesbian couple who had lived together for some 10 years but whose relationship ultimately broke down. M sought financial provision from H. Had the couple been married, such financial provision could have been claimed under the Ontario equivalent of s 9 of the Family Law (Scotland) Act 1985; had the couple been heterosexual, similar though more limited financial provision could have been claimed because the Ontario legislation permitted "spouses", which it defined to include unmarried cohabiting couples, to seek such provision. And herein lies the lesson for Scotland. The proposals presently being considered in the Scottish Office Consultation Paper that cohabitants be able to seek financial provision on the break up of their relationship, based on a similar principle to that contained in s 9(1)(b) of the 1985 Act, are limited (as the Ontario provisions were) to heterosexual couples. The exclusion of same-sex couples was held by the Supreme Court, on a majority of 8 to 1, to be unconstitutional and that part of the statute was struck down.

Now, the Supreme Court of Canada has been noticeably more proactive in the advancement of gay equality than has the European Court of Human Rights and for that reason it does not follow that if, against expectation, the Scottish Parliament decided to discriminate against homosexuals, such legislation would necessarily fall, but the reasoning in both the majority and the minority judgments is revealing and illuminating. Both examined the purpose of allowing a support obligation. As a general principle, no person is obliged to support another – each person must support him or herself. Nevertheless the law does occasionally make, for good reason, exceptions to this general rule. The most obvious one is the support obligation imposed on parents, with the reason, again obvious, being the inability of children to support themselves. The next most obvious support obligation is that of married persons, though the justification for that support is rather less natural. Originally the obligation was on the husband to support the wife, but that was complementary to the common law rule that on marriage the wife's property transferred to her husband. In consideration for this the husband was obliged to maintain his wife. Though that particular legal rule disappeared in the early years of the 20th century, the social position of women remained such that they were (at first) almost completely unable to support themselves in the job market and (latterly) their earning power within that market was noticeable lower than that of their husbands. This imbalance in earning capacity is exacerbated when the woman, married or unmarried, becomes a mother – for it is typically she who, for the benefit of the child, voluntarily allows her earning capacity to be severely compromised. As heterosexual cohabitation increased, the support obligation was extended in most Canadian provinces to unmarried couples – crucially, for the same reasons as justified such obligation between married couples. The question before the court was basically whether it was unconstitutional to deny this support obligation to same-sex couples (discrimination on the basis of sexual orientation having previously been identified by the court as contrary to the Charter of Rights and Freedoms).

The majority held that there was no justifiable reason to exclude same-sex couples from the protections (and, depending on your point of view, liabilities) of "spousal" support. The minority judge, however, considered that the obligation of support was there to tackle the "systemic imbalance" in economic power that characterises opposite-sex relationships and that since the evidence showed that same-sex couples did not typically suffer from such imbalance there was no need to extend the system of spousal support. This is, of course, illogical. The social imbalance in earning power remains heavily in favour of men and against women but, notwithstanding a lack of systemic imbalance to men's detriment, spousal support may be claimed by a man who, in his particular circumstances, suffers in relation to his female partner. The majority judges saw, for this reason, spousal support as designed to tackle particular individuals' needs and not a social, or systemic, imbalance. In addition, there was no rational connection between the claimed statutory objective of protecting the economic well-being of children and women and the exclusion of same-sex couples. In reality, the majority held, the purpose of the Act was to provide for the equitable resolution of economic disputes, and to reduce the burden on the public purse. Those who had been dependent on their ex-cohabitants should be able to turn to the ex-cohabitant rather than to the state for continued support. Both these true purposes would be enhanced rather than inhibited by extending the rights to same-sex cohabitants. Thus if a person in a same-sex relationship could establish the dependency and sacrifice necessary to trigger the support obligation then that person was no different from such a person in an opposite-sex relationship, and ought not to be treated any differently.

Lessons in human rights

There was much in the case about the appropriate judicial approach to equality cases. Some of that is unique to the constitutional structure of Canada. But much of it will give valuable lessons to Scottish courts dealing with claims that legislation of the Scottish Parliament infringes some right guaranteed by the European Convention on Human Rights and in particular the requirement that these rights be afforded without discrimination. For reasons elaborated (at some length) in my Response to the Scottish Office Consultation Paper, reprinted in this issue, it is to be hoped that when the improvements to Scottish family law are enacted, no such challenge will be necessary because the rights and protections suggested for cohabiting couples will be extended to all cohabiting couples, regardless of sexual orientation.

Update

What a difference 10 years makes. When this commentary was written in 1999 it was not discrimination against gay and lesbian people that needed justification, but granting them the same legal rights and obligations. Since then, the legislation that (eventually) followed the Discussion Paper Improving Scottish Family Law fully included same-sex couples. The Scottish Parliament has been punctilious in not discriminating on the basis of sexual orientation, and of course the jurisprudence of the European Court of Human Rights has significantly developed in this area. The occasional, usually religiously motivated, objection to treating gay and lesbian people as if they were as good as heterosexual people is still sometimes heard (see, for example, the cases discussed at Commentary No 36 below) but the law is now robustly resisting such objections.

M *v* H *was, with hindsight, a very conservative judgment. The female couple there were treated as an unmarried couple. The fact that they had no access to marital rights, whether via marriage or a civil partnership regime, was not raised as an issue. A mere 6 years later, Canada became the second country in the world to open marriage itself to same-sex couples as the only means of ensuring true equality irrespective of sexual orientation. The UK, of course, went down the civil partnership route, but it remains to be seen whether that is the end of the story here: see Commentary No 46 below.*

Commentary No 3: October 1999

Maternal Liability for Ante-Natal Injury

No apology is, I hope, necessary for this column returning to the Supreme Court of Canada, after last quarter's discussion of the lesbian "spousal" support case, for that court continues to produce judgments of impressive analytical depth on questions which have not yet been, but sooner or later will be, faced by the Scottish court. Unlike last time, however, I am by no means convinced of the absolute rightness of the decision that I want to discuss here. The question before the Supreme Court in *Dobson* v *Dobson* [1999] 2 SCR 753 was this: Should a child be able to sue his or her mother for injuries that she causes before the child's birth? This question arose in the context of injuries received *in utero* by a child as a result of a car crash caused, allegedly, by his mother's negligent driving, but it could arise in many other contexts. The case is one of those arising from the tension between a desire to protect the vulnerable and the need to ensure that a woman's freedom of action is not limited merely because she has become pregnant. The Court of Appeal for New Brunswick in the present case ((1997) 148 DLR (4th) 332) had attempted to balance these competing aims by holding that a mother could be held liable for pre-natal injuries, but only when the injuries she causes her unborn child occurred within the ambit of a duty she independently owed to third parties. So, for example, holding a woman liable to her unborn child for negligent driving is no extra limitation on her freedom of action since her duty to other road users imposes the obligation to drive carefully in any case. The New South Wales Court of Appeal had adopted a similar approach some years previously in *Lynch* v *Lynch* (1991) 25 NSWLR 411, holding that liability should be recognised in circumstances in which the mother is required to be insured. The Supreme Court of Canada, however, overturned the New Brunswick Court of Appeal by a majority of 7 to 2 and held that Canadian law did not recognise maternal liability for pre-natal injury in any circumstance.

The Canadian approach to liability

Sensibly, the Canadian courts approach the question of whether to recognise new forms of liability by adopting an *Anns*-type analysis (see *City of Kamloops* v *Nielsen* [1984] 2 SCR 2). They ask, first, whether there is a relationship between the plaintiff and the defendant of sufficient proximity to establish a duty of care and, secondly, whether, if there is such a relationship, there are any policy considerations which negate that duty of care. The first question in the present case was simple and clearly to be answered affirmatively and the real dispute concerned the second. Liability was denied because the majority perceived two policy considerations which determined the case. The first was the fear that recognising liability even in the limited circumstances in which the Court of Appeal had done would open the door to potential liability for so-called lifestyle choices, such as smoking, drinking and adopting an unhealthy diet, thus imposing an undue burden on women who become pregnant. Here the Supreme Court seems to have fallen into the trap that has seriously ensnared the House of Lords over the past two or three decades: the assumption that recognising or not recognising a duty of care is the only way of avoiding liability in unjustifiable circumstances. Yet in truth liability can be denied, even when a duty is recognised, on the ground that in the circumstances of the case the duty has not been breached or on the ground that the breach of duty did not cause the injury complaind of. Smoking may not be an unreasonable action for a nicotine addict, and the search for proof that it actually caused the child's actual injury is likely to be vain. The second policy objection was the perceived difficulty in drawing an appropriate judicial standard of behaviour to be expected of pregnant women – an odd objection since courts are called upon to determine appropriate standards of behaviour on a daily basis.

Who makes the law?

Underlying the decision is another tension – that between legislative and judicial legal development. Whose role is it, in other words, to recognise new forms of liability and to introduce exceptions thereto? In England, Parliament laid down the rule (Congenital Disabilities (Civil Liability) Act 1976, s 1) that a mother is exempt from liability to her child for pre-natal injuries, unless these injuries are caused by her negligent car driving. The exception to the maternal exemption was designed to avoid the unborn child being the only victim of road accidents who was unable to access insurance funds for compensation. The New South Wales Court of Appeal held that the court itself could fashion, for similar reasons, a similar rule. The Supreme Court of Canada, on the other hand, has held that it would be a matter for the legislature to create a remedy, with such limitations as is considered appropriate. Which approach should the Scottish courts take? The very failure to extend the 1976 Act to Scotland might be taken to indicate a Parliamentary intention to leave the matter to judicial development. But judicial development does have its limits. The Supreme Court saw maternal liability as an extension of the general principle of liability for pre-natal injury. Perhaps they ought to have regarded it as an application of the general principle, leaving it to the legislature to make such policy curtailments as that body considered appropriate. In my view, that is the approach that ought to commend itself to the Scottish courts.

Commentary No 4: January 2000

The Adoption (Intercountry Aspects) Act 1999

Deep in the human psyche and widespread across cultures is the belief that children should be brought up by their parents. That this is not just a claim to parental right but a faith in the natural order of things is clear from the extent to which ancient and not so ancient myths, legends and stories tell of the harmful consequences when that order is subverted. From Oedipus to Tom Jones, from Moses to Huckleberry Finn the lesson is the same: that society as well as individuals suffer, sometimes tragically, when children are brought up by blood strangers. The difficulties are all the greater when children are brought up not only by blood strangers but by cultural strangers. While Joseph seemed to have no difficulty adapting to the Egyptian culture that was not his own, Moses in the same circumstances never really settled and eventually he led "his people" home. Perhaps there is some wisdom in Islam's prohibition (or at least non-recognition) of adoption (notwithstanding that the pre-Islamic practice of tabanni was common within societies that are now Islamic). The Prophet's marriage to the repudiated wife of Zaid, his adopted son, would be valid only if the tabanni were not recognised.

Yet for a variety of reasons in modern society children are left parentless or require, for their own welfare, to be permanently removed from their parents; and the orthodoxy today is that such a child is best dealt with by being integrated into another family. However, there is no international orthodoxy as to how far that integration should go – which is hardly surprising since even in the domestic law the acceptance that full integration is appropriate has been a long and gradual process. The understanding of "adoption" lacks the universality that, by and large, characterises the people of the world's understanding of "marriage".

The new Hague Convention

This lack of universality makes recognition and enforcement of foreign adoption orders one of the most awkward areas of international family law. The legal position is made more difficult by the modern shortage of children available for adoption, creating a temptation, to which too many people succumb, to seek a child in a country other than their own. Different countries have different standards of supervision of the adoption process for ensuring that the child's best interests are the paramount consideration in adoption, and for striking an appropriate balance between that and the rights of the parents. Some desperate Westerners are willing to pay large sums for healthy children and many poorer countries, seeing a way of earning hard currency, are less rigorous in protecting the rights of natural parents than they might otherwise be. Checks on suitability of prospective adopters are not always possible in the intercountry context and occasionally prospective adopters who have been disappointed at being rejected as unsuitable by Western adoption agencies turn to countries where such checks are either non-existent or less rigorous. It was to tackle potential dangers (and even abuses) of intercountry adoption such as these, and others, that the Hague Conference on Private International Law concluded on 29 May 1993 a new Convention on Protection of Children and Co-operation in Respect of Intercountry Adoption. This Convention will be given the force of law in this country by the bringing into force of the Adoption (Intercountry Aspects) Act 1999, which received Royal Assent (as, incidentally, a "pre-commencement enactment" within the meaning of the Scotland Act 1998) on 27 July 1999. The Act sets out a structure allowing for the better regulation of intercountry adoptions, though the precise details remain to be enacted in regulations permitted under the Act.

The teeth of the Act, which is aimed to force prospective adopters to utilise official rather than unofficial channels to adoption, is the creation of a new offence. This is to be found in s 14, which adds into the Adoption (Scotland) Act 1978 a new s 50A. After the Act is brought into force (probably at some time in the year 2000), it will be an offence for a person habitually resident in the British Islands to bring into the UK for the purposes of adoption a child who is habitually resident outside with British Islands. The only exception is when requirements to be specified in the regulations have been satisfied. These requirements will be based on the design contained in the Hague Convention itself. For ease of reference that Convention is set out as Schedule 1 to the Act. The Convention applies (Art 2(1)) only to intercountry adoptions, that is to say adoptions in which the prospective adopters and the child do not share the same habitual residence. It also applies (Art 2(2)) only to those adoptions which create a permanent parent–child relationship. This means that fostering relationships and other institutions which do not last life-long are not covered, even if called, formally or informally, "adoption". There are requirements under Art 4 on the competent authorities of the state of origin (ie the state of the child's habitual residence before placement with prospective adopters) to ensure that the child is adoptable, that intercountry adoption is in the child's best interests, and that the appropriate consents have been obtained, after counselling, and that those who consent are fully informed about the effects of adoption. Article 5 requires the competent authorities of the receiving state (ie the state of the prospective adopters' habitual residence) to ensure that the prospective adopters are eligible and suitable, that they have been properly counselled and, importantly, that the child will be permitted to enter and reside permanently in the receiving state. The receiving state must prepare a background report on the prospective adopters and send this to the state of origin (Art 15); the state of origin must prepare a background report on the child and send this to the receiving state, together with proof of all the necessary consents (Art 16). In addition the child may not be entrusted to the prospective adopters until the state of origin has ensured that the prospective adopters agree, that the relevant authorities of the receiving state have agreed (where necessary), and that the relevant authorities of both states have agreed that the adoption should go ahead (Art 17). There is also provision to protect the child, including the power to remove the child from the prospective adopters and return him or her back to the state of origin, if the receiving state comes to the view that the placement with the prospective adopters is not in the child's best interests.

The Convention also makes provision for the recognition of Convention adoptions, and for their effect. Basically, so long as the adoption is appropriately certified as having been made in accordance with the Convention, it will be entitled to automatic recognition in all other contracting states (Art 23). The only exception is when recognition would be manifestly contrary to public policy, taking account of the best interests of the child (Art 24). The necessary implication of recognition is that the child and the adopters have a parent-child relationship that lasts for life and which involves the imposition on the adoptive parents of parental responsibilities during the child's childhood. It also includes the termination of the original parent–child relationship but only if this is one of the effects of adoption in the state where the adoption takes place. If the adoption does not have this terminating effect then the receiving state may convert the limited adoption into a full adoption if that state permits it and if the necessary consents are obtained.

This new Hague Convention on Adoption replaces the 1965 Hague Convention on Adoption, which had proved unweildy and attracted few signatories. It is to be hoped that the new Convention is ratified far more widely. Vulnerable children will be protected if it is.

Update

A large number of countries have indeed ratified this Convention. Regulations passed under the 1999 Act include SSIs 2003/19, 2009/182 and 2010/173.

Commentary No 5: April 2000

Mothers who Love Women

There are two issues that deserve our attention this quarter: entirely separate in principle, but with a coincidental factual link.

Early v *Early* is dead

In *Early* v *Early* 1989 SLT 114 (OH); 1990 SLT 221 (IH) an 8-year-old male child was removed from his mother with whom he had always lived and custody awarded to the father with whom he had never lived and who had two convictions for child neglect. A major part of the reason for doing so was that the mother had entered into a lesbian relationship and the Lord Ordinary felt that this created two disadvantages for the child: it deprived him of any male role-model in his upbringing, and if the truth of his home life became known to his school friends he might be subjected to teasing at school. The first reason is insubstantial – any award of sole residence to a single mother deprives the child of a male role model. The second reason is speculative – it is as absolutely true that the child might suffer teasing as it is that the child might be horribly mutilated and ritualistically killed by his or her parent, but the courts should not take such truth into account unless there is reason to suggest that the fear is relevant in the instant case. Nevertheless, on appeal the Inner House held that the judge's reasoning was not such that no rational judge could have considered these reasons to outweigh the father's convictions and the child's settlement with the mother. The case has always left the impression that the judges were influenced by unspoken but very real prejudice against the mother's lifestyle. The case received a significant blow 6 years later in *T, Petitioner* 1997 SLT 724 where the First Division warned judges very strongly against allowing their own prejudices against lesbians and gay men to influence them. It was no longer acceptable, the court held, to assume that a child living in a homosexual environment would be harmed, though it is of course always open to any party to lead evidence to prove that harm is likely.

Early has now been killed off completely by a recent decision of the European Court of Human Rights: *Salgueiro da Silva Mouta* v *Portugal* (2001) 31 EHRR 47. The long term significance of this case will lie in the fact that, for the first time, the European Court has held that discrimination on the basis of sexual orientation (rather than simply on the basis of sex) is prohibited by Art 14 of the ECHR.

In *da Silva Mouta* the father was a gay man who, on the break-up of his marriage, was granted parental responsibility for (in our terms, residence of) the child of the marriage. The mother then abducted the child and appealed to the Lisbon Court of Appeal. That court granted parental responsibility to the mother and limited contact to the father. The child, the Court of Appeal held, "must live in a traditional Portuguese family". Homosexuality, they held, was an abnormality and children "must not grow up in the shadow of abnormal situations". The father was permitted contact with his child, but on the condition that he hid the nature of his relationship with the man with whom he lived from the child.

The European Court of Human Rights unanimously held that the Portuguese court's decision constituted a violation of Art 8 (right to respect for private and family life) taken together with Art 14 (prohibition of discrimination). Regarding a homosexual orientation less favourably than a heterosexual orientation in a child custody dispute was not justified by the legitimate aim of protecting the child's health and rights since there was no evidence to suggest that the child would be in any way harmed by the father's homosexuality. For the same reason *Early* v *Early* would be considered a breach of Arts 8 and 14, for there the mother's lesbian orientation was assumed to be a negative factor in the custody dispute while the father's heterosexuality was assumed to be a positive factor. But as in *da Silva Mouta*, no legitimate aim could be served by making these assumptions in the absence of any indication of (likely rather than speculative) harm.

Section 11 orders: title and onus

Lesbians featured also in an unreported decision from Dunfermline Sheriff Court, *R* v *F* (discussed by J Fotheringham at 1999 SLT (News) 337). Here, the sheriff questioned whether a lesbian ex-cohabitant had title to seek a s 11 order in relation to a child her ex-partner had given birth to while the two women lived together (though after debate he was persuaded that she did have title). So resurfaces that hoary old question whether persons other than parents have title to seek an order relating to parental responsibilities and parental rights. The pre-1995 answer was clearly yes, though much judicial ink was spilt getting to that result (see, in particular, *F* v *F* 1991 SLT 357). Most people (including me) have assumed that the Children (Scotland) Act 1995 did not change this – indeed made it clearer by providing that any person who claims an interest has title. Yet obviously some doubt remains, as is clear both from this case and from certain statements of Sheriff Principal Nicholson in *White* v *White* 1999 SLT (Sh Ct) 106, discussed below.

The problem seems to be that while s 11(3) permits any person claiming interest (other than those expressly denied title under s 11(4) and (5)) to seek an order under s 11(1), s 11(1) itself limits the court's power under s 11 to make orders relating only to "parental responsibilities, parental rights, guardianship or the administration of a child's property". An order designed to deal with any other matter is not a s 11 order and so an applicant cannot rely on the liberal title provisions in s 11. The question is whether an order relating to contact between a child and a stranger is an order relating to "parental responsibilities" when, *ex hypothesi*, the stranger – be it ex-cohabitant, grandparent, sibling or whomsoever – has no parental responsibilities. On innumerable occasions before the 1995 Act, and doubtless often since, grandparents and even blood strangers have sought and obtained orders relating to, typically, contact. A careful (if somewhat convoluted) approach to statutory interpretation supports the competency of strangers seeking an order regulating the contact they have with children, or any other s 11 order.

Section 11(2)(d) of the Children (Scotland) Act 1995 permits an order regulating the arrangements for maintaining personal relations and direct contact between a child and a person with whom the child is not living. This reflects the parental responsibility contained in s 1(1)(c) but in itself s 11(2)(d) is not limited to that particular parental responsibility. The problem, as explained above, lies in s 11(1) which limits the scope of s 11 to (*inter alia*) parental responsibilities. But what are "parental responsibilities" in this context? Section 15, the interpretation section for Pt I of the 1995 Act, provides that "parental responsibilities" has the meaning given by s 1(3); s 1(3) defines the phrase to mean "the responsibilities mentioned in paragraphs (a) to (d) of" s 1(1). The escape for grandparents, ex-cohabitants and the rest is the fact that these paragraphs are merely descriptive and "parents" do not appear except before the paragraphs open. In other words, paragraphs (a)–(d) describe what parents have but do not limit their effects to parents.

A rather simpler approach is to remind ourselves of what the First Division said in *Girvan* v *Girvan* 1988 SLT 866 at 871D: "In a case such as this when the welfare of a child is the paramount consideration procedural and legal niceties must give way to common sense and reality." The traditional approach of the Scottish courts has been to be more concerned with the substantive issue of welfare rather than the procedural niceties of title and interest. So the Gordian knot tying title into the concept of "parental responsibilities" can simply be cut, by recognising that there is no necessary connection between "parents" and "parental responsibilities". The phrase "parental responsibilities" is simply shorthand to describe what parents do and have but it contains no implication that only parents can do and have these things.

Sheriff Principal Nicholson adopted a rather different approach in *White* v *White* 1999 SLT (Sh Ct) 106 where he interpreted s 11 to require a person, who did not have parental responsibilities and parental rights but who sought a s 11 order relating to contact, to seek an order granting such responsibilities and rights before seeking an order for their regulation. This strikes me as clumsy and unnecessary if an open view of title is taken. Contact is both a factual and a legal matter, and both, in my view, may be regulated by an order under s 11(2)(d). So grandparents who are being denied contact in fact with a grandchild by a parent can seek a s 11 order regulating the arrangements for factual contact and there is no requirement that the grandparents first seek an order conferring upon them the legal responsibility and right of contact.

Apart from that *obiter* oddity, Sheriff Principal Nicholson's careful analysis of the issue of onus, the real point of the case and another hoary old problem discussed interminably under the pre-1995 law and not changed by the 1995 Act, deserves close attention. The case involved a father who after divorce from the mother sought contact with his child which the mother was, in fact, not permitting. As a divorced father, statute imposed upon him the responsibility and right to maintain personal relations and direct contact with his child on a regular basis. The sheriff had taken from this statutory imposition of responsibility a presumption that contact between a father (at least one with parental responsibilities) and a child was in the child's interests with the result that the onus was on the mother (as the resident parent in this case) to show why a contact order should not be made. On appeal the sheriff principal disagreed with this approach. He found nothing in the 1995 Act that created a presumption in favour of contact such as would shift the onus to the party wishing to deny it. In this he is right.

The first thing to note is that the father was not seeking an order conferring the responsibility and right of contact on him, for statute had already done so. Rather, the order he was seeking was one to force the mother, who was refusing to allow him to fulfil his responsibilities, to give him access to the child. One might argue that prima facie the mother was in the wrong and it may be that this is the element which encourages the belief that she it is who should have the onus to justify her position. But the 1995 Act does not place the onus on the party "in the wrong". Rather, it places the onus on the person seeking the order, in this case the father. The no-order principle contained in s 11(7)(a) – often overlooked, though not by Sheriff Principal Nicholson – places the onus not on the person who cannot rely on a presumption but on the applicant to show why the order is necessary. The real presumption is in favour of making no order. Now, one of the effects of this is that the distinction between the married and the unmarried father, so deliberately and maliciously made by Parliament in 1995, is rendered (at least for purposes of onus) illusory. The married father who is, in fact, being denied contact by the residence parent has the same onus as the unmarried father who is seeking contact with his child: both must show why making an order would be better for the child than making no order at all. A married father would not satisfy this onus simply by saying "I have an obligation to maintain contact; my ex-wife is not permitting it; I therefore need an order to force her to permit it". Such a father is likely to need to show something further and in particular some good accruing to the child. The assumption of benefit from contact between children and their parents, statutory in the case of mothers and married fathers, and judicial in the case of unmarried fathers (*Sanderson* v *McManus* 1997 SC (HL) 55) will play but little role in establishing a benefit from contact between a particular child and a particular person. The onus is firmly on the applicant to show why there is good for the child who is the subject of the application. This is not new law and was effectively the position as stated in *Porchetta* v *Porchetta* 1986 SLT 105. One drawback with this approach is that it gives greater practical power to the residence parent than the opposite approach would do; one advantage is that it minimises one of the iniquities of Scottish child law, the difference in treatment between the married and the unmarried father. Either way, it is an inevitable consequence of the no-order presumption.

Update

The European Court of Human Rights has subsequently built upon the foundations laid in da Silva Mouta *and has held, in particular, that especially serious reasons need to be put forward by the state which seeks to apply different legal rules to people depending upon their sexual orientation:* Karner *v* Austria *(2004) 38 EHRR 24. A mere 10 years after* da Silva Mouta, *Portugal so moved away from its position on homosexuality that it became the fourth European country to open marriage to same-sex couples.*

Title to seek a s 11 order continued to trouble the courts well into the new decade. In X *v* Y *2002 SLT (Sh Ct) 161 the mother's lesbian partner was held by the sheriff to have no title to seek an order granting her parental responsibilities and parental rights, because same-sex couples did not have a right to family life under Art 8 of the European Convention. This is a* non sequitur, *because the determination of title to seek a s 11 order is not dependent on possessing Art 8 rights, and in any case the European Court has now held that same-sex couples do indeed have Art 8 "family life" rights:* Schalk & Kopf *v* Austria *24 June 2010, ECtHR.*

White *v* White *went to the Inner House, which produced a hugely important judgment: see Commentary 8 below. They held that the no-order principle did not create any presumption one way or another and that there was no onus on either party in a dispute over a s 11 order: the matter was to be determined by the welfare of the child and not on the issue of who had the onus of proving their case. Courts remain reluctant to accept that a s 11 order is available to people who are not parents,but in* Authority Reporter *v* S *2010 SLT 765 the Inner House accepted that a s 11 order could be made so long as it "relates" to parental responsibilities and parental rights and that an order regulating contact arrangements between a child and someone who had no parental responsibilities and parental rights was, therefore, a competent s 11 order.*

Commentary No 6: July 2000

A Habit That Brings Scots Law Into Disrepute

The Scottish Executive, in response to last year's consultation paper *Improving Scottish Family Law*, have announced that they are minded to retain the concept of marriage by cohabitation with habit and repute, on the basis that it continues to serve some useful function. Perhaps someone can explain what that useful function is, for it is beyond me.

The Court of Session has twice recently been asked to grant a declarator of marriage on the basis of cohabitation with habit and repute, in one case granting the declarator, in the other refusing it. These cases together illustrate well that the concept is illogical and unfair.

Repute missing

In *Ackerman* v *Logan's Executor* 2002 SLT 37 the pursuer, Mrs Ackerman, had lived from about the middle of 1994 with a gentleman, Mr Logan, until shortly before his death in 1998. In February 1996 Mr Logan had asked her to marry him and she had agreed. Thereafter they went to a jewellers and purchased a diamond ring. A month later, while staying in a hotel in Auchterarder, he put the ring on her finger and, she claimed, they treated the rest of their time in Auchterarder as their "honeymoon". However, the relationship thereafter soured and they had separated by early 1998. Mr Logan was then unexpectedly killed in an accident while hill walking. Mrs Ackerman's claim was based on the assertion that she and Mr Logan considered themselves to be married. Her claim failed, however, because she could not establish the necessary habit and repute. The friends, relatives and acquaintances of the couple believed them to be engaged to be married, and that they planned to have a ceremony of marriage some time later, perhaps after the wedding of Mr Logan's son. But the pursuer was unable to produce witnesses who believed the couple were anything other than a cohabiting, unmarried, couple. This was fatal to Mrs Ackerman's claim. Lord Nimmo Smith in the Outer House put it thus: "I think therefore that in the case of a couple such as the pursuer and Mr Logan, no less than with any other couple, it is necessary to seek evidence of habit and repute which is general and consistent, so preponderating as to leave no substantial doubt. It appears to me that in the present case such proof is conspicuously lacking."

Repute existing

In *Vosilius* v *Vosilius* 2000 Fam LR 58, the pursuer, Mrs Cunningham, had lived with Mr Vosilius from 1976 until his death in 1995. While living together they had slept together, had sexual relations and, she alleged, regarded each other as husband and wife. Though his children tried to establish that Mr Vosilius lived with Mrs Cunningham as her lodger, Lord MacFadyen found on the evidence that the relationship was conjugal. The couple were both divorced and, as Roman Catholics, believed that were they to marry in a civil ceremony they would be excluded from the communion of their church. Close relatives knew that the pair had never gone through a ceremony of marriage, but acquaintances and friends did not. They were known by neighbours and friends either as Mr and Mrs Cunningham or as Mr and Mrs Vosilius. Her children referred to him as "Dad". Lord MacFadyen held that they were married by cohabitation with habit and repute.

The law

Both judges accepted as accurate, and applied, the description of the doctrine as stated in Clive, *Husband and Wife*, 4th edn. Clive says (at para 05.025) that marriage requires both a mental element (mutual consent to marry) and an outward or factual element. This outward element is usually a regular marriage ceremony, but it is sometimes constituted by cohabitation with habit and repute. This passage is important in making plain that marriage in Scots law, even irregular marriage, does not require any ceremony at all. The doctrine of marriage by cohabitation with habit and repute is not based on an evidentiary presumption that sometime in the past a ceremony has been gone through (as is the case in England). Rather, the status of marriage itself is created by the combination of the mental element and the cohabitation with habit and repute. Both Mrs Ackerman and Mrs Cunningham knew that they had not undergone any ceremony of marriage: they knew that they were, in one sense, not "married". Yet in law Mrs Cunningham was able to access the benefits of marriage, while Mrs Ackerman was not, because the former had sufficiently shown the necessary outward element but the latter had not.

Mrs Cunningham succeeded in her claim because people misunderstood her true situation. While her children were at school she allowed people to assume that Mr Vosilius was the father of her children, and while with his associates she let herself be introduced as his wife. Mr Vosilius, who had worked for British Rail, obtained a spouse's travel pass for her by describing her (fraudulently?) as "Sarah Vosilius, spouse". Yet she too, like Mrs Ackerman, knew that no marriage ceremony had taken place – she did indeed call herself Mrs Cunningham on the voters' roll, believing that it would be a criminal offence for her to claim to be married in that context when she knew that she was not.

These cases show that one can access legal benefits (in both cases, succession rights) so long as, knowing the truth, one allows others to assume that which is not so. If people generally know the truth one loses access to benefits. But how is the truth to be conveyed? Many married couples today keep their own names, though that remains unusual. Many unmarried couples take the names of their partners. Though both judges emphasised that the mere use of names was not determinative, this is one of the most potent means by which strangers and new acquaintances make assumptions about the nature of any relationship. And it is these assumptions upon which the application of the doctrine depends. Acquaintances assumed Mrs Cunningham had married Mr Vosilius; acquaintances assumed that Mrs Ackerman and Mr Logan had not married. Mrs Cunningham won, Mrs Ackerman lost.

The reality

Why does the doctrine continue to be regarded as part of the law of marriage? In reality it is an aspect of the law of succession. What is really happening in the vast majority of cases is that a cohabitant, on the death of their partner, is informed that she or he has no claim to any portion of the estate; but that the law will grant a claim if she or he can prove that they had tacitly agreed to be married (even although they never went through with a ceremony) and that they were generally reputed to be married. In other words, the law is attempting to ameliorate the otherwise harsh and unfair position that cohabitants would otherwise find themselves in – that of having no claim against the estate of the person with whom they have spent a "considerable period" (remembering that cohabitation has to be for a considerable period) and who may be assumed to have wished that they benefit from their estate on death. Of the cases in the last decade, the defenders have been executors or heirs on intestacy in *Mullen* v *Mullen* 1991 SLT 205, *Donnelly* v *Donnelly's Executor* 1992 SLT 13, *Gow* v *Lord Advocate* 1993 SLT 275, *Kamperman* v *MacIver* 1994 SLT 763 and, of course, the two cases under discussion. In only two, *Dewar* v *Dewar* 1995 SLT 467 and *Walker* v *Roberts* 1998 SLT 1133 was the dispute between the cohabitants themselves at the end of their relationship (in *Dewar* the claim was for aliment and in *Walker* the claim was for financial provision on divorce). This is the reality of these claims. They are, however, successful or unsuccessful on the basis of facts irrelevant to the real issue. The real issue is whether it is fair, just and reasonable (to coin a phrase) that one person should have a claim out of the estate of another, or whether it is reasonable to assume that the deceased would have wanted a portion of the estate to go to the surviving partner. Whether the parties' acquaintances believed them married or not may be one small element in the reasonableness of the claim, but it can hardly be determining. Of the two cases being discussed here, determining the succession issue on that basis would probably not have led to different results. In *Ackerman* the relationship had come to an end before Mr Logan's death and it would not be reasonable to assume that he would have wanted Mrs Ackerman to succeed to a portion of his estate; in *Vosilius* the 19-year relationship was no different from that of a married couple – or, and this is the point, of that of a couple who either could not or had deliberately decided not to get married but who had a conjugal relationship – and the assumption that Mr Vosilius would want Mrs Cunningham to succeed to part of his estate would be entirely reasonable, in both situations.

Similarly with claims for financial provision at the end of the relationship. These should depend on the factors identified by the Scottish Law Commission who recommended (*Report on Family Law*, May 1992, para 16.23) that cohabitants should have such claims, on the basis of contributions made to the relationship and disadvantages suffered in its interests, and not on the irrelevancies of how acquaintances saw the relationship. "Marriage" by cohabitation with habit and repute should be abolished forthwith and the rights of cohabitants should be extended in a logical and reasonable fashion which addresses the real issue rather than diverting it into the law of marriage.

Update

Marriage by cohabitation with habit and repute was partially abolished by s 3 of the Family Law (Scotland) Act 2006. It survives only to preserve the validity of marriages contracted abroad which, for some technical reason, are otherwise invalid. This means of preserving legal relationships contracted abroad is not extended to civil partnerships contracted abroad. It is difficult to see what legitimate aim is served by withholding this benefit from same-sex couples that is available to opposite-sex couples and it is vulnerable, therefore, to challenge. Abolition was not retrospective and so cases still occasionally arise in respect of relationships that existed before the coming into force of the 2006 Act: see, for example, Toner-Boyd *v* Secretary of State for Work and Pensions *[2010] CSIH 7. Cases like this may continue to appear for some decades yet.*

The major importance of the 2006 Act is that it rendered irregular marriage entirely pointless by creating proper claims for financial provision for cohabitants, both when the couple separate and when one dies. These claims do not depend, as irregular marriage depended, on the parties being economical with the truth. Whatever flaws there are in the 2006 Act, the legislation is far more principled and far better reflects today's society than does the old common law doctrine, which had long outstayed its welcome.

Commentary No 7: October 2000

Title to Seek Contact: Grandparents, Welfare and Constitutionality

The United States of America, like the past, is a foreign country: they do things differently there. In their legal system this is true not only in the obvious sense that the constitutional framework within which US law operates is very different from our own, but also in more subtle ways in which very different perceptions and attitudes are sometimes revealed. An example of the latter is the application of the welfare test (or, as American lawyers tend to put it "the best interest test") in child law. While all states accept that test as paramount, its application is skewed (to European eyes) by the strong presumption that parents act in the best interests of their children. In reality that presumption has grown out of the very different proposition that parents have a right to bring up their children as they think fit, and while that latter proposition is usually hidden it happens occasionally that the mask of welfare slips and the ugliness of unfettered parental right shows through. A well-known example is *Wisconsin* v *Yoder* 406 US 246 (1978), in which the US Supreme Court held that a parent's right to withdraw a child from education after the age of 14 was, at least when this was done for reasons of "religious" conviction that children should not be educated beyond that age, more important than any individual child's right to be educated. More recently the Supreme Court has decided that state statutes dealing with child law are unconstitutional if they do not contain a presumption of parental goodness and, further, that they are unconstitutional if they grant title to any person to seek to persuade a court to make an order against the wishes of the parent merely on the court's assessment of the child's welfare.

Grandparents seeking contact

On June 5, 2000, the US Supreme Court handed down its decision in the case of *Troxel* v *Granville* 530 US 57 (2000), in which the appellant challenged the constitutionality of a child law statute from the state of Washington. Neither the facts nor the statute at issue were particularly unusual. After their son's death, Mr and Mrs Troxel sought a significant amount of contact (or "visitation", in the American term) with their grandchildren. The mother of the girls was willing to permit a certain amount of contact, but not the amount their grandparents sought. So the grandparents went to court. The Washington statute (Washington Rev Code ss 26.10.160(3)) permitted "any person" to petition the court for visitation rights "at any time" and authorized the court to grant such rights whenever visitation may, in the court's view, serve the child's best interests. Because the grandparents "can provide opportunities for the children in the areas of cousins and music", it granted the visitation sought by the grandparents.

Now, had this decision been reached in Scotland under s 11 of the Children (Scotland) Act 1995, the mother's only option (other than compliance) would be to appeal against the order. But here a decision of a fact finder on a child's welfare can be disturbed by an appeal court only if it is demonstrated that the sheriff or other first instance judge had failed to take account of a significant factor or had reached a conclusion that was so plainly wrong as to demonstrate that he had not properly exercised his discretion. However, in the US, and in the future in Scotland if the decision is made under an Act of the Scottish Parliament, the unsuccessful party has two options: appeal the decision in the normal way, or challenge the constitutionality of the statute upon which the decision was based. It is the latter approach that Mrs Granville adopted.

The Washington State Court of Appeals and then the US Supreme Court struck down the visitation statute, on the ground that it was an unconstitutional infringement of the Due Process Clause of the Fourteenth Amendment to the US Constitution. That provides heightened protection against governmental interference with certain fundamental rights, of which a parent's right to make decisions concerning the care and control of their children is one. The statute at issue permitted the court to overturn a decision by a fit parent merely by substituting its own assessment of welfare for that of parent. (So, be it noted, does the Children (Scotland) Act 1995). The Washington statute contained no presumption that parental decisions are in children's best interests, with the result that the original court gave no special weight to the decision of the parent. All that was before the court was a simple disagreement between a mother and the grandparents of a child as to what was in the child's best interests, and for the court (the state) to the substitute its own views for that of the parent was an unconstitutional infringement of the parent's rights.

Human rights and family rights

The equivalent provisions in the Children (Scotland) Act 1995 would not survive in the US: can they survive challenge under the European Convention on Human Rights, Art 8 of which provides a right to respect for private and family life? A parent might argue that his or her family life may be interfered with only when this is necessary in a democratic society and when the interference is proportionate to the aim sought to be achieved (ie the welfare of the child); and that it is not "necessary" to interfere with parental decision-making unless some positive harm can be shown to arise from the parent's decision. Many, if not most, disputes under s 11 concern not a choice between good and bad but between two alternatives which are both reasonable and acceptable and the court's role under s 11 is to identify which of the two is, on balance and sometimes marginally so, better. In these circumstances, a parent might argue (though only if the dispute is with a non-parent) that his or her private and family life is being interfered with if his or her reasonable and acceptable assessment of the child's welfare is not given effect to.

I do not think this argument works. Parental freedom and parental rights are given a far higher value in the US Constitution than they are in the ECHR (as seen both in the present case and in the dreadful *Yoder* decision mentioned above). The so-called liberty interest at stake in *Troxel* was described as "the interest of parents in the care, custody, and control of their children – perhaps the oldest of the fundamental interests recognized by this court" (per O'Connor J). This is not the fundamental right that is protected by Art 8 of the ECHR, which is "family-life" rather than "parental rights". In any case, it is not only parents who have a right to family life. Family life has been held to exist between children and grandparents (*Marckx* v *Belgium* (1979) 2 EHRR 330 at para 45), between siblings (*Moustaquim* v *Belgium* (1993) 13 EHRR 802 at para 36) and between children and step-parents (*Soderback* v *Sweden* (1998) 29 EHRR 95). When a grandparent seeks contact with a grandchild in order to maintain an existing relationship, both the grandparent and the grandchild can validly argue that there is a family relationship between them, and they may even argue that the parent's attempt to limit contact amounts to an interference with that family life.

Presumptions of parental goodness

Should the court presume that a parent's decisions are in the best interests of his or her children, so placing the onus on those who seek to go against the parent's wishes? The no-order presumption is not based on the proposition that parents act in the interests of their children – long experience has told us that, unhappily, this is so often not so that any such presumption would be unhelpful in the extreme. Rather, it is based on the proposition that it is better for the child that parties be encouraged to sort out their differences themselves and that a child's life should not, except in cases of necessity, be governed by the formality of a court order. The Scottish courts have long resisted, and rightly so, deciding welfare cases on the basis of onus and there is nothing in either Art 8 or the jurisprudence of the European Court of Human Rights which requires a presumption of parental goodness.

It is interesting, finally, to note that English law seems to be developing just such a presumption. *In Re D (Care: Natural Parent Presumption)* [1999] 1 FLR 134 the Court of Appeal held that in a dispute with a local authority as to whether what we would call a "looked after" child should be cared for at home or by his grandparents the court should first examine whether there was any reason to displace the parent: only if there was could the court then move on to weighing up the disadvantages and advantages between two competing solutions. This was followed (more disturbingly) in a purely private dispute in *Re D* [1999] 2 FLR 1023. And in *Re J (Specific Issue Order: Child's Religious Upbringing and Circumcision)* [2000] 1 FLR 571 the Court of Appeal held that when parents disagree as to whether to subject their baby boy to genital mutilation the court should apply the best interests test, but when parents agree to such mutilation they are entitled to so subject the child. Of course in England title to seek an order relating to a child has long been much more limited than in Scotland (see *Re H (Residence Order: Child's Application for Leave)* [2000] 1 FLR 780, where the child himself was denied leave) and so it may not be surprising if the law there develops differently and more in line with the US position. But the point remains good that nothing in Art 8 of the ECHR requires the Scottish courts to adopt such a parental preference. If a dispute is submitted to a Scottish court it is entitled and obliged to weigh up all the circumstances and to make a decision giving paramountcy to the welfare of the child. Parental wishes are, like the child's wishes, an important element to be taken into account but they do not create a presumption. There is no presumption in Scots law that parents' decisions on the upbringing of their children are in the best interests of these children. Nor should there be.

Update

Any presumption in favour of parents has been comprehensively rejected by the UK Supreme Court. The issue in all cases is the welfare of the child, and its determination is not affected by any claimed parental "right": Re B (A Child) (Residence Order: Biological Parent) *[2009] 1 WLR 2496. Title to seek a s 11 order inheres in any person who "claims an interest", subject to the stated exceptions in s 11(4) and (5). Grandparents will satisfy this test without difficulty, though the claim they make must be one relating to parental responsibilities and parental rights, or guardianship, or the administration of a child's property. A contact order sought by someone who is not a parent and who does not have parental responsibilities and parental rights is nevertheless an order relating to parental responsibilities and parental rights:* Authority Reporter *v* S *2010 SLT 765.*

Commentary No 8: April 2001

Whither the No-Order Principle?

Some years ago Professor J M Thomson, discussing the case of *Porchetta* v *Porchetta* 1986 SLT 105, asked whether a "right" of access existed in Scots law in any jurisprudentially meaningful sense, and he answered No ("Whither the "Right" of Access?" 1989 SLT (News) 109.) This was because *Porchetta* had held that a married father who sought access to his child had to do more than claim access on the basis of paternity – he had to show that making an order allowing him access would do some good for the child. This effectively put the married father in the same position as the unmarried father, notwithstanding that the former but not the latter had statutory "parental rights" under the Law Reform (Parent and Child) (Scotland) Act 1986 which included the "right" of what was then termed access. *Porchetta*, which was decided under the pre-1986 law, was approved by the House of Lords in *Sanderson* v *McManus* 1997 SC (HL) 55, which was decided under the pre-1995 law. The First Division of the Court of Session has now decided a case under the Children (Scotland) Act 1995, *White* v *White* 2001 SLT 485, which, again, follows *Porchetta*, subject to one crucial qualification.

The facts and the decisions of the sheriffs

Mr and Mrs White married in 1984 and divorced in 1997, having had two children, born in 1985 and 1991. They had separated in 1995. No order for contact was made at the time of the divorce since the parties' informal arrangements under which Mr White had regular contact were proceeding satisfactorily. However, when Mr White entered into a relationship with another woman Mrs White decided that she was no longer willing to allow contact between the children and their father. He therefore sought an order permitting him to spend time with the younger child, the effect of which would be to force the mother to allow it. The sheriff granted the order sought, holding that since s 1(1) of the Children (Scotland) Act 1995 imposed upon parents who did not live with their children a duty to maintain direct contact and personal relations with their children, the person opposing contact would have to establish "the strongest competing disadvantages" before contact would be refused. In other words, in a case like the present, the onus rested with the residence parent to show why the non-residence parent should be denied contact. In the present case Mrs White had failed to do so. The sheriff was overturned by the Sheriff Principal (Nicholson) who held, rather, that the onus rested with the person seeking the order to show that it would be better for the child that the order be made than that no order should be made at all. The sheriff principal was following the approach (though not, of course, the statutory background) adopted by Lord Dunpark in *Porchetta*, who had said "A father does not have an absolute right to access to his child. He is only entitled to access if the court is satisfied that that is in the best interests of the child. The onus is on the defender [the father] to show that". Shortly after that decision the Law Reform (Parent and Child) (Scotland) Act 1986 enacted (s 3(2)): "In any proceedings relating to parental rights the court shall regard the welfare of the child involved as the paramount consideration and shall not make any order relating to parental rights unless it is satisfied that to do so will be in the interests of the child". The 1995 Act repeats and strengthens these words by providing in s 11(7)(a) that the court "shall regard the welfare of the child concerned as its paramount consideration *and shall not make any such order unless it considers that it would be better for the child that the order be made than that none should be made at all*".

The italicised words have come to be referred to as "the no-order principle" or the "no-order presumption" or, sometimes, the "minimum intervention principle" and they have been interpreted by commentators (myself included) as creating a presumption which has an effect on the onus of proof: the court should start with the presumption that it will make no order, with the result that the onus of dislodging this presumption lies with the person seeking the order (see, for example, Wilkinson and Norrie, *Parent and Child* (2nd edn) at pp 344–346). This is the approach the sheriff principal followed, and in this column last year I commended him for doing so ((2000) 5 SLPQ at 171). This approach is now revealed as error.

Correcting the Commentators

The Lord President gave the lead judgment. He started by accepting the commonly held belief, given judicial expression particularly by Lord Hope of Craighead in *Sanderson* v *McManus*, that children generally benefit from continued contact with absent parents and (like Lord Hope) he made no distinction in this respect between fathers who were or had been and fathers who never had been married to the mother (other than saying that this understanding applies "at least as powerfully" to the former as to the latter). He described this understanding as a "general principle" which is used as a "point of reference" in helping judges decide cases. The point of reference both "represents the consensus of society" and, through s 1(1) of the 1995 Act, represents the views of Parliament as to where the interests of children lie. There is no need to hear evidence from experts to establish this. But, he points out (again following Lord Hope in *Sanderson*), this is "nothing more than a general principle which must be applied with discrimination". Given the terms of s 11 of the 1995 Act, it cannot impose any legal onus. This is because s 11(3) permits the court to make an order either when a party seeks an order or when a party does not seek any order: since no question of onus can guide the court when it is considering whether to act *ex proprio motu* it would be illogical to apply an onus when there is a party seeking an order. Lord McCluskey elaborated on this, holding that a case in which the court is to determine the welfare of the child can never be decided on a matter of onus. He said that it would be "inconceivable" that a court after hearing evidence would make its judgment on the basis of the failure of one party or the other to discharge the onus of proof. Rather, the court having heard the evidence must decide whether or nor the order sought is likely to further the child's interests: questions of onus raise technical considerations that have nothing directly to do with the interests of the child.

So, rather as the High Court of Australia did last year (see *A & A: Relocation Approach* [2000] FamCA 751, August 1, 2000, and *H & L* [2000] FamCA 752, decided on the same day), the First Division has held in the clearest possible language that the judge, faced with opposing options, may not require one side or the other to prove his or her case but must instead weigh the options on offer and make a positive decision one way or another. The welfare test, dependent as it is on both the evidence presented and the judge's assessment thereof in the light of his or her own common understandings, is in and of itself inconsistent with the imposition of an onus of proof. Lord Dunpark's statement on onus was not expressly disapproved, but clearly it can no longer stand.

The no-order understanding

Now that is all very well, but where does it leave the so-called "no-order principle"? Clearly, that principle can no longer be interpreted as creating a presumption with the effect of placing the onus on the person seeking the order. The structure of s 11(7), which contains what have come to be called "the three overarching principles" is to be noted. Only the principle concerning the child's views stands alone in s 11(7)(b), while the welfare principle and the no-order principle are both expressed in s 11(7)(a). This might be taken to indicate that the latter is no more than an elaboration of the former. This is giving the no-order principle a far more limited scope than commentators have hitherto allowed it, but it seems that the First Division sees no more scope for the principle than this. Only the Lord President referred to the second limb of s 11(7)(a), describing the formulation as one "designed to give effect to Parliament's view that, wherever possible, matters should be regulated by the parties without the intervention of the court". But if this is all that it says then it has no effect whatsoever when a party to an action seeks an order, for the very raising of the action indicates that attempts at private regulation have not worked (as illustrated well in the present case, where Mr White had attempted to persuade Mrs White to allow contact, but to no avail). Might the words, which no longer amount to a principle, have more effect if the court is considering whether to make an order *ex proprio motu*? In that situation Parliament's view that matters are better left privately regulated can have little more effect than the general principle that children are better maintaining contact with both their parents: in other words, the courts should hesitate in making orders which they are not asked to make (to reflect the general consensus that unnecessary orders over children are bad for their subjects). That does not amount to a presumption that they will not do so, but is merely a common belief that has to be taken into account.

The no public law order principle

It may be, and indeed it is to be hoped, that this limited conception of the role of the no-order principle is restricted in its application to Pt I of the 1995 Act, for very different considerations come into play in Pt II, dealing not with disputes between private persons but with disputes between the state and its citizens. The court in a private law dispute must resolve the issue on the basis that the child's welfare is paramount, and this involves the court balancing the available options and determining which is better – often marginally so – for the child.

But in public law cases the dispute is not between private individuals but between individuals and the state. In balancing the options in such a dispute, the court cannot apply only the welfare test with its sometimes fine distinctions. For there is another consideration – the right of individuals to respect for their private and family life, as protected by Art 8 of the European Convention on Human Rights. The European Court of Human Rights has held that a state cannot interfere with family life unless it can show that it has a legitimate aim in interfering and that the interference goes no further than is necessary to achieve that aim. This is the principle of proportionality. It is submitted that a pure application of the welfare test, without any onus, which might be acceptable in private law disputes, is entirely inappropriate in public law disputes. For in the latter the court cannot simply balance, for example, care by foster carers and care by natural parents and hold that, since the former is, marginally, better for the child, the child should be removed from the parents. Proportionality requires that the state prove some greater necessity for action than a marginal improvement in the child's life. Human Rights law requires, in other words, that the onus be on the interfering state in public law disputes to justify the infringment of respect for private and family life. Interpreting the no order principle as it appears in s 16 to impose such an onus would render Scots domestic law consistent with the ECHR. Nothing in *White v White* precludes such an interpretation, for the structure of s 16 is very different from the structure of s 11(7). As we have seen, the no order (now non-) principle in s 11(7)(a) is an elaboration of the welfare principle in the same paragraph, but in s 16 it is set out in a separate and independent subsection (s 16(3)). This gives it a separate existence independent of the welfare principle (s 16(1)), so permitting a different interpretation from the similar but now more limited principle in s 11(7)(a).

Incorporation of the UN Convention

There is one other important point of interest in this case. Both the Lord President and Lord McCluskey made much reference to the UN Convention on the Rights of the Child. Indeed, the latter elevated that Convention to the status that the ECHR had before the coming into effect of the Human Rights Act 1998. He said that before then the presumption (at least since *T, Petitioner* 1997 SLT 724) was that in interpreting ambiguous legislation the court had to assume that Parliament intended it to be in conformity with the ECHR: and he stated that "the same general approach has to be taken when construing and applying legislation dealing with the subject matter of the UN

Convention, which the United Kingdom ratified in December 1991." This is the strongest statement of support for that Convention that a Scottish court has yet made, and has given it practical force that it never had before.

Commentary No 9: April 2001

Tales from Abroad

Too much has been happening in Scots family law recently to comment on all the current issues. There is no time here to talk about the long awaited decision of the Inner House in *S* v *Miller* 2001 SLT 531 where the children's hearing system was challenged under the Human Rights Act 1998. Nor is there time to talk about a recent Outer House decision (*D, Petitioner*, April 21, 2001) in which Judge Coutts returned children wrongfully removed from California to their drug using and dealing mother. (The father, in bringing the children to Scotland, was not exactly "clean" himself, having jumped bail in the US where he was due to appear charged with various drug offences.) The temporary judge held that it was for the court of the child's habitual residence to determine the competing claims of these less than ideal parents. Good. That is what the Hague Convention is all about. And there is no time to do other than mention in passing Sheriff Craik's interesting decision (*City of Edinburgh Council* v *H* 2001 SLT (Sh 9 Ct 9) 51) in which he refused to make a parental responsibilities order in favour of the local authority notwithstanding the mother's agreement because the child (a boy aged 10 and a half) opposed the making of the order.

This quarter's column, instead, is going to take one of its occasional excursions abroad, first to South Africa, and then to Australia.

Parental love and court orders in South Africa

There is presently within the Law Schools of Scotland a growing collaboration with their counterparts in South Africa, and though so far this has concentrated on property and obligations law, family law too will repay comparative study. South African family law was neglected in that country by the legislature for a lot of years and from the perspective of Scots and English law at the start of the 21st century, the law there looks to be about 50 years out of date. There is still illegitimacy; there is still a requirement on married couples to adhere; there is still "custody" and "access" and "parental rights"; there is still, believe it or not, the Roman law ages of capacity to marry (12 for girls and 14 for boys). Yet legislative and constitutional change, as well as the ratification of the UN Convention on the Rights of the Child in 1995, has begun the long process of turning South African family law into a modern body of rules. The constitutionalisation of private law is a recurring theme throughout current legal literature in South Africa and this is making itself felt in family law also. It was given particular impetus by s 8 of the South African Constitution, which obliges the courts to develop the common law in a way that gives effect to the rights contained in the Constitution. These rights are both more extensive and more specific than those contained in the European Convention on Human Rights, but the way the South African courts deal with them in private disputes provides lessons for domestic courts here applying the ECHR in such disputes. An interesting recent case is that of *Jooste* v *Botha* 2000 (2) SA 199.

This case involved what South African law continues to call an "illegitimate" child, born to a woman 11 years prior to the court case. The father, Botha, is apparently a famous sportsperson in South Africa and the pregnancy came about as a result of a one-off incident of what the judge called "carnal intercourse" between Botha and the boy's mother. Botha had always refused to acknowledge the child as his, or to have anything to do with his upbringing. However, paternity was established and Botha contributed financially to the child's upbringing. Family law could do little more, but the case was raised in delict, the boy seeking damages against his father.

Breach of common law duty of care

The action was raised by the child himself (though the judge, at the end of the judgment, indicated that the child could understand nothing and that the real plaintiff was the mother – he speculated as to her motives, believing the court case against the famous person could do nothing but harm to the child). The boy (through his mother) alleged that he had suffered an injury at the hands of his father, being emotional distress at the father's failure to acknowledge him or to have anything to do with him, and for his loss of amenities of life. The claim was based on the proposition that the defendant had a legal duty to render the plaintiff attention, love, cherishment and interest, either under the common law or under the South African Constitution. The claim was (in our terms) dismissed as irrelevant.

The common law claim was doomed to failure. The court pointed out that there was no duty at common law on a father to care for an "illegitimate" child, beyond the statutory obligation to pay maintenance. The boy's argument, that he had a right to be cared for and that there can be no right without a remedy, was dismissed as misconceived: the common law imposed many obligations through family relationships (eg the duty on spouses not to commit adultery) without giving a right of action for damages when the obligation was breached. Van Dijkhorst J said this: "Neither can conjugal rights be enforced by order of court nor love kindled by the sheriff's writ".

Breach of the constitution

The constitutional claim was the more interesting. Section 28 of the Constitution lists various children's rights (which the court accepted had to be interpreted in light of the UN Convention), including the right to "parental care" and to "be protected from maltreatment, neglect or abuse". The question was whether these created rights in the delictual sense. The boy argued that these provisions would have no effect unless the Court followed its obligation to develop the common law in line with the Constitution and the UN Convention: the only remedy for infringement of these rights, he argued, was a delictual one for damages. The Court disagreed. The question resolved into whether these rights had "vertical effect" or "horizontal effect" – whether, that is they were enforceable against the state alone, or enforceable against individuals. The Court held that this constitutional provision had vertical effect only: "It is aimed at the preservation of a healthy parent-child relationship in the family environment against unwarranted executive, administrative or legislative acts". The notion of "parental care" did not require all "parents" to provide care for the child: rather it required the state to protect, and not interfere with, the parental care the child was in fact receiving from the legal custodian.

Lessons for Scotland

There seems little doubt that the Scottish court would similarly dismiss such a claim as irrelevant – at least if pleaded as it was here. The ECHR's requirement on states to protect "family life" is designed to protect social reality rather than genetic inheritance. There was no "family" relationship such as Art 8 would protect in these facts. The current proposals before the Scottish Parliament to confer parental responsibilities on (some) unmarried fathers will place them in the same position as married fathers and mothers in terms of legal obligation, but that does not in itself mean that they can be sued for damages for failing to fulfil their obligations. For it depends both on the nature of the obligation and on the nature of the loss said to result from the failure. The Children (Scotland) Act 1995 and the Adoption (Scotland) Act 1978 provide various consequences for a failure to fulfil parental responsibilities but neither mentions damages. Yet an action for damages by a child against a parent is not entirely unarguable, given the peculiar little provision that is s 1(3) of the 1995 Act. That provides that "The responsibilities [mentioned in s 1(1)] ... are in this Act referred to as 'parental responsibilities' and the child ... shall have title to sue, or to defend, in any proceedings as respects those responsibilities". That provision cannot be limited to giving the child title to sue or defend a s 11 application, for s 11(3) and (5) does so directly and s 1(3) would therefore be robbed of meaning. Certainly the provision gives the child title to defend an action for one of the Pt II orders (as in *City of Edinburgh Council* v *H*, above, where the child entered the process as a party minuter) but that does not explain the words "shall have title to sue", which a child cannot do under Pt II. I have previously suggested (*The Children (Scotland) Act 1995* (revised edition, 1997, at p 9) that the words must refer to the child's title to sue in delict, the wrong being a breach of the parent's parental responsibilities, but also that liability therefor must come from the common law rather than statutory words conferring title to sue the liable party. So the question is what *injuria* Scots law would recognise as flowing from a breach of the parental responsibilities listed in s 1(1) of the 1995 Act. If a parent neglected the child's health (for example by not seeking appropriate medical treatment) then there would seem to be little difficulty in the child suing for any direct physical loss caused thereby. Similarly a parent acting as the child's legal representative who enters into a legal transaction on the child's behalf which is not reasonable and which causes the child economic loss could be sued (a conclusion fortified by the terms of s 10 also). But could the child sue for emotional distress at being rejected or unloved? The courts are more and more having to deal with claims for emotional distress that constitute "illness" and while for the most part feeling unloved is unlikely to be considered an illness it is not entirely inconceivable that a discovery of one's parentage or the realisation of the lack of interest that one's parent has could lead to severe emotional disturbance. Such an illness might, in some circumstances, sound in damages.

Update on the Australian Children (Scotland) Act 1995

A couple of years ago this Journal carried my article on the Australian Family Law Reform Act 1995 ("The Australian Children (Scotland) Act 1995" (1998) 3 SLPQ 15), which basically did for Australian law what our own 1995 Act did for Scots law. There has now been published by the Family Court of Australia a Report by Rhoades, Graycar and Harrison into the operation of that Act in its first three years of operation. It may be found at http://www.familycourt.gov.au/papers/pdf/famlaw.pdf It does not make comfortable reading for those who had high hopes that legislation could effect a culture shift for the benefit of children.

The Report highlights a number of drawbacks in the reforms. In Australia, as in Scotland, the idea was to encourage separating parents to continue with shared responsibility for the upbringing of their children. The evidence suggests that little has changed in reality: that mothers continue to carry the bulk of caregiving after parental separation and that the numbers of fathers who contribute to caregiving has not varied to any noticeable extent. The Report suggests that the certainty of the old law has been replaced by confusion and disappointment. Fathers, particularly, saw the new law (quite erroneously) as one designed to give them equal time with their children, but of course there is no presumption of equal sharing in child law. There is, however, a presumption (informal and non-statutory and very similar to what is now the approach of the courts in Scotland) that contact between the child and the non-resident parent is good for the child, but the Report's findings suggest that this presumption is applied even in cases of domestic violence with the result that (i) the safety of residence parents is being put at risk and (ii) the effects on children of witnessing domestic violence are being underplayed more often than they were before 1995.

Perhaps the most disappointing finding is the significant increase in disputes being taken to court. The Australian Act contains no "no-order presumption" (but then neither, now, does Scots law – see my comments in this column last quarter) but it did introduce the concept of "parenting plans" under which parents were encouraged to come to private arrangements for the post-separation care of children. These have not proved popular and the concept of continued parental responsibility has had little effect other than to give the non-resident parent "a new tool of control", or a method of disrupting the life of the resident parent: the exercise of this control and attempts to avoid it has led to many more cases going to court than prior to the implementation of the 1995 Act.

Another disappointing feature – which is certainly reflected in Scotland – is the fact that the new terminology of parental responsibilities, residence and contact, has not sunk in, either for parents or the media, or even for practicing lawyers (a glance at many Scottish firms' websites will show how many solicitors continue to advertise their willingness to take on "custody and access" disputes). Moving away from the winner-takes-all concept of custody to the less contentious residence dispute can only work if disputants, and their advisers, see the conflict in that way.

An in-depth examination into the practical consequences of the legislation, in terms of both children's lives and court practice, is essential for a proper assessment of the success or otherwise of the Act. A study in Scotland would do well to take the Australian Report as a model.

Commentary No 10: July 2001

Transsexual Law

It occasionally happens, and in family law no less than in other areas of the law, that a whole jurisprudence is built up around a single case which in itself is palpably a product of its time but which continues to rule the law notwithstanding that its reasoning, mode of expression and, sometimes, result would almost certainly not be followed today if the issue came before the court for the first time. But one of the drawbacks of a system based on judicial precedent is that it does not allow for a clean slate, even when the precedent itself arises from a lowly court. One such case is *Corbett* v *Corbett* [1971] P 83, a first instance decision of the English high court (Queen's Bench Division), which decided that a sex-change operation would not be recognised for the purposes of the English law of marriage. Surprisingly, there has been no case since, in England or in Scotland, in which claimants seek the recognition (or, as in *Corbett*, non-recognition) of a marriage, though there have of course been a number of cases coming to the court with increasingly tedious regularity in which change of sex is sought to be recognised (or not) for a variety of other legal purposes. The *Corbett* rule was accepted as being not contrary to the European Convention on Human Rights by the European Court in *Rees* v *United Kingdom* (1986) 8 EHRR 56, *Cossey* v *United Kingdom* (1990) 13 EHRR 622 and *Sheffield and Horsham* v *United Kingdom* (1998) 27 EHRR 163, though with an ever-decreasing majority and growing signs of impatience by that Court. The European Court of Justice, on the other hand, held that discrimination on the basis of transsexualism was contrary to the Equal Treatment Directive which prohibits sex discrimination in employment (see now the Sex Discrimination (Gender Reassignment) Regulations 1999 (SI 1999/1102) enacted under s 2(2) of the European Communities Act 1972 and amending the Sex Discrimination Act 1975).

The Court of Appeal has recently been faced with a direct challenge to *Corbett* on facts similar to, but altogether more benign than, those in that case. Since *Corbett* was a first instance decision it was open to the Court of Appeal to overrule the case and put English law onto a quite different path, had it been minded to do so. A majority of the court was not so minded.

A challenge to *Corbett*

In *Bellinger* v *Bellinger* [2002] 1 All ER 311 (Court of Appeal) Mrs Bellinger sought a declaration from the court that her marriage to Mr Bellinger was valid at its inception and was currently subsisting. There was no dispute between the parties (unlike the antagonistic pair in *Corbett*) but an intervening Attorney-General found time from a busy schedule (and public money) to oppose the petition. The Bellingers had gone through a ceremony of marriage in 1981, Mr Bellinger being perfectly aware of the fact that Mrs Bellinger had been born a male and had previously undergone gender re-assignment surgery. They challenged the criteria for defining "male" and "female" which had come from *Corbett*, on grounds well rehearsed in the literature and which do not need repeating here. Of interest is (i) how the majority decided; (ii) how the minority judge decided; and (iii) the approach to the issue the government has taken of late.The majority judgment was given by Butler-Sloss P, joined by Robert Walker LJ. After an extensive examination of the evidence, *Corbett* and subsequent cases, they held that the appeal revolved around two questions. First, was Mrs Bellinger male or female? Curiously they do not directly answer this question, though the answer they give is clear enough, for having asked it they conclude "we would therefore dismiss the appeal" (against the first instance judge's holding that Mrs Bellinger was male). They also hold that the *Corbett* criteria cannot be challenged, at least for determining sex at birth; but the real issue is whether criteria which manifest themselves later (primarily of a psychological nature and surgical intervention) can be brought into the equation in determining continued gender status. That brings them to the second question, which is: "At what point would it be consistent with public policy to recognise that a person should be treated for all purposes, including marriage, as a person of the opposite sex to that to which he/she was correctly assigned at birth?" This is obviously the crucial question, for in essence it is asking whether a change of sex from that correctly recorded at birth can be given any legal effect. But they purport to refuse to answer this question: "The second question cannot be properly decided by the court"; "the second question is for Parliament". But in fact the answer to the question of whether a change of sex can be recognised is given loud and clear: it will not be recognised until such time as Parliament acts.

Lord Justice Thorpe dissented. He attacked head-on the decision in *Corbett*. It is, he says, "no longer permissible in the light of scientific, medical and social change" to restrict the definition of gender to biological and physiological criteria and ignore the pyschological factors. This is especially so after surgery when the only remaining biological factor pointing to the original sex is chromosomal. He said this: "To make the chromosomal factor conclusive, or even dominant, seems to me particularly questionable in the context of marriage. For it is an invisible feature of an individual, incapable of perception or registration other than by scientific test. It makes no contribution to the physiological or psychological self. Indeed in the context of the institution of marriage as it is today it seems to me right as a matter of principle and logic to give predominance to psychological factors just as it seems right to carry out the essential assessment of gender at or shortly before the time of marriage rather than at the time of birth". He also held that it is no more usurping the function of Parliament to develop the meaning of the word "male" as it appears in a statute than it was for the House of Lords to develop the meaning of the word "family" in *Fitzpatrick* v *Sterling Housing Association* [2001] 1 AC 27 (where the House of Lords held that a same-sex couple could now be included within the term "family" for the purposes of succession to tenancies). He concluded by adopting a passage from an unpublished paper recently given by the Court of Session judge, Lord Reed, who said: "For the law to ignore transsexualism, either on the basis that it is an aberration which should be disregarded, or on the basis that sex role should be regarded as legally irrelevant, is not an option. The law needs to respond to society as it is. Transsexuals exist in our society, and that society is divided on the basis of sex. If a society accepts that transsexualism is a serious and distressing medical problem, and allows those who suffer from it to undergo drastic treatment in order to adopt a new gender and thereby improve their quality of life, then reason and common humanity alike suggest that it should allow such persons to function as fully as possible in their new gender".

The Government's response

And what of the Government? The European Court has long been signalling (without yet holding the UK in breach of the ECHR) that the law in this country needs to change. In *Cossey* v *United Kingdom* in 1990 the Government undertook to the court that it would look at the matter again. But it did nothing, attracting much criticism in 1997 when the next case went to Strasbourg (*Sheffield and Horsham* v *United Kingdom*). As a result of that criticism the Government did this time act, but to little effect (the cynic might regard this as intentional). It set up an inter-departmental working group, which eventually reported in April 2000. That Report suggested that there were three options: (i) do nothing, (ii) allow the reissue of birth certificates, (iii) recognise for all purposes the reassigned gender (the cynic might say, well we knew that). The Report recommended, in astounding weasel words: "we suggest that ... the government may wish to put the issues out to public consultation". The Government did not so wish and, as it made plain to the Court of Appeal in *Bellinger*, it has no plans to do so. This leaves it wide open to further criticism by the European Court. There is little doubt that the law will change, sooner or later, for the reasons spelt out by Lord Reed. But the Government seems to be adopting the approach of waiting until it is forced to do so: is it easier to say to a still queasy public: "we changed the law because we were told to, not because we wanted to or considered it right to do so"? Yet Lord Reed's words as quoted above are, surely, unanswerable.

Update

There was not long to wait before the changes adverted to here occurred. In Goodwin *v* United Kingdom *(2002) 35 EHRR 18 the European Court finally lost patience with the United Kingdom and unanimously held the UK to be in breach of both Art 8 and also (to the surprise of many) Art 12.* Bellinger *shortly thereafter was decided by the House of Lords which rejected the appeal for the same reasons as the Court of Appeal did – that it was for Parliament and not the courts to change the law in this manner – but, in light of* Goodwin *the House of Lords had no option but also to grant a declaration of incompatibility under s 4 of the Human Rights Act 1998. The Gender Recognition Act 2004 was passed in 2004 and came into effect in 2005. See Commentary No 20 below.*

Commentary No 11: October 2001

Suing Local Authorities for Child Protection Failures

The European Convention on Human Rights has already become a central source of law in relation to the legal processes involved in the care and protection of children. Most of the cases decided by the European Court have involved the issue of proportionality, that is to say, whether or not the actions taken by the state in interfering with family life were in the event justified by the need to protect the child of the family from the perceived harm. The two most recent cases from the European Court did not concern that particular issue, but they resolve some matters of importance, for the law of delict as well as for family law.

Both cases arose out of the House of Lords decision in the English case of *X* v *Bedfordshire County Council; M* v *Newham LBC* [1995] 2 AC 633. That was the case in which it was held that local authorities could not be sued for their negligence in the performance of their child care and protection duties. The plaintiffs went to the European Court, and both decisions were handed down on 10 May 2001.

TP and KM v *United Kingdom*: Arts 6 and 8

In *TP and KM* v *United Kingdom* [2001] 34 EHRR 42 a mother and daughter had sued the London Borough Council of Newham in negligence. The daughter was suspected of having been sexually abused. She was, at the age of 5 years, examined and interviewed, and the interviews were videotaped. Abuse was highly likely to have taken place and the little girl disclosed the first name of the man involved. The mother's current boyfriend (of whom she had what were described as a "steady stream") had that name. The mother was told that her boyfriend was the likely culprit, but was not given any indication of the evidence upon which that implication rested. She refused to eject the boyfriend from her home and as a result the little girl was removed. That would have been unchallengeable – and entirely appropriate – had the boyfriend been the abuser. The problem was, the boyfriend was entirely innocent, and it was another man, with the same first name, who was the real abuser. And he did not live in the family home so there was in fact no need to have removed the child: this was only discovered after the child had been kept away from home for over a year. Both mother and daughter sued for negligence in the English courts. They lost. The House of Lords held, founding on *Hill* v *Chief Constable of West Yorkshire* [1989] AC 53 (the Yorkshire Ripper case), that there were policy reasons why local authorities should not be sued for failures in their child protection system. It may have been the reference to *Hill* which caused the subsequent difficulties, but the case has been interpreted as giving local authorities a blanket immunity from civil suit in relation to their child protection failures. The applicants before the European Court argued that such a blanket immunity amounted to an infringement of their Art 6 right to a fair trial (because they were absolutely barred from any trial of their claims) and an infringement of their Art 8 right to family life because the interference had, in the event, proved to be unjustified.

The Art 6 claim concerned the mother and daughter's inability to sue under English law. They founded particularly on the well-known *Osman* decision in which the blanket immunity from liability that English law seemed to grant to the police was held to be contrary to Art 6 (*Osman* v *United Kingdom* [1999] 29 EHRR 245). However, they lost this claim. The European Court held that English law had developed since *Hill* v *Chief Constable* and that there was in fact no immunity but simply an application of the "fair, just and reasonable" test which has now come to dominate the law of tort (and delict). Given the difficulties inherent in any system of child protection, and the subtle and impressionistic judgments that social workers have to make, the English court could not be criticised for striking out the claim for damages as being not fair, just and reasonable. The court, incidentally, pointed out that the applicants had received a fair hearing, all the way to the House of Lords, and they could not, therefore, be said to have been denied access to the courts.

The more interesting claim for family lawyers was that under Art 8. The Court accepted that the system of child protection operating in England was "in accordance with the law" and had a "legitimate aim". As usual, the real question was whether the removal was "necessary in a democratic society". The court commenced its consideration of this question by reminding itself that its "task is not to substitute itself for the domestic authorities in the exercise of their responsibilities ... but rather to review, in the light of the Convention, the decisions taken by those authorities" (para 70). It stated that "the margin of appreciation to be accorded to the competent national authorities will vary in accordance with the nature of the issues and the importance of the interests at stake ... Authorities enjoy a wide margin of appreciation, in particular when assessing the necessity of taking a child into care. However, a strict scrutiny is called for in respect of any further limitations, such as restrictions placed by those authorities on parental rights of access and of any legal safeguards designed to secure an effective protection of the rights of parents and children to respect for their family life. Such further limitations entail the danger that the family relations between the parents and a young child would be effectively curtailed" (para 71). The court reminded itself that a failure to disclose relevant documents to a parent was an interference with the parents' interests as safeguarded by Art 8 (*McMichael* v *UK* (1995) 20 EHRR 205). It then held that since the video recording of the interview in which the child had named her abuser had never been shown to the mother, the opportunity had been lost for the mother to point out that the man named was not her boyfriend but someone else. Thus the local authority had infringed the mother's protections under Art 8 and there was therefore a breach of her human rights. It was not proportionality that was the problem here but the failure to effect the justified interference in a manner that protected the mother's right to be involved in the decision. A procedural flaw infringed Art 8 even while it did not infringe the right to a fair trial in Art 6. There was not a breach just because in the event and with hindsight the removal was unjustified: rather there was a breach because that mistake could have been avoided by involving the mother more.

Z v *United Kingdom*: Arts 6 and 3

The second case, also arising from the same House of Lords decision, is *Z* v *United Kingdom* (2001) 34 EHRR 97 which in many respects was the reverse of the case just considered. Here a local authority ought to have acted but it did not. The case involved four young children who were subject to truly appalling neglect at the hands of their parents. The children were not fed regularly, had never been toilet trained, and were frequently locked in a bedroom for days. They slept in urine-sodden and soiled bedding; their mother left used sanitary towels around the house. The children would appear at school with various unexplained bruises. The local authority knew this, but decided not to place the children on the Child Protection Register: instead, voluntary help would be offered to the family. The parents divorced when the children were between the ages of 10 and 4, and a couple of months later the mother delivered up her children to the social services, saying that she could no longer cope with them. By now all the children were severely emotionally, and physically, damaged and it was immediately plain that the local authority had made a dreadful mistake – one indeed amounting to negligence – in not acting sooner. The children were adopted and fostered and their guardians then sued the local authority. The local authority did not – could not – deny negligence but the House of Lords held, in the same judgment as in the previous case, that they could not be sued. So again the applicants took their case to the European Court.

Their first claim was under Art 6 and the European Court held as they had held in *TP and KM*: there was no immunity, merely a proper application of the "fair, just and reasonable" test. Much more interesting was the children's other claim. They could have claimed under Art 8(2) with its implicit right of protection imposing a duty on the local authority. But instead they went for a quite different article: Art 3 which provides that "no one shall be subjected to torture or to inhuman or degrading treatment or punishment". Now, the applicants may well have chosen to use this article because it might be an easier one than Art 8 to establish since it is both explicit and (unusually for the ECHR) unqualified. The problem was the constitutional distinction between "horizontal" and "vertical" application of the Convention. It was not the state that was torturing these children or subjecting them to inhuman and degrading treatment or punishment, it was other individuals. Could the state be held liable for the actions of one private individual against another? The court held that it could, and in so holding it confirmed that the ECHR can have effect in respect of the relations between citizens as well as relations between the citizen and the state.

The UK Government did not attempt to deny that the sort of treatment meted out to these unfortunate children reached the level of severity prohibited by Art 3. The important point was that the court held that Art 3 did more than impose an obligation on the state to refrain from torturing or treating inhumanly its citizens but in addition imposed a positive obligation on the state to ensure that its citizens were not so treated by other citizens: in this case this amounted to an obligation on the state to act appropriately to ensure that children were not tortured or inhumanly treated by their parents. This is not the first time the court has so held: it did so earlier in *A* v *United Kingdom* [1998] Fam LR 118, one of the corporal punishment cases. The court held in the present case that the local authority was under a statutory duty to protect the children and had a range of powers at its disposal to do so. Its failure to do so (which was negligence though not such as to create civil liability) rendered the state itself in breach of its obligations, created by Art 3, to protect its citizens from torture. So a child's implicit right to protection imposes a duty on the local authority to interfere with the parents' explicit right to family life.

Lessons for the future

The European Court in *Z* v *United Kingdom* did acknowledge (at para 74) that local authorities have a difficult and sensitive decision to make in balancing their duty to protect children with their other duty not to interfere unjustifiably in family life, but they gave no indication as to how to reconcile these conflicting duties. Perhaps this was not the case in which to attempt to do so, given the extreme horror to which the children had been subjected. The balance was utterly obvious. But it does leave the application of the law, if not the law itself, in some doubt. There are some lessons to be learnt, however, from these two cases. First and most obviously, in applying the rules contained in the Children (Scotland) Act 1995 local authorities must be careful to ensure that they involve parents at every stage. This is not only to protect the parents' rights to be involved in the decision-making process, but also in order to allow mistaken judgments to be identified and rectified (as the facts in *TP and KM* v *United Kingdom* show). Secondly, the minimum intervention principle must not be used as an excuse for lack of action when action is palpably necessary: it can only justify no action when such an approach is reasonable. Thirdly and following on from this, the margin of appreciation given to states means that local authorities are afforded an element of discretion within which they can take a range of decisions – and they will be at risk of civil liability only when the decision they take, as in *Z* v *United Kingdom*, was clearly outwith the range of reasonable decisions. Fourthly, it would appear that these judgments might amount to a re- imposition of civil liability even when the law of delict does not do so. Section 8 of the Human Rights Act 1998 provides that a court which finds a public authority in breach of the ECHR may grant such relief or remedy, including damages, as it considers just and appropriate. Whether this will be interpreted identically with the fair, just and reasonable test is a matter yet to be determined.

Update

Two cases from the European Court followed soon after this Commentary originally appeared. In E *v* United Kingdom *(2003) 36 EHRR 31 the*

United Kingdom was found to be in breach of Art 3 for the local authority's failure to refer children to a children's hearing, notwithstanding their awareness of the fact that the mother's cohabitant subjected her and the children to sustained physical and sexual abuse. In DP *and* JC *v* United Kingdom *(2003) 36 EHRR 14, on the other hand, there was held to be no breach where the local authority had similarly failed to act but had had no reason to be aware of the seriousness of the abuse being visited upon the children.*

The House of Lords returned to the question of public authority liability for child protection failings in D *v* East Berkshire Community Health NHS Trust *[2005] 2 AC 373. Parents in three separate cases sued health care authorities and a local authority for the psychiatric harm they suffered as a result of the authorities having acted on unfounded allegations that the parents were abusing their children. The judge found no duty of care and that decision was affirmed by both the Court of Appeal and the House of Lords. It was not fair, just and reasonable to impose a duty of care towards parents which would put child protection professionals in a position where they had conflicting duties – to the parents being investigated for alleged child abuse and to the child who is the subject of investigation. The application of the fair, just and reasonable test did not amount to a blanket immunity from liability, such as the European Court had found to be contrary to Art 6 in* Osman. *Where, however, there was no conflict of interests between parent and child, for example where there is no allegation of abuse against the parent, there is nothing to prevent the local authority owing a duty of care to both parent and child: see* Merthyr Tydfil CBC *v* C *[2010] 1 FLR 1640.*

Commentary No 12: January 2002

"Family Life", Same-Sex Couples and Damages for Non-Patrimonial Loss

In December 2001 the State of Virginia announced that bereaved partners of those who lost their lives in the Pentagon on September 11, 2001, would receive state compensation for their loss, but only if the deceased partner was of the opposite sex to the bereaved partner.

In October 2001 the Scottish Law Commission issued a discussion paper on *Title to Sue for Non-Patrimonial Loss* (DP 116) in which they ask, *inter alia*, whether the definition of "immediate family" to whom damages are currently awarded under the Damages (Scotland) Act 1976 when a person is negligently killed ought to be extended to same-sex couples.

The Ghost of Christmas Yet to Come (Or, It doesn't need to be this way)

Charity v *Scotland* (Application No. 76245728/05)

Before the European Court of Human Rights

STRASBOURG December 24, 2005

The Facts

The applicant, Faith Charity, is a Scottish national, born in 1961. She lives in Glasgow, Scotland. In 1983 she entered into a conjugal relationship with Hope Everlasting who was then 30 years of age and who was the mother of a 10-year-old child. The two women brought the child up to adulthood; they continue to cohabit in an admittedly sexual relationship.

The Damages (Scotland) Act 1976 allows the "immediate family" of a person killed as a result of another's negligence to sue the negligent party for, *inter alia*, non-patrimonial loss.

As originally enacted the only conjugal relationships to come within the definition of "immediate family" were those based upon marriage. In 1981 the definition was extended to include unmarried couples who lived together "as husband and wife". In 2003 the Scottish Law Commission recommended further extending that definition to include unmarried couples of the same sex, but the Scottish Government subsequently announced that it had no intention of introducing legislation to give effect to these recommendations. The 1976 Act, being a statute of the now-abolished Parliament of Westminster, is not open to challenge in the domestic courts; it is accepted between the parties that the words "living together as husband and wife" cannot be interpreted to include a same-sex cohabiting couple. The applicant has therefore applied to this Court alleging a violation of Art 8 of the Convention, taken alone or in conjunction with Art 14. The Scottish Government disputes the allegation, arguing, first, that the applicant is not a "victim" of any alleged infringment since her partner remains alive and well; secondly, that the rule in the 1976 Act does not concern a matter relating to the applicant's private or family life; thirdly that if the applicant is a victim and the 1976 Act does concern private or family life then the interference thereof is necessary in a democratic society; and fourthly, that any difference of treatment between opposite-sex and same-sex couples is not discriminatory for the same reason.

Judgment

I. The Government's Preliminary Plea

The applicants are overlooking, in the Government's submission, the fact that it is not the Court's function to rule *in abstracto* on the compatibility with the Convention of certain legal rules … The Court does not share the Government's view. Article 25 of the Convention entitles individuals to contend that a law violates their right by itself, in the absence of an individual measure of implementation, if they run the risk of being directly affected by it … The Court recalls in this respect that the question of the existence of prejudice is not a matter for Art 25 which, in its use of the word "victim", denotes a person directly affected by the act or omission which is in issue (*Marckx v Belgium* (1979) 2 EHRR 330 at paras 26–27).

II. Applicability of Article 8

A. Family Life

By guaranteeing the right to respect for family life, Art 8 presupposes the existence of a family. The Court concurs … on a crucial point, namely, that Art 8 makes no distinction between the "legitimate" and the "illegitimate" family. Such a distinction would not be consonant with the word "everyone" [as it appears in Art 8]. (*Marckx* at para 31). The Court recalls that the notion of the "family" in this provision is not confined solely to marriage-based relationships and may encompass other de facto "family" ties where the parties are living together outside of marriage (*Keegan* v *Ireland* (1994) 18 EHRR 342 at para. 44).

B. Private Life

There can be no doubt that sexual orientation and activity concern an intimate aspect of private life. (*Laskey, Jaggard and Brown* v *UK* (1997) 24 EHRR 39 at para 36).

The Court does not consider it possible or necessary to attempt an exhaustive definition of the notion of "private life". However … respect for private life must also comprise to a certain degree the right to establish and develop relationships with other human beings (*Niemietz* v *Germany* (1992) 16 EHRR 97 at para 29).

III. Compliance with Article 8

The Court recalls that although the object of Art 8 is essentially that of protecting the individual against arbitrary interference by the public authorities, it does not merely compel the State to abstain from such interference: in addition to this primarily negative undertaking, there may be positive obligations inherent in an effective respect for private or family life. These obligations may involve the adoption of measures designed to secure respect for private life even in the sphere of the relations of individuals between themselves (*X and Y* v *Netherlands* (1985) 8 EHRR 235 at para 23).

An interference with the exercise of an Art 8 right will not be compatible with paragraph 2 unless it is "in accordance with the law", has an aim or aims that is or are legitimate under that paragraph and is "necessary in a democractic society" for the aforementioned aim or aims … It has not been contested that the first of these three conditions was met (*Dudgeon* v *UK* (1981) 4 EHRR 149 at paras 43–44.)

The Government does not deny that the present law favours the traditional family, but they maintain that the law aims at ensuring that family's full development and is thereby founded on objective and reasonable grounds relating to morals and public order. The Court recognises that support and encouragement of the traditional family is in itself legitimate and even praiseworthy. However, in the achievement of this end recourse must not be had to measures whose objects or result is, as in the present case, to prejudice the "illegitimate" family; the members of the "illegitimate" family enjoy the guarantees of Art 8 on an equal footing with the members of the traditional family (*Marckx* at para 40).

The cardinal issue arising under Art 8 in this case is to what extent, if at all, the maintenance in force of the legislation was "necessary in a democratic society" for those aims (*Dudgeon* at para 48).

"Necessary" in this context does not have the flexibility of such expressions as "useful", "reasonable" or "desirable", but implies the existence of a "pressing social need" for the interference in question ... It is for the national authorities to make the initial assessment of the pressing social need in each case; accordingly a margin of appreciation is left to them. However, their decision remains subject to review by the Court (*ibid* at paras 51–52).

Finally, in Art 8 as in several other Articles of the Convention, the notion of "necessity" is linked to that of a "democratic society". According to the Court's case law, a restriction on a Convention right cannot be regarded as "necessary in a democratic society" – two hallmarks of which are tolerance and broadmindedness – unless, amongst other things, it is proportionate to the legitimate aim pursued. (*ibid* at para 53).

The Court recognises that it is for the national authorities to make the initial assessment of necessity, though the final evaluation as to whether the reasons cited for the interference are relevant and sufficient is one for this Court. A margin of appreciation is left open to Contracting States in the context of this assessment, which varies according to the nature of the activities restricted and of the aims pursued by the restrictions. Accordingly, when the relevant restrictions concern a most intimate part of an individual's private life, there must exist particularly serious reasons before such interferences can satisfy the requirements of Art 8(2) of the Convention (*Lustig-Prean* v *UK* (2000) 29 EHRR 548 at paras 81–82).

On the issue of proportionality, the Court considers that such justifications as there are for retaining the law in force unamended are outweighed by the detrimental effects which the very existence of the legislative provisions in question can have on the life of a person of homosexual orientation like the applicant (*Dudgeon* at para 60).

The Court therefore finds that the reasons put forward as justifying the interference found are not sufficient to satisfy the requirements of para (2) of Art 8. There is accordingly a breach of that Article (*Norris* v *Ireland* (1991) 13 EHRR 186 at para 47).

IV Article 14
A distinction based on considerations regarding the applicant's sexual orientation … is not acceptable under the Convention (*da Silva Mouta* v *Portugal* (2001) Fam LR 2 at para 36). [However], the Court considers that, in the circumstances of the present case, the applicants' complaints that they were discriminated against on grounds of sexual orientation … amounts in effect to the same complaint, albeit seen from a different angle, that the Court has already considered in relation to Art 8 of the Convention. Accordingly, the Court considers that the applicants' complaints under Art 14 in conjunction with Art 8 do not give rise to any separate issue (*Lustig-Prean* at paras 108–109).

Update

This little piece of fantasy never came about, of course, for civil partnership was invented and civil partners brought within the terms of the Damages (Scotland) Act 1976 by the Civil Partnership Act 2004. Same-sex cohabitants were subsequently given equality of access to legal rights and liabilities by the Family Law (Scotland) Act 2006. The European Court has subsequently held that such cases can be argued on the basis of "family life" as well as "private life" under Art 8: Schalk and Kopf *v* Austria, *24 June 2010, ECtHR.*

The Scottish Law Commission followed up its Discussion Paper (which motivated this commentary) with a Report on Title to Sue for Non-Patrimonial Loss (Scot Law Com No 187 (2002)) which was partly given effect to, though in places ineptly, by the Family Law (Scotland) Act 2006. *See Commentary No 28 below.*

Commentary No 13: March 2002

Legal Representation at Children's Hearings: The Interim Scheme

On 23 February 2002 the Children's Hearings (Legal Representation) (Scotland) Rules 2001 (SSI 2001/478) came into effect. These Rules were passed as a result of the decision of the Inner House in *S* v *Miller* 2001 SLT 531 and 1304 in which the court held that certain aspects of the children's hearing system in Scotland were incompatible with Art 6 of the ECHR (right to a fair trial). In particular the unavailability of paid legal representation of children in any circumstances was held incompatible, as would have been a total ban on providing papers to children. The latter issue was dealt with by SCRA introducing a policy whereby all children over the age of 12 years will automatically receive the same papers as every other active participant (12 is the age at which, remember, children are presumed to be able to take part in hearings and to hold and express views: Children (Scotland) Act 1995, s 16(2)). In addition, children younger than 12 will receive reports if so recommended by report providers. It is expected that this policy will be given full effect (after assessment of a pilot scheme) later in 2002.

Representation for limited purposes

In relation to legal representation, it is important to remember that the Court of Session did not require that this be made available to all children at every hearing. Rather, they identified two circumstances in which the Art 6 right to a fair trial requires that children who appear before a hearing should have access to legal representation, paid for by the state: (i) when there is a possibility that the outcome of the hearing will be to deprive the child of the right to liberty, and (ii) when the child is not otherwise able, due to the complexity of the issues involved, effectively to participate at the hearing. Both these circumstances have now been given statutory effect in the scheme of the new Rules, and both need to be interpreted in the light of the decision in *S* v *Miller* and the flaws identified by the court there. So while it might be pointed out that, technically speaking, deprivation of liberty is a possibility in nearly every case (for the issue of secure accommodation – the only form of deprivation of liberty relevant – can arise unexpectedly during the course of virtually any hearing), the Rules, in order to address the real concerns of the court, need to be interpreted restrictively, covering only those hearings in which secure accommodation is under active consideration. For panel members this is likely to be the less troublesome circumstance (though if the issue does arise unexpectedly there is a fairly serious practical difficulty of adjourning or continuing the hearing until such time as a legal representative can attend).

Effective participation

Legal representation in order to allow the child's effective participation in the hearing is similarly to be interpreted with the history and purpose of the Rules firmly in mind. The Rules themselves do not specify the nature or form of the child's participation and it is to be remembered that there already exist provisions to allow the child to participate fully. First, it is expected that panel members themselves will do their utmost to afford the child a realistic opportunity to take part in the discussion at the hearing. Secondly, the child has for long been able to bring a "representative" to the hearing "for the purpose of assisting the child ... at the hearing" (Children's Hearings (Scotland) Rules 1996, r 11(1)). And thirdly, a safeguarder may be appointed for the purpose of safeguarding the child's interests (1995 Act, s 41(1)). The new Rules would achieve nothing if the legal representative's role were limited to assisting the child or safeguarding the child's interests or even ensuring that the child gets an opportunity to talk, and it must therefore follow that the role of the legal representative – and the criterion for his or her appointment – is the need to assist the child in any legal discussion at the hearing or safeguarding the child's legal interests. In other words, appointments are appropriate only if the hearing raises a matter of legal complexity. The expectation is that no more than a small number of hearings will raise issues of legal complexity, but if, as would be appropriate, "complexity" were atuned to a child's rather than a lawyer's assessment of the matter, then that expectation may well turn out to be illusory. For it seems likely that, from the child's point of view, there is a whole host of circumstances that are legally complex but which are mundane from the point of view of the adult participants. The grounds of referral themselves, for example, nearly always raise legal issues, particularly when they are offence based and defences may not be apparent or "art and part" guilt may not be understood or when they concern those obscurely worded grounds referring to other legislation (and where the Rehabilitation of Offenders Act 1974, an Act obscure to many lawyers as well as children, is always relevant). In addition, adoption is always a complex legal issue, as is, to only a slightly lesser extent, contact and residence – for these issues involve the notion of family and private life and its protection under the ECHR, requiring thought to be given to human rights concepts such as proportionality and the state's margin of appreciation. Similarly, whether a warrant is justified and, if so, under which provision of the 1995 Act, is always complexedly legal and few panel members, far less children, are aware of all the variations between the different and overlapping warrants. All these matters are bread and butter issues at children's hearings. It is right and proper that a child should be assisted in participating in these discussions with significant legal consequences, and it is, surely, their right to have someone able to identify, on their behalf, when such an issue might arise (if for no other reason than that lay panel members may not themselves be able to do so).

Who are legal representatives?

The appointment must be made from one of the lists of either safeguarders, curators *ad litem* or reporting officers (which lists have – finally – been established by Regulations: see the Panels of Persons to Safeguard Interests of Children (Scotland) Regulations 2001, and the Curators Ad Litem and Reporting Officers (Panels) (Scotland) Regulations 2001, SSI 2001, 476 and 477). It is important to remember that the appointment is made by the hearing rather than by the child and so there can be no implication from the purpose of the appointment (to ensure effective participation) that the child has the capacity to instruct a solicitor on his or her own behalf. It is factual inability to participate, due to the complexity of the issues involved, rather than legal capacity to instruct a solicitor (as determined, by a different test, under the Age of Legal Capacity (Scotland) Act 1991) that justifies the appointment. It may indeed follow from this that the younger the child is, the more necessary an appointment might become. Rights do not arise only on the achievement of capacity to understand them, and it is to protect the child's rights to participate that the whole scheme was set up.

Gaps in the scheme

A number of matters are left unresolved or, at best, to implication. It is not specified how long the appointment lasts though it may be presumed that it lasts until a dispositive decision has been made and the time for appeal has passed. It is unclear whether the legal representative (paid for under the new Rules) can appeal on behalf of the child or take a proof hearing before a sheriff: he or she may have to appoint another (paid for, this time, out of the legal aid fund) to do so. It would seem that there would be nothing to prevent the child appointing as his or her legally aided solicitor the person who previously acted as the hearing-appointed legal representative to take a proof or appeal. It is also unclear whether the decision to appoint or not appoint is itself appealable. Section 51 of the 1995 Act appears to permit an appeal against "any decision" of the hearing, though that, presumably, would apply only when there is an express and recorded decision, after discussion, not to make the appointment rather than when the issue is simply not raised. But if the issue is not raised the child might appeal against the dispositive decision on the ground that the failure of the hearing to recognise that the issue had to be addressed had the effect of depriving the child of necessary legal advice. Entirely different considerations arise if the child is unwilling to accept an appointment: it may be that the imposed appointment is unappealable on the basis that the child cannot be prejudiced thereby. It would be sensible, in my view, for hearings to take the view that whenever a child considers he or she needs legal representation then legal representation is needed, and to be reticent in the extreme about imposing legal representation when it is not wanted.

Left for another day entirely is the issue of the parents' right to legal representation (remembering that their civil rights are as much at issue at a hearing as the child's). This is a result of legislation reflecting court decisions but refusing to go any further, however logical it would be to go further. The same phenomenon was seen after *McMichael* v *United Kingdom* (1995) 20 EHRR 205 when the UK was held by the Strasbourg court to be in breach of Art 6 in not permitting parents to have access to the papers available to panel members before hearings. Legislation followed shortly thereafter but, since the actual decision in *McMichael* concerned only parents, the right to receive papers was not extended to children (leading to the subsequent successful challenge on the matter by the child in *S* v *Miller*). The failure to extend legal representation in the present Rules to parents makes a future claim by parents, and future amendments to the legislative scheme, inevitable (as well as leaving us presently in the absurd situation whereby children can get paid legal representation but not always access to papers while parents will always have access to papers but not legal representation).

The new Rules set out an interim scheme which, it is to be hoped, does not turn into a long-term scheme. It is designed to meet the concerns of the Court of Session and nothing more. But the Scottish Executive do realise that a more principalled approach is necessary and they are currently consulting on a variety of suggested ways forward such as hearings rights officers or automatic legal aid for specialised child lawyers. Doubtless cost will enter into the calculation and in order to ensure that as much money as possible is made available to whatever new scheme replaces the interim scheme described here, it is important that hearings take a very wide view of what constitutes a complex legal issue justifying the appointment of a legal representative, and appoint as many as they possibly can.

Update

In the event, it took 7 years for a challenge by parents to be made, alleging an infringement of their Art 6 rights by the failure to afford them paid legal representation at hearings. The challenge was, inevitably, successful: K *v* Authority Reporter *2009 SLT 1019, where the Inner House described it as an "inbuilt systemic flaw" in the children's hearing process that paid legal representation was not available to parents. The Scottish Government knew it would lose this case, for 4 months previously it had passed the Children's Hearings (Legal Representation) (Scotland) Amendment Rules 2009 which amended the 2002 Rules so that parents ("relevant persons") were included. This remained the "interim scheme" until the coming into force of the Children's Hearings (Scotland) Act 2011 which included amendments to the Legal Aid (Scotland) Act 1986 to ensure that legal representation is accessible by parents and children, and in specified circumstances will be paid for by the state.*

Commentary No 14: July 2002

Freeing Orders and Fathers who are not Parents

The unmarried father always has been more trouble than he is worth and he really ought to be abolished as soon as possible. This was illustrated yet again in three recent adoption cases. It will be recalled that under the Adoption (Scotland) Act 1978, s 65(1), "parent" is defined to mean the mother or the father who has parental responsibilities and parental rights; and that under the Children (Scotland) Act 1995 parental responsibilities and parental rights are conferred on all mothers but only those fathers who are or have been married to the mother, who have a court order conferring such responsibilities and rights on them, or who have persuaded the mother to sign a s 4 agreement to share such responsibilities and rights. The result is that the father who has neither married the mother nor obtained a court order or a s 4 agreement is not a parent and has no right to be heard in the adoption process. But an awkward situation can arise if such a father attempts to become a parent by any of these means during the adoption process.

A likely lad

In *G* v *City of Edinburgh Council* 2002 SLT 828 a local authority petitioned the court for a freeing order in relation to a child whose parents were unmarried but whose father had raised proceedings seeking to have parental responsibilities and parental rights conferred upon him. In a freeing case that brought into play the clumsy little provision contained in s 18(7) of the 1978 Act, under which a court must satisfy itself, before making a freeing order, that any person claiming to be the father has no intention of applying for parental responsibilities and parental rights, or if he does have such an intention that it is likely he would be refused, and that he has no intention of entering into a s 4 agreement with the mother, or, if he does have such an intention, that such an agreement is unlikely to be made. This is designed to ensure that if an unmarried father is "likely" to become a parent and thereby obtain parental responsibilities and parental rights before the making of the adoption order then the right to be heard that he would thereby acquire is not prematurely prejudiced. In the present case the sheriff held that the unmarried father was unlikely to obtain responsibilities and rights and he made the freeing order. The father then appealed the decision that he was not likely to obtain responsibilities and rights but Sheriff Principal Nicholson held (2002 SLT (Sh Ct) 58) that the appeal was incompetent on the basis of the father's lack of title. Basically, the sheriff principal was holding that the unmarried father only had title (both to be heard at first instance and to take an appeal) if the court held it "likely" that he would obtain responsibilities and rights. This would have the effect of rendering a decision that a man is "unlikely" unappealable, which is an inherently suspicious outcome. The Court of Session overruled the sheriff principal, holding that if a father has locus to be heard as to whether he is "likely", then he has locus to appeal a decision that he is "unlikely".

Sheriff Principal Nicholson also and interestingly speculated what would happen if the court held that it was in fact "likely" that the father would obtain responsibilities and rights. The Act does not actually tell us – it merely requires that the court be satisfied that the father is not likely to obtain responsibilities and rights. The sheriff principal concluded that the appropriate course would be to adjourn the freeing proceedings to await the father's obtaining of responsibilities and rights; but at least as plausible is the conclusion that the freeing order should at that point simply be refused on the ground that the statutory conditions for its granting have not been met. The Inner House did not discuss the point, other than accepting (para 9) that "there is some obscurity" in the statutory provisions.

A respectable lad

In *North Lanarkshire Council* v *AW* (April 4, 2002, Sheriff I C Simpson) the father proposed to become a parent by marrying the mother before the freeing order was made. Sheriff Simpson referred to Sheriff Principal Nicholson's views in *G* v *City of Edinburgh* but doubted whether it would be practicable to adjourn proceedings, particularly if the parties repeatedly "threatened to marry" (in the sheriff's wonderfully revealing words) without ever actually going through with the threat. The sheriff held that in the circumstances before him he ought to make a decision as to whether he would grant the father parental responsibilities and parental rights had a s 11 order been sought, and only adjourn the hearing on the freeing petition if he considered it likely that he would. In other words, he imported the philosophy of s 18(7) concerning a father attempting to become a parent to the one situation to which that provision does not apply. Since he held that it would be "unlikely", the sheriff found that the father had no locus in the case, notwithstanding the "threat" to marry the mother.

An agreeable lad

In *West Lothian Council* v *M* 2002 SLT 1155, another freeing case, the father became a parent a year after the termination of contact between the children and their parents, this time by entering into a s 4 agreement. It is an unattractive feature of s 4 agreements (observed previously in England) that a disturbingly high percentage of them concern not the nice, stable cohabitants for whom they were designed but volatile and erratic parents who have had their children removed into local authority care and who can cause extra difficulties by requiring, through the agreement, the local authority to deal with two awkward people instead of one. In the present case, having become a parent as well as a father, the father's consent to the freeing order needed to be dispensed with. The sheriff held that his consent could be dispensed with both because it was being unreasonably withheld and also because of his failure to fulfil parental responsibilities. On the former ground the Inner House agreed, but on the latter the sheriff was overruled. The father did not have parental responsibilities until he became a parent and he did not become a parent until after his children had been removed from his care and his contact with them had been terminated. He could not, therefore, be accused of failing to fulfil those responsibilities that the law did not require of him.

Another issue that arose in this case was whether the freeing process was inconsistent with the ECHR. (In fact, the issue was not directly relevant since the original order had been made 6 months before the Human Rights Act 1998 came into force). The perceived problem was that, unlike with an adoption order, there is no statutory mechanism by which a freeing order can be made subject to any conditions, such as contact. The parents argued that their inability to seek to preserve their contact with their children through a condition attached to a freeing order was a breach of their right to respect for family life. Lord Reed expressed the view that if the inability to make a freeing order without a condition of contact were indeed incompatible with the ECHR (which he did not hold) then the freeing order 'should not be made' (para 11). This is careful language. As the issue was not live in the present case Lord Reed made no definitive decision, but it may well be that not only should the court not make the order but it cannot do so. If a freeing order without conditions is contrary to the ECHR then the court, being a public authority and so barred from acting contrary to the ECHR, is barred from making the order, for there is no countervailing statutory requirement that the order be made. Whether a declaration of incompatibility is in addition necessary may be open to doubt – there is no requirement that the freeing process be pursued by the local authority (another public authority, be it remembered) and little is lost by avoiding it completely. If a local authority wants to acquire parental responsibilities and parental rights before the full adoption order is made, they have the choice of doing so by means of either a freeing order under s 18 of the 1978 Act or a parental responsibilities order under s 86 of the 1995 Act. The latter does not only permit conditions of contact to be attached but requires contact to be allowed (subject to the sheriff's power to make such order in relation to contact as he considers appropriate: s 88(3)).

Whether courts will simply not apply provisions considered contrary to the ECHR and thereby avoid the need for declarations of incompatibility remains to be seen; whether the legislature finally abolishes the unmarried father depends upon political will to stand up to those who consider his continued existence an essential bulwark in the law's efforts to bolster marriage.

Update

The unmarried father's position was, of course, substantially improved by the Family Law (Scotland) Act 2006, under which such a father obtains parental responsibilities and parental rights on being registered (on or after 4 May 2006) as the father of the child. The Adoption (Scotland) Act 1978 was replaced by the Adoption and Children (Scotland) Act 2007, which abolished the concept of "freeing for adoption" as well as parental responsibilities orders, with the result that most of the issues discussed in the above cases will no longer arise. Permanence orders, which in some respects are the successors to freeing orders (and in others the successors to parental responsibilities orders), do not affect parental status and are not a necessary precursor to adoption.

Commentary No 15: October 2002

Paternity and Reproductive Technology

It never ceases to surprise (though by now it should) that, however carefully statute tries to provide for every conceivable scenario, unforeseen problems will eventually emerge which require judicial input to resolve. This is shown yet again with the rules for imposing paternity on men whose partners become pregnant through artificial reproductive technology. Parliament laid down rules which seemed clear and were intended to be comprehensive, in ss 27–29 of the Human Fertilisation and Embryology Act 1990. With hindsight, these rules do contain a number of gaps, which can only be filled by such common law rules as exist; and their application might not be as clear as was originally supposed. Though neither has yet led to judicial determination, the press became terribly excited in the summer of 2002 about two quite different cases which expose some of the gaps and lack of clarity. Though both are from England they do provide interesting hypotheticals for Scots law also.

The wrong child

In the first case [now reported as *Leeds Teaching Hospitals NHS Trust* v *A* [2003] 1 FLR 1091], a child born after *in vitro* fertilisation was of a different colour to its parents, which was fairly conclusive evidence that in the process the husband's sperm had not been used as had been planned. Rather, due to error, someone else's sperm had been used, who was of different racial origin. No-one knows how often such mistakes occur but it is inconceivable that this was the first such in this country: it would not have come to light had not the child's skin colour made the mistake immediately obvious. One of the questions (and the only one I am going to consider here) is: who are the child's parents? There is no difficulty with the child's mother (notwithstanding the press's palpable relief – or was it disappointment? – when DNA analysis showed that the woman who gave birth was what they called the "real" mother). Section 27 of the 1990 Act defines "mother" in gestational and not genetic terms and s 29(1) provides that where a person is defined as "mother" by s 27 "that person is to be treated in law as the mother ... of the child for all purposes". So, a white woman who gives birth to a black baby is that child's mother, for all purposes of law. Her genetic connection or otherwise to the child is not relevant to the question of legal maternity. And nor, it should be noted, is her consent to her impregnation (just as a rape victim who conceives is the mother if she continues with the pregnancy).

Becoming a father

The issue of the husband's paternity is, of course, much more difficulty. Had the husband's own sperm been used, the 1990 Act would not be relevant (for the paternity provisions in ss 28 and 29 apply only when a stranger's sperm is used) and he would be presumed father (in Scotland) by the normal *pater est quem nuptiae demonstrant* rule in s 5(1)(a) of the Law Reform (Parent and Child) (Scotland) Act 1986. But palpably his sperm was not used (though, somewhat strangely perhaps, he would have the benefit of the 1986 presumption until a court decree rebuts it) and so the 1990 Act is potentially applicable. Section 28(2) provides that if at the time of the placing in her of an embryo or of sperm and eggs or of her artificial insemination, the woman who becomes pregnant was married, the other party to the marriage (ie her husband) is the father of the child born through this procedure. And again, s 29(1) provides that where a person is defined as "father" by s 28 "that person is to be treated in law as the ... father of the child for all purposes". However, this rule suffers an exception (not found in the maternity provision): the rule applies "unless it is shown that [the husband] did not consent to the placing in [his wife] of the embryo or the sperm and eggs or to her insemination (as the case may be)". So the husband in our case can escape paternity only by showing that he did not consent, but a difficult question is this: what exactly is it that the statute requires him not to have consented to? A husband seeking to avoid paternity might argue that he did not give consent to the events which took place: he consented to the implantation of an embryo created with his sperm but not to the implantation of an embryo not so created. However, this is a difficult argument to sustain in the light of the words of the Act, which requires consent to the treatment and not the outcome. All that is required is that the husband consent to "the placing in [his wife] of the embyro or the sperm and eggs or to her insemination (as the case may be)". What is "the" embryo? Is it the embryo that was in fact implanted, or the hypothetical embryo he thought was being implanted? The use of the definite article "the" refers us back to the embryo mentioned earlier in the section, being the one which was actually implanted in the married woman, with the result that if the husband consented to that embryo being implanted then he is the father of the subsequent child notwithstanding that he was mistaken as to its characteristics.

A more plausible argument for the husband who wishes to escape paternity in these circumstances is for him to argue that any purported consent is vitiated by extraneous factors. If a man is deliberately lied to as to the genetic provinence of the embryo, in order to obtain his consent, the matter seems clear: a fraud is being perpetrated against him which will have economic consequences for the man (in terms at the very least of an alimentary or child support obligation). And such a fraud would almost certainly vitiate his consent (thereby preventing paternity being imposed upon him). But would negligence act so as to vitiate consent? Almost certainly it would not. An analogy is provided by the law of informed consent to medical treatment. All medical treatment without consent is assault. Consent given on the basis of negligently provided flawed or incomplete information (for example in relation to risks and possible outcomes) is valid consent sufficient to provide a defence to a charge of assault, though the failure to provide proper information might in itself lead to an action for negligence to recover any loss suffered thereby. But s 28 is not about loss but paternity and paternity is determined by the validity of consent and not any flaw in the information upon which it is based. So the consent is not compromised by a negligent failure to provide full information, but it may be by a fraudulent failure. On the assumption that the error in the present case was a genuine mistake (whether negligence or not) the husband's consent is still valid consent and he therefore remains the father.

The only alternative would be for the husband to show that his consent was conditional, that is to say that he was consenting to the placing in his wife of sperm or an embryo only if it was his sperm or the embryo was created with his sperm. But such a condition would have to be imposed very explicitly by the husband. An expectation and an unspoken understanding is not, it is submitted, such conditional consent. So in the normal case, a husband will be the father unless he can show that he expressly informed the treatment provider that he would positively and unequivocally withhold consent if the outcome was his wife becoming pregnant with a child that was not genetically his. This would be a heavy onus, unlikely to be discharged except in the clearest of circumstances.

There are good policy reasons for limiting a husband's ability to challenge the validity of consent actually given. For one thing, there is a risk that challenges might be made for contemptible reasons, such as discontent at the outcome (the child is disabled, or of a different colour from what was wanted and expected). And for another thing unless challenges to consent are kept within the very narrowest possible bounds, the law would deal with unmarried couples differently from married couples. The rules imposing paternity on an unmarried male partner are very different: under s 28(3) paternity is imposed not by the man giving consent but by the service-provider providing treatment to a couple "together". Had the white couple been unmarried there would be no doubt that the man could not escape paternity because the treatment was most certainly provided to the couple "together". Married men, in principle, should not be able to escape paternity easier than unmarried men.

A final point to note in this context is that a child's parentage is not affected by considerations of welfare: it is a matter of genetic fact or of legal definition. Whether the child will face difficulty as a result of its being brought up by parents of a different race is irrelevant to who, in law, the parents are.

Whose sperm is it anyway?

The second case which caught the attention of the press [now reported as *Evans* v *Amicus Health Care Ltd* [2005] Fam 1] was that of a couple who had created embryos which were frozen for later use and who then separated. The woman wanted to use these embryos so that she could become pregnant; the man wanted the embryos destroyed. Parenthood is (relatively) straightforward (on the assumption that the woman attempts to act without a new partner). If the woman obtains the embryos and eventually gives birth, she is clearly the mother. As for the man, the 1990 Act would be inapplicable since it applies only when the embryo is created with sperm that did not come from the woman's partner, but the common law rule of genetic fatherhood imposes paternity on him in any case, and it does so whether or not he consents (and whether or not this consent can be said to be vitiated by fraud). There are only two ways in which a child can be born without any legal father: (i) where donor sperm is used, with consent of the donor and in the context of licenced treatment, to bring about a pregnancy (1990 Act, s 28(6)(a)) and (ii) if sperm, or any embryo created with his sperm, is used after the death of the sperm provider (1990 Act, s 28(6)(b)). Neither scenario operates here. So we must fall back on the common law: if the woman becomes pregnant and we know who the genetic father is, it is that man who is the legal father, notwithstanding that he does not consent to the use of the embryo in this way.

So the question of legal significance is not parenthood but whether the man can prevent the woman using the embryo, or to put the same question another way whether the woman can use the embryo without the consent of the man. This is a question that has arisen abroad (see the cases discussed in Wilkinson and Norrie, *Parent and Child* (2nd edn, 1999) at 41–42), though never in this country. But the legislation is clear: Sch 3, para 6(3) of the Human Fertilisation and Embryology Act 1990 provides that "an embryo the creation of which was brought about in vitro must not be used for any purpose unless there is an effective consent by each person whose gametes were used to bring about the creation of the embryo to the use for that purpose of the embryo and the embryo is used in accordance with those consents".

Of course in *R* v *HFEA, ex parte Blood* [1997] 2 All ER 687 Mrs Blood was able to get around the consent provisions by arguing on the basis of European law that free movement of services required that she be allowed to export her dead husband's sperm to a country that did not require his consent. But there are at least three vital differences between that case and the present: (i) Mrs Blood sought to export sperm while the present case concerns embryos and it is not apparent that the provision of an embryo can be regarded as a service in the way the provision of sperm was; (ii) Mrs Blood's problem was mere lack of consent (because her husband, from whom the sperm had been taken – non-consensually on his death bed, – was dead) while in the present case there is positively withheld consent; (iii) Mrs Blood's subsequently born child had no legal father against whom any claim flowing from paternity could ever be made while in the present case there would be a father with a very much more direct interest in opposing the treatment than the HFEA had in Mrs Blood's case. It is to be hoped that the courts are not once more duped by the sympathy they might feel towards a childless woman into further subverting the careful balance of interests contained in the Human Fertilisation and Embryology Act 1990.

Update

The courts were not so duped. The Court of Appeal in Evans *held that the consent provisions depended on ongoing consent and that either party was free to withdraw their consent at any time before implantation; the*

European Court of Human Rights subsequently ((2008) 46 EHRR 34) held that the woman's right to found a family was no stronger than the man's right not to found a family. Ms Evans could still become pregnant, with donor eggs, and she is in no worse position than any other single woman wanting to become pregnant: she needs to find a man. It is an odd (and irredeemably masculine) conception of "real" motherhood to see it in terms of genetics.

The 1990 Act was replaced by the Human Fertilisation and Embryology Act 2008 (see Commentary No 39) and many, but not all, of the rules discussed above were amended. Neither of the cases discussed here would, however, have been decided any differently had they arisen subsequent to the commencement of the 2008 Act. The main aim of the parentage provisions in the 2008 Act was to avoid the extensive litigation that the 1990 Act had led to. Section 27 of the 1990 Act (definition of mother) is replicated without change in s 33 of the 2008 Act. Section 28(2) of the 1990 Act (fatherhood imposed on husbands) is replicated in s 35 of the 2008 Act, and no change to the position that led to the result in Leeds Teaching Hospitals NHS Trust *has been effected. It might be noted, however, that the court did not follow the argument in this commentary, and held instead that the husband was not the father since he had not consented to his wife being impregnated with another man's sperm. The rules in s 28(3) of the 1990 Act, imposing paternity of the unmarried partner of the mother, are now contained in ss 36–38 of the 2008 Act, though the test for parenthood changes from "treatment together" to "consent to being a parent". The provisions are extended to include same-sex couples. Consent to storing gametes or embryos remains governed by the 1990 Act and that consent continues to be an on-going concept that can be withdrawn by either party at any time.*

Commentary No 16: January 2003

Extensive New Rights for Same-Sex Couples

The Scottish Law Commission, in their *Report on Title to Sue for Non-Patrimonial Loss* (Scot Law Com No 187) recommended that same-sex couples should have the same right to claim damages under the Damages (Scotland) Act 1976 as opposite-sex cohabitants. It seems that this has been the law all along, only no-one realised. A decision of the English Court of Appeal handed down on 5 November 2002 shows this to be the case at least in England. In *Mendoza* v *Ghaidan* [2002] EWCA Civ 1533 the phrase "living together as husband and wife" was held to include same-sex couples, this being the only interpretation of the phrase which avoided discrimination outlawed by the European Convention on Human Rights and, therefore, avoided being unlawful under the Human Rights Act 1998. The phrase "living together as husband and wife" is the long-standing statutory formulation for describing unmarried couples when they are to be granted the same or similar rights (and obligations) as married couples under various statutes. Before *Mendoza* the clear understanding was that this phrase limited the rights (and obligations) contained in such statutes to opposite-sex unmarried couples because the normal everyday meaning of the phrase indicated a relationship between a male and a female. That understanding received the imprimatur of a unanimous House of Lords in *Fitzpatrick* v *Sterling Housing Association* [1999] 4 All ER 707, where it was held that a same-sex couple could be a "family" but could not be said to be "living together as husband and wife". Symbolically important in terms of its recognition of the legitimacy of same-sex relationships, the practical effect of that decision was minimal since very few statutes gave rights to (or imposed obligations on) "families" (see Norrie, (2000) 4 Edin LR 256). Lord Slynn had suggested that the exclusion of same-sex couples from the phrase "living together as husband and wife" might well require reconsideration once the Human Rights Act 1998 came into force: and so it has come about.

Living together as husband and wife

The actual issue in *Mendoza* was almost the same as in *Fitzpatrick*. The Rent Act 1977 confers the right to succeed to a "statutory tenancy" on the tenant's partner who was living with the tenant at the time of his or her death "as his or her wife or husband", and a right to succeed to the rather less well protected "assured tenancy" on the tenant's partner who was a member of the tenant's family. Mr Fitzpatrick succeeded to an assured tenancy as a result of the House of Lords decision, but he was denied the extra protections of a statutory tenancy. Mr Mendoza also succeeded to an assured tenancy (because he was a member of his deceased same-sex partner's family) but he wanted the extra protection of a statutory tenancy (which he would only get if he had been "living with the original tenant as his or her wife or husband"). He asked the Court of Appeal to depart from a decision of a unanimous House of Lords. They had no hesitation in doing so, for the Human Rights Act 1998 had changed everything.

Mr Mendoza claimed discrimination under Art 14 of the ECHR. Now, to activate article 14 the claim had to come within the ambit of one of the substantive articles, and Mr Mendoza (unsurprisingly) founded upon Art 8. He argued that the Rent Act 1977 impinged on his interest in his home, since he would after the death of his partner have a less secure position in the tenancy than he would have had if the partnership had been a heterosexual one. The court held that the case clearly came within the ambit of Art 8, "home" being more than bricks and mortar but including the rights and security of tenure attaching to these corporeal items. The protection of "home" would be greater for heterosexual than for homosexual couples if the phrase "living together as husband and wife" were limited to the former, and it followed that there would be an infringement of the Convention unless the distinction had an objective and reasonable justification. The landlord put forward two arguments. First, that the state had a margin of appreciation in striking the appropriate balance between the legitimate interests of landlords and of tenants. The court held that they were not concerned with the state's margin of appreciation but with whether the state could justify discrimination. The second argument of the landlord was that the Rent Act gave effect to the policy of the Convention, which was the protection of the family; "family", it was argued, was limited in Convention terms to heterosexual units. This argument could not, of course, survive *Fitzpatrick* but in any case it was not logical. The court could not see how an aim to "promote the family" could be said to be achieved by the difference in treatment between same-sex and opposite-sex couples, for "it has not been suggested that heterosexual couples, whether married or unmarried, are more likely to live together or to do so for longer *because* [the crucial word] homosexual couples are denied the equivalent right of succession under the Rent Act" (at para 42). So even if the Convention is about strengthening (heterosexual) families, it does nothing to further that aim for the law to disadvantage same-sex couples.

This being so, the court had to, if it could, interpret the phrase at issue in such a way as did not make the unjustified (and therefore illegitimate) distinction between same-sex and opposite-sex couples. "That duty", said Lord Justice Buxton, "can be properly discharged by reading the words 'as his or her wife or husband' to mean 'as *if they were* his or her wife or husband' ... It is quite true ... that the words 'husband and wife' are in their natural meaning gender-specific. They are also, however, in their natural meaning limited to persons who are party to a lawful marriage ... Parliament having swallowed the camel of including unmarried partners within the protection given to married couples, it is not for this court to strain at the gnat of including such partners who are of the same sex as each other" (para 35).

Applying the Convention

This case is notable for the readiness with which the judges accepted that "sexual orientation is now clearly recognised as an impermissible ground of discrimination" (para 32), and also for the ease with which the attempted justification for the discrimination was dismissed. Its practical effect is likely to be far greater than *Fitzpatrick* since cohabitants' rights are more extensive than the "family" rights there at issue. But the case does not mean that same-sex couples will be able to access all the statutory rights and duties presently conferred on opposite-sex cohabitants. There are four questions that must be asked:

(i) Is a Convention right at issue?
(ii) Is the treatment of same-sex couples different from opposite-sex couples in relation to that right?
(iii) Is such differential treatment justified?
(iv) Can the court reinterpret the statute to remove the discrimination?

The answers the court in *Mendoza* gave to (ii) and (iii) (yes there is discrimination and no it is not justified) are unavoidable in all statutes conferring rights on opposite-sex couples but withholding them from same-sex couples; but question (i) depends upon the rule of law contained in the statute and question (iv) depends upon the precise terms in which the couple are described. A Convention right is clearly at issue when dealing with security of tenure of one's home, and so statutes like the Rent (Scotland) Act 1984 and the Matrimonial Homes (Family Protection) (Scotland) Act 1981 would satisfy this first hurdle. The Damages (Scotland) Act 1976 does so less obviously since the Convention right at stake is likely to be "family life" which might be argued to have come to an end on the death of the partner that led to the claim under the 1976 Act in the first place. But since damages are awarded under that Act to reflect the interference in family life that the death causes it is likely that that statute will be held to come within the ambit of Art 8 as well.

Applying the Human Rights Act 1998

The issue of reinterpretation is more problematic. There would be little difficulty with statutes worded like the Damages (Scotland) Act 1976, which talks of "any person … living with the deceased as husband and wife". The *Mendoza* approach allows that phrase to include same-sex couples. But the Matrimonial Homes (Family Protection) (Scotland) Act 1981 grants rights "if a man and a woman are living together as if they were man and wife". Can that phrase be rationally interpreted under s 3 of the Human Rights Act 1998 to mean "if a man and a woman *and his or her partner* are living together as if they were man and wife"? It is necessary to add the italicised words to prevent discrimination but it would be illegitimate to do so if the addition *changed* the meaning of the statute, and the court's only option (for a Westminster statute like the 1981 Act) would be to issue a declaration of incompatibility or (for a Holyrood statute) to strike the provision down. But a declaration of incompatibility "is a measure of last resort. It must be avoided unless it is plainly impossible to do so" (per Lord Steyn, *R* v *A (No 2)* [2001] 2 WLR 1546 at 1563). In accordance with s 3 of the 1998 Act, "it will sometimes be necessary to adopt an interpretation which linguistically may appear strained. The techniques to be used will not only involve the reading down of express language in a statute *but also the implication of provisions*" (*ibid*, emphasis added). Given the "family protection" policy underlying the 1981 Act, together with the House of Lords-endorsed recognition of same-sex families and their strong encouragement to avoid interpretations which risk incompatibility, the only coherent approach is to accept the legitimacy of adding the words suggested above. If so, then the full panoply of cohabitants' occupancy rights, exclusion orders and matrimonial interdicts under the 1981 Act can now be accessed by same-sex couples.

On the other hand, there are some statutes which are too unambiguously gender-specific to make reinterpretation possible. An example is the Social Security Contributions and Benefits Act 1992 which defines an unmarried couple as "a man and a woman who are not married to each other but are living together as husband and wife" (s 137). To bring same-sex couples within that phrase would be to change its meaning rather than to reinterpret it.

So, while many statutory consequences of living together in a sexual relationship must now be extended to same-sex couples, there is not yet any general rule that they are to be given all the rights and obligations of unmarried opposite-sex cohabitants. It still depends on the terms of each statute. But *Mendoza* requires courts to do their very best to remove discrimination which they accepted absolutely to be not justified. Let us hope that our two parliaments accept this as clearly.

Update

Mendoza, *of course, went to the House of Lords which affirmed the decision of the Court of Appeal discussed here: [2004] 2 AC 557. The crucial issue before the House of Lords, and the reason that the case will remain of great import even although statutory development has now minimised the discrimination between same-sex and opposite-sex couples, was the extent to which the court can change the meaning of a statutory provision in order to fulfil the interpretative requirements of s 3 of the Human Rights Act 1998. The House of Lords held that courts can and indeed must change the meaning of words and indeed go against the clear intention of Parliament, if this is necessary to ensure ECHR compliance. What they cannot go is to give to the words a meaning that they will not bear: if doing so is the only way of ensuring ECHR compliance then the correct approach is to make a declaration of incompatibility, as the House of Lords did in* Bellinger *v* Bellinger *[2003] UKHL 21 (see Commentary No 22 below).*

Commentary No 17: April 2003

Wrongful Adoption

Parenthood is always a risk, which those seeking to become parents have no choice but to accept. Things can go wrong, either in terms of the quality of the child or the quality of the relationship thereby created. You cannot return the child as damaged goods nor seek a replacement, and you can only claim damages for your loss if there is someone to blame (such as for example the obstetrician who negligently injured the child in the course of delivery). When the parent–child relationship is created by law, ie by the process of adoption, there are more third parties involved who may bear the blame, but also more judicial control – and more, let us not deny, in the way of parental choice – which suggests that allocating blame or shifting losses from the parents is inappropriate. The Americans (who have legal imaginations second to no other nation) some years ago created a delict which they call "wrongful adoption", designed to provide redress when a parent-child relationship created by adoption has gone wrong, and caused loss, due to fault that can be attributed to the adoption agency (for a brief discussion, see Wilkinson and Norrie, *Parent and Child* 2nd edn (1999) at pp 123–124). The English court has recently been faced with such a case, for (everyone thought) the first time.

A hard case

In *A* v *Essex County Council* [2003] 1 FLR 615, a married couple sought damages from an adoption agency, Essex County Council, for the agency's failure to provide them with full information about a child placed with them for adoption. The child was severely emotionally disturbed and his presence in his new family turned their lives into a misery. The claimants argued that had this information been given to them before the placement, they would not have adopted the child:

they framed their case as one of "lack of informed consent" (the analogy being with cases of medical negligence in which a patient consents to recommended treatment which subsequently has a bad outcome, and who claims damages on showing that had proper information been given he or she would not have consented to the treatment and so thereby would have avoided the bad outcome: see in particular *Chatterton* v *Gerson* [1981] QB 432 and *Thake* v *Maurice* [1986] QB 644). The claimants alleged that social workers employed by the Council possessed information about the child but had been negligence in failing to disclose this information before the adoption order was made. The judge, Buckley J, held that the social workers did indeed have a duty to pass the information on to the prospective adopters and that their failure to do so rendered the Council vicariously liable for any loss caused by the breach of duty.

Breach of duty

That a duty of care existed between the social workers and the claimants was not a major issue in the judgment, though perhaps it ought to have been. More contentious in the event were the issues of breach of duty and causation. As regards breach of duty, the question was what standard of information-giving ought the social workers to have reached? In the medical informed consent cases there had been a long-standing debate as to what level of information was required to be given by doctors to patients before the latter could be said to be in a position to give "informed consent". The standard of full information (ie all the information that the doctor himself had) was generally regarded as impractical since medical knowledge is so highly specialised, and eventually the House of Lords settled on the standard of information that would be given by the reasonable doctor: *Sidaway* v *Bethlem Royal Hospital* [1985] AC 871. Buckley J does not discuss the medical cases, though he implicitly rejects the approach followed therein. At para 26 he says "I do not need to attempt to define the scope of the duty, it is enough to hold that it includes taking reasonable steps to provide all relevant information about [the child] to [the claimants]", and at para 76 he defines "sufficient relevant knowledge" to mean "such knowledge as informed them of the substance of the information that would have caused them to refuse the placement". The fact that specialist training is not required to understand background information concerning a child's life suggest that the *Sidaway* standard is not necessarily appropriate here.

Causation

The final, and perhaps most interesting, feature of the case was the issue of causation. The claimants were able to show that they would have refused to accept the child into their household (ie would have refused the placement) had full information about his background and his behavioural problems been given to them. But for that failure, their loss (the disruption to their family life) would have been avoided. But the adoption order was not made until 14 months after the placement, by which time the claimants had had direct personal experience of the child's difficulties. They had still not received the full information from the Council, but they were by then aware that there was information that they needed to know. Nevertheless they went ahead with the adoption. Indeed even now, the child having been removed from their care and placed in a specialist unit which could more appropriately meet his needs, they were not rejecting their parenthood of the child nor seeking the reduction of the adoption order. But was it the breach of duty or their own decision to proceed with the adoption order that caused the post-adoption losses? The claimants argued that by the time of the court hearing they had become emotionally and morally committed to the child and could not for that reason refuse consent to the making of the adoption order. Thus, they argued, their losses after the making of the adoption order sounded in damages as much as those losses during the placement but before the making of the adoption order. The judge rejected this argument. The negligence of the social workers had caused them to accept into their household a child which they would not have accepted had there been no negligence and they had been given sufficient information, and for that they deserved compensation. But notwithstanding their emotional and moral commitment once the placement had occurred, it was still their choice to go ahead with the adoption, and as a result damages were limited to the losses that were referable to the 14 months of the placement before the adoption order. Though the judge does not explore it, the analogy with medical negligence cases (and in particular the wrongful birth cases) is once again instructive. In *Emeh* v *Kensington, Chelsea and Westminster Area Health Authority* [1985] QB 1012 a woman fell pregnant due to the negligence of a surgeon performing a sterilisation operation. She discovered this at the 17th week of pregnancy and the judge at first instance held that since she then chose to continue with the pregnancy her damages should be limited to the losses during these 17 weeks, but not thereafter. He was overruled in the Court of Appeal on the basis that to expect her to choose an abortion at that stage was unreasonable. Buckley J's judgment in the present case suggests that a decision by prospective adopters not to proceed with an adoption after a placement cannot or ought not ever to be characterised as unreasonable. This must surely be right, for otherwise the law would regard prospective adopters as adopters, and the placement as, effectively, a point of no return. The Adoption Act structures the process very differently and one of the very points of the court hearing is to give the adopters the chance to change their minds. Their own feelings of obligation do not affect this legal position.

So in the end the case was not really one of wrongful adoption, because damages were given for the consequences of the placement but not of the adoption itself. The case is more nearly analogous (and therefore is unexceptional) to *W* v *East Essex County Council* [1998] 2 FLR 278 where damages were awarded to foster carers who had not been informed when a child was fostered with them that the child constituted a risk (which eventuated) to their own children.

Dealing with causation in this manner allowed the judge to avoid a further analogy with wrongful birth cases like *Emeh, Thake*, and (of course) *McFarlane* v *Tayside Health Board* 2000 SLT 154. Are wrongful adoption cases to be treated the same as wrongful birth cases, in that damages should be limited to pre-birth or pre-adoption losses and not include costs of upbringing? Or is *McFarlane* distinguishable on the ground that there the post-birth losses were economic and in the present case they were inconvenience and distress? It is true that economic losses are traditionally dealt with more strictly than non-economic losses in negligence, but the balance of policies in both types of case is, in my view, so similar that it ought not to be considered fair, just and reasonable to expect adoption agencies to pay for post-adoption losses. It should in particular be remembered that adoption is a court process, judicially controlled. There would be something distinctly odd in allowing damages for the result of a judicial decision which is not, itself, challenged.

A Scottish precedent

One final point: this is not, as was reported in the press and as the judge thinks, the first wrongful adoption case in the United Kingdom. Glasgow Sheriff Court dealt with such a case over 25 years ago. In *M and M* v *Glasgow Corporation* 1976 SLT (Sh Ct) 45 an action for damages was raised by adoptive parents some years after the adoption against the adoption agency for their negligence in failing to discover before the adoption that the child was seriously and permanently brain damaged. The action was dismissed as irrelevant since the defenders had carried out their statutory duties – in other words, there had been no breach of a duty of care. The sheriff did not hold that there was no duty of care in the first place and he accepted that the claim might be relevant if the pursuers had pleaded that the adoption agency had negligently ignored some medical warning in the medical report on the child (which was effectively the claim in *A* v *Essex County Council*). These comments were, however, long before either the development of the fair, just and reasonable test or the creation and then restraining of the action for wrongful birth. Both that test and that restraining suggest strongly that "wrongful adoption" has no future in UK jurisprudence. And this, in my view, is as it should be.

Update

A v *Essex County Council went to the Court of Appeal: [2004] 1 WLR 1881. That court affirmed the decision discussed above. Both the council and the claimant had appealed and both appeals were rejected. The award of damages against the council for their failure to supply proper information was affirmed because, once they had decided to pass on information, they had a duty to ensure that this happened and that information was received by the prospective adopters. And the limitation of these damages to events prior to the making of the adoption order was also affirmed since by then the claimants were fully aware of the child's behavioural problems.*

Commentary No 18: July 2003

Arranged Marriages, Forced Marriages and Consent to Sham Marriages

A large number of successful and happy marriages have been contracted by parties brought together by their parents with the express purpose that they agree to marry each other. In many cultures, including some that are well represented in modern Scotland, this is the traditional and common way of doing things. There is, however, a crucial difference between what are commonly called arranged marriages (which are perfectly legitimate and serve a useful social purpose) and forced marriages (which are not and do not): the former, but not the latter, involve the true consent of both parties. It follows that forced marriages are not valid marriages, because of the lack of that element, deemed utterly and definitionally essential by Scots law (and indeed most other legal systems). So a marriage may be annulled if one of the parties can show that their purported consent had been forced out of them by threats and was not therefore true consent. This rule must be applied with some care, however, because a party to a marriage who would prefer not to get married will be held to have given true consent if he or she submits to pressure and does, in fact, agree to get married. As Lord Sutherland put it in *Mahmood* v *Mahmood* 1993 SLT 589: "the consent which has to be given to marriage need not be enthusiastic consent, but even reluctant consent will suffice provided that the consent is genuine". A person who, acceding to his or her parents' wishes, consents much against his or her own better judgment and much preferring to do something else, will be married. But a person who in saying "I do" is stating someone else's desire, and not indicating his or her own matrimonial intent, will not be married. The difference is sometimes subtle.

A marriage in Scotland may also be annulled by one party because the other had a mental reservation, or ulterior motive for saying "I do".

Annulment will only be granted in these circumstances if there is no true consent to be married. So parties will be married if they consent in order to achieve one of the benefits of marriage, but they will not be married if they consent to obtaining the benefit by going through an empty ceremony but not to being in any real sense husband and wife: see for example *Akram* v *Akram* 1979 SLT (Notes) 87. The difference here is also sometimes subtle.

Videoing the ceremony

There have been two recent cases illustrating these points and exploring the nature of the consent necessary to constitute marriage. In *Sohrab* v *Kahn* 2002 SCLR 663 a marriage was arranged between the parents of the parties thereto. The girl was 16 and she was informed of the arrangements only a week before the ceremony was due to take place. Thereafter, according to the judge (para 10) "there was a convincing body of evidence about threats ... The evidence showed there was a number of scenes with crying, shouting and things being thrown, refusals and threats of increasing severity to send [the pursuer] to Pakistan, to disown her and the mother threatening that she would take her own life ... At the age of 16 the pursuer was wholly dependent on her parents and was not forisfamiliated". The actual ceremony was videotaped, and the judge, Lord McEwan, noted that "the pursuer never smiled throughout the ceremony although at the proof she demonstrated frequently and often that she could smile beautifully. The video supported her own evidence that she was in a sense silently protesting on the day of the wedding and how she looked was how she felt. Later scenes in videos show her as unhappy". Other than the unhappy assessment of the pursuer's smiling beauty, this passage is significant and reflects a crucial piece of evidence in the next case, discussed below. All in all, the judge was able to conclude, fairly readily, that "the pursuer here did not give any genuine consent to this marriage but was put under such duress by her parents that whatever semblance of consent was exchanged at the [ceremony] was vitiated" (para 77).

That conclusion was, in a sense, *obiter*. For the ceremony that took place lacked, in addition to effective consent, another essential ingredient – a marriage notice and schedule. Once someone realised this error, a couple of weeks after the ceremony, a marriage notice was obtained, and a schedule registered which purported to relate to a ceremony which, in fact, never took place. The actual ceremony could not create a marriage because there was no schedule to be registered; and the schedule that was registered referred to a fiction. Such a fundamental defect was not open to correction under the terms of s 23A of the Marriage (Scotland) Act 1977.

Enjoying the benefits

A more recent case raising a similar issue but in a different way is that of *Hakeem* v *Hussain* 2003 SLT 515 (OH). The pursuer, like Ms Sohrab, was 16 when her mother, through a friend, arranged for her to meet a man in his mid 20s who had come to Scotland from Pakistan on a 6-month visa. But in the present case the pursuer was altogether more enthusiastic at the prospect of marrying. She found the defender attractive, as he found her, and (at their first meeting) they agreed to marry each other, to the delight of both families. This was an arranged and not a forced marriage. The arrangement was that a civil marriage ceremony would take place but that the parties would not commence living together as husband and wife until a religious ceremony had taken place – for only then would they consider themselves to be truly married. But the completion of the civil ceremony would allow the defender to apply for and obtain a visa allowing him to remain in Scotland indefinitely; in the meantime the pursuer could finish her schooling. So the civil ceremony took place and, as in the previous case, was videotaped, though this time the bride looked happy (as well she might). The defender obtained his visa but he then changed his mind about being married to the pursuer and he refused to undergo the religious ceremony. The wife then sought to have the marriage annulled, not on the basis that she had been forced to consent but that neither she nor the defender had consented before the district registrar to be "married" in any sense that they understood the word. She adopted this tactic rather than seeking a divorce, which would have been open to her on the ground of non-cohabitation, because she preferred to be treated as never having been married rather than as divorced, believing that she would be more likely to attract another husband as an unmarried person than as a divorced person. Her case was doomed, and not just because of her videoed happy face.

Sensible judge

Lord Clarke dismissed as a *non sequitur* the argument that a marriage with an ulterior purpose is void. He said this: "The *non sequitur* and misconception is as follows: when a man and woman enter a regular marriage but do not, because of their religious beliefs, consider themselves to be married in the eyes of their god, or according to their religion until they undergo another ceremony of a religious character, the regular marriage is void and has no legal effect. The regular form of civil marriage in compliance with provisions of the Marriage (Scotland) Act 1977, provides for parties, who follow the procedures there prescribed to be regarded, according to the law of Scotland, as husband and wife, with all the legal consequences that flow from that. It has nothing to say about the religious significance, or otherwise, of the parties' relationship" (para 30). The happy video was evidence of the pursuer's state of mind – which was to be lawfully married, and so Lord Clarke found.

This is an important judgment. It illustrates clearly that marriage is both a religious and a secular legal concept, but that the law is concerned with marriage only in its legal aspects. "Marriage", as a concept and an institution, has a variety of meanings. Some sections of society see cohabitation as the equivalent of what is (to a lawyer, mistakenly) called "common law marriage". Some religious groups consider it a sacrament, the sanctification before a higher authority of a personal relationship between two individuals. The law is disinterested in these notions. For the law, marriage is a relationship entered into by legally established methods and it has legally defined consequences. The fact that the legal concept of marriage can trace its roots to the religious concept is, today, not relevant to the essential nature of the former. The secularisation of marriage has been an essential precondition to the multiculturalism which characterises modern society, but it means that the religious and the legal concepts no longer have any symbiosis, and the one exists quite independently of the other. It follows that if the parties to a legal marriage do not regard themselves as "married" for religious purposes then that is of no concern to the law. If they are unwilling to commence sexual relations until their religion has sanctioned this through a ceremony it (too) calls marriage then that is their choice but is irrelevant to the law. In legal terms the marriage between Ms Hakeem and Mr Hussain was clearly not a pretended or sham marriage. It was a lawful marriage which was not a religious marriage (as many are not). The consent the parties gave was to be lawfully married, and so they were lawfully married even although they did not consent to be religiously married. The secular courts can deal only with legal institutions, and that is as it should be. The judge had little sympathy for the pursuer and that, too (in cases like this), is as it should be.

Lesson for marriage-arranging parents: keep the video-camera switched off.

Update

Unhappily, the convincingly secular judgment of Lord Clarke was overruled by the Inner House in H *v* H *2005 SLT 1025 on the ground that the parties had not given true "matrimonial consent" for the purposes of the civil law of marriage. With respect, this is exactly what they did give. They were seeking to have their religious perception of marriage trump the civil law of marriage. See Commentary No 27 below.*

"Mental reservation" as a ground for avoiding an otherwise valid marriage has been removed from the law by s 20A(4), inserted into the Marriage (Scotland) Act 1977 by s 2 of the Family Law (Scotland) Act 2006. Though the matter could have been expressed more clearly in the statute, it may well be that this provision prevents marriages such as those in Hakeem *v* Hussain *from being deemed to be void.*

The Children's Hearings (Scotland) Act 2011 creates a new ground of referral: that the child is at risk of being forced into a marriage against his or her will. Other children in the household can also be referred to a hearing. The pressure must be on a person under the age of 16, and since this is under the age of marriage in the United Kingdom the ground's main focus will be on children at risk of being taken abroad to be married off, or being pressurised to do something in the future.

Commentary No 19: October 2003

Sewel Motions, Devolution, and Family Law

Many countries in the world operate a federal system of government and so too, now, does the United Kingdom. It is in the nature of a federal system that different constituent parts of the whole will have different laws and will move at different speeds towards similar goals of law reform. It may be unfortunate if one part embraces a modern development before another part, but there is no constitutional or legal necessity for the different legislatures to move forward hand in hand. There may well be practical awkwardnesses, with individual citizens having more or less rights and responsibilities as they move from one part of the country to another but other countries with such systems of government live with these awkwardnesses as an inevitable consequence of federalism.

The UK Government (which acts as the individual government for England) has recently announced two initiatives of high significance within family law. First, on 30 June 2003 the Department of Trade and Industry published a consultation paper on the UK Government's proposals to introduce "civil partnership registration" for same-sex couples in England and Wales. And secondly, on 10 July 2003 that Government, through the Department of Constitutional Affairs (AKA the Lord Chancellor's Department) published a draft Gender Recognition Bill which will allow for the legal reassignment of a person's gender from male to female, or from female to male. These are grand proposals, overdue and welcome, and it is very nice for English and Welsh people to be afforded such a significant extension of their rights. The same pressures that exist in England and Wales to change the law in this direction exist in Scotland. Many of the practical consequences of allowing individuals to change their legal sex and of allowing same-sex partners to register their relationship are matters reserved to Westminster and Holyrood could not, therefore, legislate thereupon: these issues include immigration, income-related benefits, state pensions, life insurance and child support. But if the proposals are accepted for England and Wales, individuals and couples in Scotland will be able to access these reserved benefits. If they cannot access the devolved benefits that is unfortunate and should indicate even more strongly to the Scottish Parliament that it should act speedily, but if there is disparity between the rights and responsibilities of people north and south of the border then that simply reflects the fact that there is a border. It is in the nature of the devolution settlement.

Of course, one way to avoid the awkwardness of different laws in different parts of the UK – and, it may be, of achieving law reform rather sooner for Scotland than would otherwise be possible – is to pretend that devolution never happened. The Scottish Parliament can (and sometimes does) pass what is called a "Sewel Motion" to allow Westminster to legislate for Scotland on devolved matters. The danger, however, is that in an area of law based on very different principles, as family law is, the Westminster Parliament will, inadvertently or deliberately, apply inappropriate English ideas to Scotland. (They did this before devolution when they were a full legislature for Scotland too: see for example the Marriage (Prohibited Degrees of Relationship) Act 1986 where the new qualifications to some prohibitions on marriage between ex-relatives were extended to Scotland notwithstanding that they were designed explicitly to address certain Anglican theological concerns of the English bishops in the House of Lords). The Scottish Executive have decided to adopt this dangerous route.

The Gender Recognition Bill

In relation to gender re-assignment, the major differences between English law and Scots law relate to the rules of marriage, and in particular the concept of the voidable marriage and the role of consummation. The draft Gender Recognition Bill contains a provision that a marriage will be voidable if one of the parties had previously undergone gender re-assignment. This is an addition to the fairly lengthy (and to Scottish eyes peculiar) list of circumstances in which a marriage in England can be considered voidable (as opposed to void). But that concept has always sat uneasily within the Scots law of marriage and there has only ever been one ground upon which a marriage here is considered voidable – the incurable impotency of one or both of the parties. Any extension of this awkward concept should be resisted vigorously. What then do you do with the marriage when a wife discovers that her husband used to be a woman, or a husband discovers that his wife used to be a man? I find it difficult to see how this is any different from any other situation in which a spouse discovers something about the previous life of his or her partner which requires a radical reappraisal of the relationship (for example, discovering that the partner had a conviction for some serious offence, like murder, rape or child abuse). If the spouse does not want the marriage to continue then divorce is always available (though only after 2 or 5 years, since the other grounds all concerns events which occur subsequent to the marriage). There is no need to pretend that the marriage never was a marriage. To do so is inconsistent with the notion that the partner has, for all legal purposes, changed sex.

Another awkwardness, not actually considered in the draft Bill, is the concept of consummation. The continued requirement to perform this act in English law, and the continued requirement for ability to perform this act in Scots law, is a disgrace in any modern legal system which perceives marriage as a relationship of mutual love and support rather than one of sexual right and procreation, but unless it is abolished there also needs to be some provision in the Bill to the effect that consummation can be effected by utilising the artificially modelled genitalia of the marriage partner who changed sex. In fact, the idea of post-operative transsexuals marrying highlights the ludicrous nature of the concept of consummation. Are our legislators going to be able to ensure that a female to male transsexual who (for whatever reason) decides not to have an artificial penis created is not regarded as "incurably impotent"? Or are we going to have to rely on the clumsy idea of personal bar to ensure that this marriage is not regarded as voidable?

The Civil Partnership Bill

The second grand initiative is to follow very many other countries in western Europe and elsewhere and create an institution, analogous to marriage, for same-sex couples (tentatively to be called "registered partnerships"). Making the new institution as close to marriage as possible will inevitably mean that same-sex couples are to be treated in Scotland differently from England, just as married couples are. There are three issues of particular note:

First, parental consent between the ages of 16 and 18. This is a long-established English rule based on the notion of parental rights which, in England, last until the young person's 18th birthday. In Scotland young persons have always shaken free of parental control earlier than in England and currently parental rights disappear on the child's 16th birthday. A rule to the effect that a 16 or 17 year old needs anyone's consent but their partner's to enter into a same-sex registered partnership must be vigorously resisted in Scotland.

Secondly, as already mentioned, the grounds upon which a marriage is voidable (as opposed to void) are more extensive in England than in Scotland and include duress, mistake, one partner being pregnant by a third party, one partner suffering from venereal disease, and lack of mental capacity to consent. These are based on the notion, alien to Scots law, that a marriage conducted in ignorance of facts which, had they been known, would have changed one of the parties' minds is no marriage. These rules, therefore, should not be extended to Scotland. Indeed, it is difficult to see how the only basis upon which a marriage is voidable in Scotland (incurable impotency, or inability to achieve penile penetration of the vagina) can be applied to same-sex couples. Given that procreation is out of the question, there is absolutely no need for the law to require ability of one partner to penetrate the body of the other. If the concept of the voidable registered partnership is to be countenanced at all, then the judges (for impotency is a common law and not statutory concept) will have to spell out in clear language which parts of the male or female body needs to be penetrated by which parts of their partner's body – and they will also need to explain to the public why the registration would remain challengeable if one or other is not able to achieve such penetration. In truth, the whole notion is distasteful and ludicrous and it is highly unlikely that the judges will extend the concept of voidability to registered partnerships if it is not statutorily invented. Nevertheless, the legislative opportunity presented by civil partnership recognition ought to be taken to rid the law of marriage itself of impotency and consummation.

Thirdly, in English law same-sex couples can already seek to adopt a child, which is not possible (yet) in Scotland. This rule should be extended to Scotland even before the rule allowing cohabitants to adopt is introduced. But parenting of children does raise another important issue which has been dealt with in many other countries that have already introduced registered partnerships. The rule is presently that the husband of a woman who gives birth is presumed to be the father of the child. It might be thought that this rule needs to be explicitly excluded from application to same-sex couples (effectively, female couples), but in my view that is not necessary. It is, after all, only a presumption which could never stand in the face of incontrovertible fact. It is an incontrovertible fact that a female partner of a woman who gives birth is not the father of the child and so she would not be presumed in any circumstance to be the father of the child. Whether she should be entitled to parental responsibilities and parental rights in respect of the child is, of course, an entirely different question.

The differences between Scots and English marriage law are sufficiently crucial (in doctrinal as well as practical terms) that the Scottish Parliament is in a far better position than is the Parliament for England to legislate on the matter. There may well be, for all I know, circumstances in which a Sewel Motion is an appropriate way to achieve law reform. But the law of marriage and family relationships, self-evidently and eminently matters for a Scottish legislature, concerns no such circumstance. There is little hope for the Scottish Parliament if it sends issues back to Westminster just because of a fear of hostile headlines, and attempts to justify their action on the patently anti-devolution stance that Scots law must move in tandem with the law of its southern neighbour.

Update

The Gender Recognition Act 2004 came into effect in April 2005, and the Civil Partnership Act 2004 came into effect in December 2005. See Commentary No 20 on the Gender Recognition Bill. Both Acts were passed by the Westminster Parliament and both are extended to all parts of the United Kingdom. The English peculiarities in the original drafts were removed (for Scotland) as the Bills made their way through the legislative process. The availability of adoption was extended to same-sex (and unregistered) couples by the Adoption and Children (Scotland) Act 2007 (for which see Commentary No 31) and parenthood after infertility treatment extended to lesbian couples by the Human Fertilisation and Embryology Act 2008 (for which see Commentary No 39).

PART TWO

COMMENTARIES PUBLISHED IN THE *JOURNAL OF THE LAW SOCIETY OF SCOTLAND*

Commentary No 20: April 2004

When Girl Meets Boy

A new Bill designed to ensure that transsexual law in the UK is compatible with the European Convention on Human Rights

The Gender Recognition Bill and its effects

For some years prior to the unfortunate demise of the *Scottish Law and Practice Quarterly* I had been writing a quarterly column giving a fairly personal view of recent developments in family law, usually in Scotland, but occasionally from abroad. The editors of *The Journal* have now given me the opportunity to share my thoughts with a far larger audience than was possible with SLPQ, and this is the first of what is intended to be a quarterly update in family law where the issues are chosen for no other reason than their topicality and their interest to me: I hope that readers will usually find something of interest to them too. The first topic that I want to write about in this new forum is, neatly, an update of the topic covered in the final issue of SLPQ, the Gender Recognition Bill, currently before the UK Parliament. (For a description of the judicial activism that led to the need for such a Bill, see my commentary on *Bellinger* v *Bellinger* [2003] 2 AC 467, published in (2004) 8 Edin LR 93.)

Parliamentary progress

The Gender Recognition Bill was introduced in the House of Lords on 27 November 2003, and was originally limited to England and Wales; the Scottish Parliament gave in to its anti-devolutionary cravings on 5 February 2004, and passed a Sewel Motion (by a majority of 76 to 35) in the following terms: "The Parliament endorses the principle of giving transsexual people legal recognition of their acquired gender and agrees that the provisions in the Gender Recognition Bill that relate to devolved matters should be considered by the UK Parliament thereby ensuring a consistent UK approach and early compliance with the rulings of the European Court of Human Rights."

In the House of Lords the Bill passed its third reading 5 days later, by a majority of 155 to 57, with even opposition peers (with a couple of notable exceptions) supporting it "in principle". The Bill then moved to the Commons where on 23 February 2004 it passed its second reading by the overwhelming majority of 335 to 26. No substantive amendments were made during the subsequent debates in the Commons Standing Committee A on 9, 11 and 16 March 2004.

Recognition – and conscience

Once the Bill becomes law any person over the age of 18 may apply to a new body, the Gender Recognition Panel, for the granting of a "Gender Recognition Certificate" (a "GRC"), and if this is granted then the applicant shall for all purposes of law be treated as belonging to the gender recognised by the certificate. The basis for the granting of the certificate will be that the applicant has lived for at least 2 years in the gender other than that recorded on their birth certificate (or has changed gender under the law of another country) and intends to live in the acquired gender for the rest of his or her life. So far so uncontroversial.

If the applicant is married then all he or she can seek is an interim GRC, which has no effect other than that it can be converted to a full GRC within 6 months of the annulment or dissolution of the marriage. Many organisations supporting the Bill, and indeed the Joint (Parliamentary) Committee on Human Rights, expressed severe reservations at the requirement for a transsexual person in a stable marriage to bring that marriage to an end before they can access those rights currently denied them, but the Government held firm on the ground that to recognise the continued existence of a marriage after gender re-assignment would amount to the recognition of a marriage between two persons who were, in law, of the same sex; and it further argued that the problem would shortly be resolved by the current proposals to allow such couples to re-establish legal links by means of a registered partnership for same-sex couples. There do remain difficulties, however, in particular (though admittedly unusual) circumstances. If, for example, two transgendered people are married to each other and each seeks a GRC, they would be required to end their marriage, obtain the GRCs, and then remarry in their new genders, which seems needlessly cumbersome. (An attempt on 16 March at the Commons committee stage to deal with this problem was not pursued.)

Once granted, the GRC would result in the new gender being the holder's gender for virtually all purposes of law. The effect would be solely prospective and it would not, for example, retrospectively validate any marriage. Again, the Joint Committee on Human Rights argued in favour of some retrospective effect, but again the Government refused to budge. GRCs will be registered in a new Gender Recognition Register, maintained by the Registrar General and open to public inspection.

There is a conscience clause for clergy from the Church of England and the Church in Wales, exempting them from any obligation to solemnise the marriage "of a person whom he reasonably believes has a gender recognition certificate". This is not needed in Scotland since clergy here are under no such obligation and have the personal power in any case to refuse to solemnise a marriage. There were attempts in the House of Lords to remove the right to marry as a consequence of the granting of a GRC, but all the amendments to that effect were defeated – and would indeed have gone against one of the central thrusts of the European Court of Human Rights decision in *Goodwin* v *UK* (2002) 35 EHRR 18 which involved both the right to private life and the right to marry.

Exceptions to recognition of the new gender include (i) parenthood, so that a person's status as "mother" or as "father" of a child will be unaffected by the GRC; (ii) peerages and titles of honour, though the Queen may be petitioned to alter the form of address of any peer who obtains a GRC; and (iii) (as a Lords amendment) sporting bodies, who will be allowed to continue to make decisions about whether individuals may participate in "male" events or "female" events (where necessary to ensure either "safe" or "fair" competition). A further exception, applying only to Scotland, relates to gender-specific offences (English criminal law having gone gender-neutral a few years ago): criminal liability for a gender-specific offence will continue notwithstanding that the relevant individual has, through a GRC, changed sex.

Shades of grey

Throughout the House of Lords debates, a recurring feature (from a regular coterie of peers) was the fear that the Bill was an attack on religion, and on the family. A few peers felt that the so-called conscience clause did not go far enough – rather churches and other faith organisations should be given the right to exclude from membership or from the provision of services other than marriage persons who are in possession of a GRC. The basis of this argument seems to have been that the GRC declares a lie (that a "man" is now a woman and vice versa) and that those who adhere to religion should not be forced to acknowledge a lie. There is some judicial precedent for this odd outlook (see Lord Hope's judgment in *Bellinger* v *Bellinger* [2003] 2 All ER 593 and my comment at (2004) 8 Edin LR 93), but it fails to recognise that gender is a legal status as much as a matter of fact. The law can define that status in any way it chooses – and indeed gender as a matter of fact is not as black and white as the religious argument assumes. At the Commons committee stage on 16 March an attempt was made to extend the conscience clause to registrars, but was defeated. A further expressed fear was that not enough consideration was being given to the effects of the granting of the GRC on others, in particular family members of the certificate holder. But this is nothing to the point. The certificate can be granted only after the individual has lived in his or her new gender for at least 2 years and it is likely that it is the decision to begin living in a new gender that will have the decisive effect on others, rather than the regularisation of what will by then be the existing position by the granting of the GRC.

Accepting the gendered regime

This Bill will shortly become law. It will affect a tiny number of people, but affect these individuals in a way as profound as it is possible to imagine. The Bill is needed only because we live in a gendered society whose gendered laws are regarded as acceptable and will not themselves be changed. But this in itself makes the argument very different from that relating to gay and lesbian people: for there the aim is to change all laws that treat people differently as a result of their sexual orientation. That is an issue that this column will certainly return to in the foreseeable future.

Update

The Gender Recognition Act 2004 received Royal Assent on 1 July 2004, and most of its provisions came into force on 4 April 2005. The difficult interrelationship between the Gender Recognition Act and the Civil Partnership Act 2004, and the Byzantine provisions each of these Acts contains in order to ensure that a change of gender does not compromise the appropriate gender-mix in these gender-specific institutions, are the single most powerful practical argument for opening both marriage and civil partnership to couples of any gender-mix.

Commentary No 21: July 2004

Identity Crisis

*Two important family cases (*Chief Constable of West Yorkshire Police *v* A, and Re U (A Child) (Standard of Proof) *which have each caused some surprise*

It has been a vibrant few months in family law since my April column. The Court of Session was faced with a fascinating and unusual case in which the pursuer sought reduction of a decree of divorce on the basis that he had earlier divorced the defender, by means of a talaq in Pakistan (*Ahmed* v *Ahmed*, 31 March 2004, Lord Menzies (appeal to the Inner House reported at 2006 SC 165). However it is two English cases, which are likely to have effect in Scotland, that I want to consider this month.

One body, two sexes

I had not intended to return to transgender issues quite so soon after my last column dealt with the Gender Recognition Bill, but then I had not expected the House of Lords to depart so soon and so spectacularly from its decision last year in the transsexual marriage case of *Bellinger* v *Bellinger* [2003] 2 AC 467. The fact that their Lordships deny departing in any way at all from that case only serves to heighten the spectacle.

The respondent in *Chief Constable of West Yorkshire Police* v *A* [2005] 1 AC 51, who was a male-to-female transsexual, had her application to become a police officer rejected on the basis of her transsexuality. To discriminate in employment against a person because of their transgender status is, of course, contrary to the Sex Discrimination Act 1975 (*P* v *S and Cornwall County Council* [1996] ECR I-2143), but the chief constable sought to rely on the defence that being of one sex or the other was a "genuine occupational qualification". This defence is not unique to sex discrimination. It appears also in reg 7 of the Employment Equality (Sexual Orientation) Regulations 2003 (SI 2003/1661), which permits discrimination if being of a particular sexual orientation is a genuine occupational requirement. (Suggestions are sought as to what sort of occupation requires as a genuine qualification that the employee or prospective employee be either gay or non-gay.) The chief constable pointed to statutory rules requiring that when the police undertake intimate body searches only male police officers can search males and only female police officers can search females. He argued that as a male-to-female transsexual, Ms A in law (because of course the Gender Recognition Bill is not yet in force) remains a male and so would be statutorily barred from searching females, but could only be allowed to search males by breaching her privacy and revealing to her colleagues and the public that though she looked female she was, in law, male.

The House of Lords were unanimous in rejecting this defence, on the basis that it would have been within the operational control of the chief constable to exempt Ms A from carrying out such searches at all: this would have been a more proportionate response to the situation than the outright refusal to employ her. But they were not unanimous in deciding how to reconcile their decision with the proposition, originally enunciated in *Corbett* v *Corbett* [1971] P 83 and affirmed in *Bellinger* v *Bellinger*, that a person born unequivocally (in physical terms) of one gender remains that gender in law all his or her life. The issue will not be entirely resolved by the Gender Recognition Bill, for there will always be some transsexuals who do not seek, or are not eligible for, a gender recognition certificate.

The majority held that the words "woman" and "man" in the Sex Discrimination Act 1975 must be read "as referring to the acquired gender of a post-operative transsexual who is visually and for all practical purposes indistinguishable from non-transsexual members of that gender" (per Lord Bingham at para 11). This means that the definition of "male" and "female" might be different depending upon the issue – and a person may be male for one purpose (say, marriage) and female for another (performing intimate body searches). A transsexual's new sex is therefore recognised for the purposes of sex discrimination law even without the enactment of the Gender Recognition Bill. Lord Rodger disagreed and held (para 24) that it would be unlawful for a male to female transsexual to carry out intimate searches on a female person: in other words, if Ms A was male for the purposes of marriage she remained a male for the purposes of the rules governing searches.

Lady Hale, at para 59, suggested that it would not be rational for a person to object to being searched, or nursed (for example) by "a trans person of the same sex" (ie by a person who is now but was not always the same sex as the person being searched or nursed). Unfortunately, she added (rather gratuitously) that it may be rational to object to being nursed by a homosexual person of the same sex. This comes dangerously close to sanctioning the police using such a so-called "rational" objection to refuse to employ gay or lesbian persons as police officers on the ground that the sexual orientation which permits searches is, rationally, a genuine occupational requirement within the terms of the 2003 Regulations cited above.

Applying different standards

It has long been the rule, as understandable to lawyers as it is incomprehensible to laypeople, that a criminal charge of child abuse may fail because the prosecutor did not meet the standard of proof beyond reasonable doubt, while at the same time the child can be removed from the accused through the child protection mechanisms because the civil standard of proof, the balance of probabilities, has been met. It is this incomprehension that explains the dismay expressed in many sections of the press at the Court of Appeal's decision in *Re U (A Child) (Serious Injury: Standard of Proof)* [2004] 3 WLR 753. Earlier this year, in *R* v *Cannings* [2004] 1 WLR 2607, the Court of Appeal had quashed the conviction of a mother found guilty of murdering two of her children, three of whom had died in early infancy. Expert evidence had suggested that the statistical chances of all three children dying in the absence of parental abuse was inconceivably high but the Court of Appeal held that this was not sufficient to satisfy the burden of proof of the mother's criminal guilt. It was thought that a consequence of this decision was that very many civil cases, in which children had been removed on the basis of expert evidence, were now vulnerable to challenge. The presiding judge emphasised that it was too broad an interpretation of *Cannings* to say that expert evidence alone is insufficient to justify a conviction or, *a fortiori*, the application of child protection mechanisms.

Dame Elizabeth Butler-Sloss P, for it was she, after setting out the familiar standards of proof in criminal and civil proceedings, explained in some detail the reasons why the two processes have different standards: child protection proceedings are quasi-inquisitorial and the function is child protection rather than adult punishment; in criminal proceedings an unjust verdict cannot be analysed, while judges trying family cases make findings of fact in the course of a reasoned judgment which is open to challenge on appeal; material available to the court in child protection cases is likely to be much more extensive than that admitted in a criminal trial. It followed that child protection cases, before and after *Cannings*, remain to be determined by the balance of probabilities and acquittal on a criminal charge does not necessarily lead to the absolution of the parent in family or civil proceedings. The effect of *Cannings* on child protection proceedings had been "over-estimated" in some quarters.

Butler-Sloss P also took the opportunity to restore to its position as the guiding principle the statement of Lord Nicholls in *Re H (Minors)* [1996] 1 All ER 1 that "the more improbable the event the stronger must be the evidence that it did occur before, on the balance of probabilities, its occurrence will be established". This is consistent with the earlier statement of the Second Division in the children's hearing case of *B* v *Kennedy* 1987 SLT 765 that "the weight of evidence required to tip the scales may vary with the gravity of the allegation to be proved". It is to be remembered that if new evidence comes to light after child protection proceedings in Scotland, a re-hearing of the evidence upon which these proceedings were based can be sought under s 85 of the Children (Scotland) Act 1995. A change in scientific understanding, or the discrediting of a scientific theory, or indeed of an individual expert witness, upon which the original finding was based would, it is submitted, amount to new evidence for this purpose. But as *Re U (A Child)* shows, while such new evidence may make a criminal conviction unsafe, it may not in itself lead to a finding that a ground of referral to a children's hearing can no longer be accepted as having been made out on the balance of probabilities.

Update

That recognition of sex change was required, at least in some circumstances, even before the coming into force of the Gender Recognition Act 2004 is confirmed by Timbrell *v* Secretary of State for Work and Pensions *[2010] EWCA Civ 701 where it was held that a male-to-female transsexual was entitled to a state pension as from the female age of 60 as opposed to the male age of 65, and that this entitlement had to be backdated to the date of the claimant's 60th birthday, which was some years before the commencement of the 2004 Act. Neither the non-retrospectivity of the 2004 Act nor the House of Lords decision in* Bellinger *v* Bellinger *prevented this result since Council Directive 79/7 requires no discrimination in matters of social security and in* Richards *v* Secretary of State for Work and Pensions *[2006] 2 CMLR 49 the European Court of Justice had required gender change to be recognised for this purpose. Re U* and *Re H* were approved by the House of Lords in *Re B (Children: Sexual Abuse: Standard of Proof)* [2009] 1 AC 1, which was itself applied in the Outer House in *Wilson, Petr* 2008 SLT 753.

Commentary No 22: October 2004

What Title?

Why title to seek orders such as contact orders is not confined to those entitled to apply for an order conferring parental rights

Scottish courts have traditionally preferred to deal with questions of parental responsibilities and parental rights in a substantive rather than technical manner. The Court of Session eschewed the use of onus, for example, in favour of the real issue of the child's welfare in *White* v *Whi*te 2001 SC 689. Another technicality which ought, in my view, to be avoided is title to seek an order relating to parental responsibilities or parental rights. Before the coming into force of the Children (Scotland) Act 1995 questions of title arose fairly frequently in the context of whether grandparents, or ex-parents after adoption, could seek access to their grandchild or ex-child (see, for example *F* v *F* 1991 SLT 357; *D* v *Grampian Regional Council* 1995 SLT 519). Since the 1995 Act, this question continues to trouble the court, not so much on the point of principle but due to the structure of s 11 itself.

In *White* v *White* 1999 SLT (Sh Ct) 106, before that case reached the Inner House (which did not comment on the issue), Sheriff Principal Nicholson held that since s 11 allows the court to make orders "regulating" contact, a person who does not have the "parental right" of contact needs to seek an order under s 11(2)(b) granting parental rights before that person could seek an order under s 11(2)(d) regulating the rights acquired thereby; but Sheriff Principal Bowen disagreed with that approach in *H* v *M* 2000 SLT (Sh Ct) 88 and would have allowed the making of an order under s 11(2)(d) even when the person with whom contact was to be regulated did not have the "parental right" of contact. The implication of Sheriff Principal Bowen's approach (which, it is submitted, is correct) is that the "contact" which can be regulated under s 11(2)(d) is not limited to the "parental right" of contact but might include contact between the child and a person who does not have any "parental right" (such as, for example, a grandparent).

"How" is different from "who"

The same question arose in a rather different context in *D* v *H* 2004 SLT (Sh Ct) 73 before, again, Sheriff Principal Bowen. The issue here was whether a 15-year-old boy could seek an order under s 11(2)(d) regulating contact between himself and his ex-sister, a girl who had been adopted away from the family some 10 years previously. The sheriff principal upheld the view of the sheriff that since what was being sought was "in the nature of an application seeking a parental rights order" and since "parental rights" can be conferred only on persons over the age of 16, the present action was incompetent. While it is true that s 11(2)(b)(i) prohibits the imposing of parental responsibilities on a person under the age of 16, it does not follow, as was assumed by both the sheriff and the sheriff principal, that it is incompetent to make a contact order regulating the arrangements for maintaining personal relations and direct contact between a child and a person under 16 with whom the child is not living.

The problem that the sheriff and the sheriff principal perceived in *D* v *H* was that an order described in s 11(2) (residence, contact, specific issue and the rest) is in fact made under, and constrained by, s 11(1): "In the relevant circumstances ... an order may be made under this subsection in relation to (a) parental responsibilities, (b) parental rights, (c) guardianship, or (d) ... the administration of a child's property". This means, Sheriff Principal Bowen held, that the court cannot make any of the s 11(2) orders unless it concerns one or more of the four concepts listed in s 11(1). He is clearly correct here. But where it is submitted he has gone wrong is in (i) confusing who has title to seek a s 11 order with who can possess and exercise what the statute describes as parental responsibilities and parental rights, and (ii) using the terminology of "parental rights order", which is a concept that does not appear in the Act. A s 11 order must, the Act tells us, be "in relation to" such responsibilities or rights, but this does not mean that the order must involve the granting or withdrawing of such responsibilities or rights. The very existence of some of the s 11 orders makes this plain. A specific issue order under s 11(2)(e) is an order regulating a specific question which has arisen "in connection with parental responsibilities, parental rights, guardianship or the administration of a child's property". In other words a s 11 order can regulate how parental responsibilities are to be exercised as well as who is to have them. A grandparent, for example, may seek a specific issue order under s 11(2)(e) regulating "any specific question which has arisen… in connection with" the parent's exercise of parental rights, such as for example whether the child is to receive religious instruction or attend a particular school or be provided with particular medical treatment, even when that grandparent is not seeking to be conferred with the "parental right" to determine the child's religion, education or medical treatment. The rule that a s 11 order must "relate to" parental responsibilities and parental rights does not imply that an order can be granted only to those to whom parental responsibilities and parental rights can be granted (ie persons over the age of 16). Were this not so then artificial persons such as health boards or education authorities could not seek any order under section 11. But the terms of ss 11(5) and 15(4) indicate that artificial persons can apply for an order relating to parental rights, even although they cannot have parental rights conferred upon them.

Not just for grown-ups

If the above is correct, might it be that a contact order is different? The wording of s 11(2)(d) clearly implies that a contact order can regulate contact in fact as well as confer or withhold the legal right of contact (as Sheriff Principal Bowen held in *H* v *M*). But in the present case Sheriff Principal Bowen concluded that the use of the words "parental rights" means that only those eligible to hold "parental rights" have title to seek what he described as a "parental rights order". This is not so. Section 2(4) defines "parental rights" as those listed in paragraphs (a)–(d) of s 2(1). Section 2 defines which rights parents have in order to fulfil their responsibilities, but paragraphs (a)–(d) list rights without limiting them to, or even mentioning, parents. In other words, "parental rights" is simply the phrase used as shorthand to describe a set of rights which parents have – but there is no implication that only parents can have these rights. One so-called "parental right" is the right to maintain personal relations and direct contact with the child on a regular basis. Parents have this right (s 2(1)(c)). Others might have this right, or seek it, or seek to have it vested in another, or seek to have another's exercise of the right regulated by a s 11 order. The regulation of contact between a child and another person with whom he or she is not living will, whoever makes the application, always affect (and in that way relate to) how the parents' parental responsibilities and parental rights will be exercised – at least to the extent that the parent loses complete discretion over who the child has contact with. So regulation of contact between a child and a third party relates to parental responsibilities and is therefore competent under s 11(1).

Keep to the welfare question

It may have been that the sheriff and the sheriff principal were concerned that the present application was being used to subvert the adoption legislation. The 15-year-old applicant had spent some time away from home, and his ex-sister had been adopted away from the family. The applicant was now back with his mother and, 10 years after having last seen his sister, he sought an order seeking that contact which the 1995 Act explicitly prohibited his mother from seeking. There is no indication in the case that this influenced the sheriff's or the sheriff principal's decision or reasoning, but it is difficult to believe that the same result would have been reached had the 15-year-old brother been seeking contact with, say, a 14-year-old sister whom he had not seen since his parents divorced a year previously.

The same effective result could – and ought to – have been achieved by eschewing technicalities and exploring the substantive issue: was it in the welfare of the child to re-establish a connection with a family she had been adopted away from and had had no contact with for a decade? The court took a detour before it got to that question, but it ended up in a blind alley. It is submitted the decision is wrong.

Sheriff Crowe at Dundee in *E* v *E*, 12 August 2004, declined to follow Sheriff Principal Bowen on this matter. He was right to do so.

Update

See Authority Reporter *v* S *2010 SLT 765, one of the implications of which is that a contact order regulating arrangements for contact between the child and a person who does not have parental responsibilities and parental rights, and is not a parent or guardian, is a competent s 11 order so long as it "relates to" parental responsibilities and parental rights (as contact does). So Sheriff Crowe is right.*

Commentary No 23: January 2005

Prevention as the Cure

The Protection of Children and Prevention of Sexual Offences (Scotland) Bill illustrates a shift of emphasis from reaction to prevention of offences against children

Protecting children from harm has at least two elements: the protective mechanisms of the civil law, now contained primarily in the Children (Scotland) Act 1995, and the punitive measures of the criminal law. However, child protection has never, until recently, been seen as a major purpose of the criminal law. That the sexual offences legislation was (and is) more about upholding a socially and morally acceptable view of sexual activity than about protecting children from early sexual activity is clear from cases like *Mohamed* v *Knott* [1968] 2 All ER 563, where a 13-year-old girl was held to be immune from child protection mechanisms because the 28-year-old man who was having regular sexual intercourse with her turned out to be her husband.

Alison Cleland, in the *Stair Memorial Encyclopaedia* reissue of *Child and Family Law* (2004, para 499), suggests that the introduction in the Children (Scotland) Act 1995 of exclusion orders heralded a shift in the civil law's focus on the child, and is evidence of what she calls "the rise of prevention and proactivity". This is seen also in the "parenting orders" provisions of the Antisocial Behaviour etc (Scotland) Act 2004, which are aimed at making parents better at bringing up their children. A similar shift in focus from reaction to prevention is also evident in recent legislation on the criminal law. The two parliaments have recently enacted various pieces of legislation aimed at both offenders and potential offenders against children. The Sex Offenders Act 1997, for example, obliged persons convicted of sex offences (both common law and statutory) to register with the police, so that their movements could be more readily traced (in the belief that recidivism by this type of offender is more common than with other offences). These rules are now contained in Pt II of the Sexual Offences Act 2003 (the part that applies to Scotland). The Crime and Disorder Act 1998 allows the chief constable to seek an order from the sheriff restricting the activities of a convicted sex offender if there is reasonable cause to believe that this is necessary to protect the public from serious harm.

Acting ahead of conviction

The preventive approach is the underlying basis also of the Protection of Children (Scotland) Act 2003, which obliges Scottish Ministers to keep a list of individuals whom they believe to be unsuitable to work with children, and obliges various organisations to refer to the list before deciding whether to employ someone in a post involving work with children. Like exclusion orders under the Children (Scotland) Act 1995, but unlike the provisions referred to above, this list can affect those who merely come under suspicion of child abuse and not just those convicted of it. The justification is the same as for exclusion orders: it is perceived to be more important to take action that might prevent children from being harmed than to ensure that an adult is not subjected to restrictions in his or her liberty which are, in the event, unnecessary.

It is this same thinking that underlies the Scottish Executive's latest proposals, contained in the Protection of Children and Prevention of Sexual Offences (Scotland) Bill, introduced in the Scottish Parliament on 29 October 2004. This will make it an offence to meet or travel to meet children for the purpose of committing a sexual offence, following "grooming behaviour". "Grooming" is the new word to describe activities which in themselves are legally (and indeed socially) innocuous but which are carried out with malign intent. Typically it involves an adult befriending a child and building up some trust in the child, but with the intention that the trust be cruelly abused by leading the child to unlawful sexual behaviour. The Bill does not use the term "grooming", but it defines the conduct it seeks to criminalise fairly precisely. A person aged over 18 (an "adult") will commit an offence if he or she (i) has met or communicated with a person under 16 (a "child") on at least two occasions, (ii) intentionally meets the child or travels with the intention of meeting the child, and (iii) intends to do anything with the child that would amount to any of the listed sexual offences. For the offence to be committed the adult must not reasonably believe the child to be over 16, and there must be a relevant connection with Scotland. So the offence is committed if there is "grooming", which is constituted by any meeting or communication with the child more than once, a bad intent, and some action which is designed to put that bad intent into action.

Proof of the pudding

The first element is much wider than "grooming" as normally understood. Simply to meet with or to communicate with a child does not indicate that trust is being built up with the intention of exploiting that trust for sexual purposes. Most adults meet and communicate with children on a very regular basis. It is when this is done with malign intent that, in common parlance, one might describe meeting with and conversing with a child as "grooming". However, the Bill does not require that the meeting or communicating be done with intent to abuse, but merely that there be, in addition to meeting or communicating, an intent to abuse. Both elements must exist, but the Bill does not require a causal connection between them. It follows that the crucial factor – the element that turns an everyday activity into a criminal offence – is intent.

The Bill does not indicate how prosecutors will be able to prove intent, but the consultation document that preceded it suggested that intent may be inferred from the nature of the communication between the adult and the child, or from other circumstances such as the adult having condoms and lubricants in his possession when he travels to meet the child. In the absence of a sexually explicit communication, in which the adult expresses his intention (unlikely in the case of true grooming in which trust is being built up, and almost certainly a criminal offence in any case), it is difficult to see how a prosecutor could ensure a conviction merely through the possession of articles associated with sexual activity, for there will always remain a reasonable doubt that the articles were possessed for the purposes of sexual activity with another adult and not with a child. It may be that the only practical effect of this provision is to remove any doubt that sexualised communication with children is an offence.

Further action against an individual who has not been convicted of any criminal offence is proposed in the Bill. It creates a new civil order, a "risk of sexual harm order", based on the English precedent contained in the Sexual Offences Act 2003, which can be made by a sheriff, on application by the police, over an adult who has done one or more of various listed acts on two or more occasions which, though criminal in themselves, may or may not in fact have led to the adult being prosecuted. The order will prohibit the adult from doing the act again, and breach of the order, without reasonable excuse, is a criminal offence.

As a civil order, the doing of the acts may be proved on the balance of probabilities, and so the major effect of the creation of this new order is to lower the standard of proof required for action to be taken against an adult who is thought to pose a risk to children.

Shaky foundations

There is no doubt that as a society we are much more conscious of the dangers of sexual exploitation of children, and it is of course right that we be proactive in seeking to prevent harmful exploitation. But important principles of the criminal law should not be sacrificed. An effective lowering of the standard of proof is worrying, as is the proposition that intent (even as wicked as to indulge in sexual abuse of children) is in itself worthy of punishment. A more pressing issue than the creation of new offences of dubious import and little likely effect is the updating of our ludicrous collection of existing sexual offences against children. Boys are given less protection than girls; same-sex sexual activity is treated more harshly than opposite-sex sexual activity; the law's understanding of "sexual activity" is too often limited to penile penetration of the vagina; marriage decriminalises unlawful abuse. Part I of the Sexual Offences Act 2003 is a model from England (albeit from a very different background) for the Scottish Executive to use to produce a criminal code of sexual offences which is gender-neutral, sexuality-neutral and (in Professor Thomson's fecund phrase) organ-neutral. The Scottish Law Commission has undertaken this as one of its imminent projects and getting the basic criminal law right will provide a more robust basis upon which to build an effective system for protecting children from sexual exploitation and harm.

Update

The Sexual Offences (Scotland) Act 2009 finally puts the law of sexual offences onto a sound and modern footing, criminalising not activities which some might find morally objectionable but activities which cause or potentially cause harm to individuals. The new law is explicitly gender-neutral and sexuality-neutral and covers a wider range of sexual behaviour than the previous law did.

The Protection of Children and Prevention of Sexual Offences (Scotland) Act 2005 received Royal Assent on 12 July 2005 and came fully into force on 7 October 2005. A sentencing appeal on a conviction under the Act is HM Advocate *v* Graham *2010 SLT 715.*

Commentary No 24: April 2005

A Wealth of Measures

Overview of some of the many important measures in the surprisingly wide-ranging Family Law (Scotland) Bill

We have waited a long time for the Bill that was presented to the Scottish Parliament on 7 February 2005. Its genesis can be traced to two reports of the Scottish Law Commission: the 1989 *Report on the Grounds of Divorce* (Scot Law Com no 116) and the 1992 *Report on Family Law* (Scot Law Com no 135). These were followed by the Scottish Office's consultation paper *Improving Scottish Family Law* (1999), the Scottish Executive's *Parent and Children: The Scottish Executive's Proposals for Improving Scottish Family Law* (2000), and finally *Family Matters: Improving Family Law in Scotland* (2004).

Within that gestation period some ideas emerged only to be dropped, including grandparents' rights and step-parental responsibilities and rights agreements. Other ideas, such as dealing with the *Wallis* v *Wallis* problem, have been added. The following is not a comprehensive description of the details of what is a surprisingly wide-ranging Bill, but identifies some of the highlights. Any opinion expressed hereafter is entirely personal, reflecting my previously published views.

Securer foundations

The Matrimonial Homes (Family Protection) (Scotland) Act 1981 is to be amended in a number of crucial ways. First, occupancy rights will be removed by the passing of 2 years during which the entitled spouse and the non-entitled spouse were not cohabiting and the home was not occupied by the non-entitled spouse. Secondly, the scope of matrimonial interdicts is to be extended so that they may cover, in addition to the matrimonial home, any other home occupied by the applicant, the applicant's place of work and the child's school. Thirdly, powers of arrest attached to matrimonial interdicts will no longer fall at the end of the marriage but will do so 3 years after their granting. Fourthly, "domestic interdicts" are created, being an equivalent to matrimonial interdicts but available to cohabitants (whether opposite-sex or same-sex).

Practicalities of divorce

The separation periods are to be reduced from 2 and 5 years to 1 and 2 years of non-cohabitation with and without (respectively) the defender's agreement. A knock-on consequence is that desertion as a ground for divorce disappears. The importance of desertion lay solely in the fact that it allowed a 2 year non-cohabitation divorce to be obtained without consent: this will now be possible whether or not there is initial desertion. Two bars to divorce are also to go: the fact that one party may suffer grave financial hardship, and collusion. Grave financial hardship lost its significance as a bar when the Family Law (Scotland) Act 1985 made it one of the justifications for granting financial provision. Collusion is to disappear in recognition of the fact that while as a bar it made sense when divorce was truly an adversarial process, today the process is often in fact collusive or at least non-adversarial, and it is indeed good social policy to encourage this.

One of the most important changes (about which the Scottish Executive took many soundings without achieving broad consensus) is that in determining financial provision on divorce, the court is to be allowed to take into account fluctuations in the value of the matrimonial property after the relevant date. This is designed to overrule the unloved decision of *Wallis* v *Wallis* 1993 SLT 1348, but the Bill as presented may well undergo redrafting before the best way to achieve that aim is identified. Another small but important practical change is that sheriff clerks are to be given the power to execute deeds necessary to ensure the transfer of property required by an order for financial provision: sheriff clerks already have this power in relation to heritable property and the Bill extends it also to moveable property.

Parenthood or welfare?

Unmarried fathers' rights was another issue upon which consensus could not be reached, though in the various consultations that preceded the Bill there was a clear preponderance of opinion to the effect that the current situation (whether or not it was consistent with the ECHR) was not sustainable. I have long argued that to distinguish between male and female parents, and between married men and unmarried men, in relation to the parent–child relationship is sexist and status-based and is therefore contrary to the UN Convention on the Rights of the Child, as well as subverting the very ethos of the Children (Scotland) Act 1995 by absolving some men of their parental responsibilities. The position of the unmarried father is very substantially ameliorated by the Bill, which grants parental responsibilities and parental rights to fathers if they are either married to the mother or registered as father. This will deal with most unmarried fathers, but it still distinguishes between male and female parents because the latter do not need to register themselves as parent before acquiring parental responsibilities and parental rights (and this distinction will survive for another 16 years since the provision is not to be retrospective).

It may be that this does not matter terribly, since registration is the means by which most unmarried fathers prove paternity. But the practical difference will lie with the man who is not registered but who claims to be the father (such as, for example, the ex-Home Secretary). Obtaining a declarator of paternity in itself brings nothing except financial obligation, and to obtain parental responsibilities and parental rights such a man would need also to seek an order under s 11 of the Children (Scotland) Act 1995 establishing that their granting would be in the welfare of the child. If proof, by whatever means, of paternity were to have the same effect as proof, by whatever means, of maternity then parental responsibilities and parental rights would follow the fact of parenthood rather than the judgment of welfare.

Cohabitants and financial rights

Cohabitants currently have a range of important private law, taxation and social security rights. The Bill grants a few more, including some highly significant rights. The definition of cohabitant, if somewhat clumsily, includes same-sex couples who have not registered their relationship as a civil partnership. The rules contained in ss 25 and 26 of the Family Law (Scotland) Act 1985 (presumption of equal share in household goods and in savings from housekeeping allowances) are extended to cohabitants. Much more importantly, an entirely new set of rules is provided for financial readjustment between the pair at the end of the relationship, either on death or on separation. When one cohabitant dies, the survivor will be able to go to court to claim a portion of the deceased's intestate estate, it being for the court to determine what portion to award, taking account of a variety of facts but being capped at the amount that a spouse would be entitled to in similar circumstances. And when the cohabitants separate for any reason before the death of one of them, either may seek a court order similar to but much more restricted than those available under s 8 of the Family Law (Scotland) Act 1985 for divorcing spouses. Putting it in the language of s 9 of that Act (which the Bill does not do), there will be two justifications for a cohabitant's claim for financial provision: (i) the sharing of any economic burden of caring after the end of the cohabitation for a child (of the cohabitants), and (ii) the harmonisation of the economic advantages and disadvantages obtained or suffered by the parties in the interests of the other or of any child of the relationship.

Same-sex couples

The Civil Partnership Act 2004 made a bit of a hash of the Scottish provisions (the blame for which lies with whoever insisted on sending the matter to Westminster). Nevertheless the opportunity has been taken in the current Bill to deal with some of the omissions and anomalies. Perhaps most importantly, the Matrimonial Homes (Family Protection) (Scotland) Act 1981, which is at present limited to married couples and opposite-sex cohabitants and which was extended to civil partners by the 2004 Act, will be further extended by the Bill to same-sex cohabitants. Other omissions are likely to be resolved as the Bill makes its way through the legislative process, such as including same-sex cohabitants in the provisions of the Civil Evidence (Family Mediation) (Scotland) Act 1995.

A long time coming

There are various other crucial amendments contained in this important Bill and doubtless more will be added during its passage, together with substantial amendment to highly complex issues. While the political climate has clearly altered since most of the changes were first mooted, the social imperative for the changes was not noticeably less pressing 15 years ago than it is today. The delay may be explained by the change of government, followed by devolution, followed by the Scottish Executive's increasing predilection for consultation. Given the consultations that the Scottish Law Commission undertakes in any case, one is left wondering whether the Executive's approach is truly based on a belief that this will lead to better law, or a belief that the process will allow it to be seen to be consulting the people. Defensive government does not necessarily create bad law, but it does mean that good law is a long time coming.

Update

Stage One of the Family Law (Scotland) Bill took place before the Justice (1) Committee of the Scottish Parliament in May and June 2005, Stage Two in November and Stage Three in December 2005. Royal Assent was given on 20 January 2006, and the Bill came into effect as the Family Law (Scotland) Act 2006 on 4 May 2006. It had been widely amended during the parliamentary process but the basic principles as described above remained in place. Consultation continued as the Bill was being debated on the best way to resolve the Wallis *conundrum, and the amended rule finally accepted is now contained in s 16 of the 2006 Act. This permits the court to set the "relevant date" for (some) financial provision on divorce purposes as either a date agreed by the parties or a date as near as possible to the date of the making of the order; this applies only for the purposes of property transfer orders.*

Commentary No 25: July 2005

Adopting a New Approach

Author welcomes the recommendations of the Cox Report on adoption, while warning against treating media coverage as representative

The long-awaited report of the Adoption Policy Review Group, chaired by Sheriff Principal Cox, was presented to the Scottish Executive on 6 June 2005. It is to be hoped that its recommendations will be accepted and that legislation will speedily follow, for the report is based on (i) a careful examination of the existing law, (ii) a realistic appraisal of how adoption operates in Scotland today, and (iii) an absolute commitment to keep the child's interests at the centre of everyone's attention. The recommendations are likely to be debated in detail by both the press and our elected representatives, and many elements are likely to change before legislation is eventually presented to the Parliament. But it is useful now to be aware of the proposals and the context in which they are made, in order that reactions to that debate (at least from the legal profession) can be informed and focused.

Increasing the number of adopters

The headline-grabbing recommendation, presented by most of the press as if this report dealt with nothing else, is the recommendation that unmarried couples, both opposite-sex and same-sex, be permitted to adopt (as in England and Wales under the Adoption and Children Act 2002, which comes into effect at the end of 2005). The whole debate on the adoption changes runs the serious risk of being hijacked by those opposed to conferring any legal recognition to unmarried couples, particularly same-sex couples. This issue ought to have been addressed (as I advised, to deaf ears) while the Civil Partnership Act 2004 was going through Parliament: it is an adults' issue on morality, the common good and how society should develop rather than a children's issue on what is best for any individual child. The rest of this article will address the children's issues that make up the vast bulk of the (bulky) Cox Report.

Where security meets flexibility

Adoption today is an all or nothing concept: it creates a new parent–child relationship through the destruction for virtually all purposes of the original parent–child relationship. It was not always thus, and adoption as introduced into Scotland in 1930 was little more than a sort of protected fostering, whereby the adoptive "parents" were given obligations of "custody, maintenance, and education". Adopters and adoptees were brought within the forbidden degrees in the 1950s; succession rights came in the 1960s; and it was not until the Adoption (Scotland) Act 1978 (coming into force in 1985) that the complete legal divorce of birth parents from adoptees was achieved.

It has long been accepted that children need above all else security, a sense of belonging, a sense of knowing that they are settled where they are and cannot be removed. It has since 1985 been assumed that this is achieved by a "clean break" that is complete for virtually all purposes. However, that assumption has never been fully justified for older children who already have established relationships with a whole family network and who have been compulsorily removed from their parents through childcare procedures.

Such children tend to be much more disparate and have a wider variety of difficulties and needs than young babies. In response to this reality the Cox Report recommends the introduction of a wholly new order that will act as an alternative to adoption and be much more flexible in meeting the needs of individual children. "Permanence orders" would allow parental responsibilities and parental rights to be shared with local authorities, carers and, if appropriate, birth parents. Children subject to these orders would be looked-after children and only local authorities would be able to seek such orders. There would be no effect on succession rights or forbidden degrees. They would be flexible enough to take account of the different needs of different children, and permit varying degrees of contact and maintained relationships with birth families. The order would be designed to provide the child with security, but without the complete destruction (in law) of existing family relationships.

The Cox Report is at pains to emphasise that it is not recommending the introduction of the European dual model of "simple adoption" as an alternative to "full adoption". This might be no more than a matter of terminology, for the effect of a permanence order will be much the same as the effect of a "simple adoption". But terminology is important as it affects people's reactions to legal processes, and for that reason the report has, in my view, adopted a sensible approach. It is easier for a birth parent to accept that his or her child has been permanently removed than to accept the legal fiction that he or she is no longer a parent. In many ways, the recommendation is that Scots adoption law returns to its 1930 roots. More accurately, perhaps, and elaborating the horticultural metaphor, the 1930s roots have thrown up a new sucker as an alternative to the main plant which is, on close inspection, a mere graft.

Dispensing with parental consent

The existing two grounds for dispensing with parental consent to adoption have generated a substantial amount of case law. The Cox Report recommends that these grounds be amended, for three reasons: to simplify them, to make them consistent with English law (where the grounds were simplified in the 2002 Act), and to meet more readily the requirements of Art 8 of the ECHR. English adoption law provides only two grounds for dispensing with consent: (i) that the parent or guardian cannot be found or is incapable of giving consent, and (ii) that the child's welfare requires the consent to be dispensed with.

The breadth of the second ground has some dangers; it justifies moderating that ground with ECHR principles. It would not be sufficient that the prospective adopters could offer to give the child a better life than the birth parents: in addition, the interference in family life that adoption undoubtedly is must be in accordance with the law and necessary to protect the health or the rights and freedoms of others. In other words, dispensing with consent must be a proportionate balance between competing but legitimate interests. The report does not attempt to draft new grounds based on the English model as moderated by Art 8, but this should not prove difficult to do.

Title and s 11 orders

The Children (Scotland) Act 1995 amended adoption law to ensure that a person whose parental responsibilities and parental rights are removed by an adoption order cannot seek the restoration of any of these responsibilities and rights by means of a s 11 order under the 1995 Act (s 11(3) and (4)). The Cox Report recommends the abolition of this rule and its replacement with a rule that a previous parent can seek a s 11 order but only with the leave of the court. Court leave is not common as a process in Scotland, but it is not unknown (for example in relation to revocation of freeing orders: s 20 of the 1978 Act). In my view this is a sensible compromise between the child's need for security and the rights of the birth parent. It always was anomalous that the birth parent is the only person in the world who cannot seek, for example, a contact order in respect of a child, and in any case the rule relates only to title and the court is perfectly free to award contact to a birth parent if sought by another person (for example the child).

To revoke or not to revoke?

The present law is strongly resistant to the notion that an adoption order once made can be revoked: this has led to some dubious results (of which *Cameron* v *MacIntyre's Executor* 2004 SLT 79, in which an adoption order made on the adoptee's 21st birthday could not be revoked over 50 years later is the most recent example). Legislation elsewhere, such as in Australia and New Zealand, permits the discharge of adoption orders for reasons such as duress, fraud or material mistake, and the Cox Report examines whether it would be sensible to follow this approach. It recommends not, even in exceptional circumstances of fraud or grave irregularity: this in order to underpin the security and stability that adoption is intended to provide. I am not convinced that this argument answers the concerns of those who would prefer revocability in cases of irregularity and gross unfairness.

Full consideration needed

The report also contains a large number of detailed procedural recommendations, including the abolition of the little-used interim adoption orders. The recommendations are primarily designed to speed the process, ensure a more robust appeal mechanism, enhance the training and role of curators ad litem, reporting officers and safeguarders, free the fostering system from unnecessary limitations and ensure that fair and appropriate regulations are in place in respect of access to information.

This is a far more wide-ranging and detailed report than the press have indicated (or even than can be described here). It needs to be read and digested in full, and it is pointless and misrepresentative and bad for children not to do so.

Update

Cameron *v* MacIntyre, *mentioned in this Commentary, was overruled by the Inner House: 2006 SLT 176. It was held that the original adoption order was incompetent, having been granted after the adopted person attained adulthood, and therefore could be reduced. Revocation of adoption orders properly made remains virtually impossible: see* Webster *v* Norfolk County Council *[2009] 2 All ER 1156.*

The Cox Report was given effect to by the Adoption and Children (Scotland) Act 2007: the Act is discussed in Commentary No 31 below.

Commentary No 26: October 2005

Tales from the Court

Recent Court of Session family law cases, where people behaving badly have made life difficult for all

Marriage by deception

Only one thing spoilt the happiness of Karen Wetherhill when she met and fell in love with Zahid Sheikh: the inconvenient fact that he was already married to someone else. But that was an arranged marriage to which Zahid was not committed, and so Karen and Zahid moved in together, started a business together, and had two children together. Zahid's parents, with whom his (proper) wife lived, would accept Karen as a member of the family only if she were married to Zahid, so they told his parents (and presumably the wife) that they were indeed married. The (proper) wife left Scotland and soon thereafter divorced Zahid. Karen was now free to marry the father of her children, but she refused to do so because she did not wish to change religion and believed that she would be trapped and would have to cover her head in public. Zahid's family continued to believe they were already married in any case.

Sadly, the relationship broke down and Karen and Zahid separated. Karen now sought financial provision on divorce from him but, of course, needed to establish that she was married in the first place. Enter the doctrine of marriage by cohabitation with habit and repute. There was clear cohabitation for some 12 years after the (proper) wife had divorced Zahid and, Lord Philip held, sufficient habit and repute: *Sheikh* v *Sheikh* 2005 Fam LR 7.

Karen may well have believed herself "married" in a social sense but she knew full well that she was not married in any lawful sense. The repute was the result of deliberate deceit to pull the wool over the eyes of a devout family – and Karen participated in that deceit as much as the unscrupulous, tax-evading, bad debtor perjurer, Zahid. As a cohabitant she probably deserved some financial provision, and the Family Law (Scotland) Bill currently before the Scottish Parliament will allow people in her position certain claims. But to regard her as "married" in order to achieve this illustrates all that is wrong with the bankrupt concept of marriage by cohabitation with habit and repute.

Two issues in forced marriages

June Kaur was 18 years old, with a boyfriend called Keith Singh, when her mother took her to India and married her off, against her will, to a man she did not know. June was taken to her new husband's house but she refused to have sex with him and a week later she returned to Scotland. She moved out of her parents' house and went to live with Keith, with whom one hopes she will be very happy.

Temporary Judge Macdonald found that June's mother had threatened to destroy her passport, leaving her stranded in India, if she did not submit. He held that this threat of immediate danger to June's liberty, causing her will to be overborne, vitiated her consent. *Singh* v *Singh* 2005 SLT 749. But he also sounded a cautionary note. The threats had to be of immediate danger to life, limb or liberty. He doubted whether the threats in the earlier case of *Mahmud* v *Mahmud* 1994 SLT 599 (that shame and degradation would be visited upon the whole family unless the pursuer submitted to the marriage arranged by his parents) satisfied this test. Lord Prosser in that case had, of course, granted the declarator of nullity but Judge Macdonald would not have done so.

There was another interesting feature in this case: choice of law. Is it the *lex loci celebrationis* (in this case India) or the law of the domicile (in this case Scotland) that determines whether a marriage is invalid due to duress? An *obiter dictum* in *Di Rollo* v *Di Rollo* 1959 SC 75 had suggested that the question of whether true consent had been given was a matter for the *lex loci celebrationis*, though an English case had come to the opposite conclusion. Judge Macdonald preferred to follow the English case. Again, the Scottish Parliament will shortly resolve the issue, for there are provisions in the Family Law (Scotland) Bill ensuring that matters of capacity and validity of consent to marriage are all to be determined by the law of the domicile, with the added safeguard that Scots law will apply in these matters for all marriages conducted in Scotland.

Insisting on the court

Mr and Mrs B were living in Aberdeen when a baby girl was born to them. When the child was 3, Mrs B removed herself and the child from the family home and went to live in London. A residence and contact dispute was played out in the English courts, the result of which was that Mrs B retained residence and Mr B was entitled to contact.

Mr B then raised an action in the sheriff court at Aberdeen, seeking divorce from Mrs B and also a residence order over the child (failing which a contact order) in terms of the Children (Scotland) Act 1995. The sheriff found that he lacked jurisdiction in the matter of residence, but the sheriff principal allowed an appeal on that question. When the case came back to the sheriff, he sisted the cause, so that the matter could be determined in England, this on the basis that the English family court was already seized of the matter. Back went Mr B to the sheriff principal, but this time that judge agreed with the sheriff. Mr B then sought to have the sist recalled but the sheriff refused on the basis that there had been no change of circumstances. Yet again Mr B went back to the sheriff principal, who again agreed with the sheriff and this time Mr B appealed further to the Court of Session. By this stage the matter had little to do with the wee girl, and all to do with jurisdiction.

The Inner House had little difficulty in holding that, since an appellate court can interfere with a discretionary decision of a judge at first instance only if the latter had misdirected himself in law, misapprehended the material facts, taken account of irrelevant facts, or reached a decision that was wholly unreasonable or plainly wrong, the appeal had to be dismissed. But they also agreed that, under s 41 of the Family Law Act 1986, the English courts had been seized of the matter before the Scottish courts and so the English courts had retained jurisdiction to the exclusion of the Scottish courts ever since. *RB* v *MB* 2005 Fam LR 49. The court ended with some finger-wagging: the appellant's obduracy in insisting that his child's future be determined in Aberdeen showed that he had little concern for the child's real welfare and was more concerned about his own sense of injustice to himself. This is not, sadly, an unusual phenomenon in family cases.

An ongoing financial saga

The saga of the divorce between Mr and Mrs Patrick Sweeney continues to entertain and inform. It will be recalled that in 2002 a divorce was granted to Mrs Sweeney with an order for financial provision against

Mr Sweeney in the order of some three quarters of a million pounds. Mrs Sweeney, who like Oliver Twist wanted more, reclaimed on the ground that the Lord Ordinary had wrongly deducted amounts payable as capital gains tax in valuing the matrimonial property to which she was entitled. That appeal was successful (2004 SC 372) and at that stage Mr Sweeney lodged supplementary grounds for a cross appeal, arguing that special circumstances existed which justified a departure from equal sharing, and that the making of an order for a capital sum was unreasonable in light of his existing resources.

The "special circumstances" that he put forward were primarily that his assets, being business interests, could not be realised without damaging their value: his wealth, he argued, was "theoretical" rather than "practical". Mrs Sweeney argued, however, that since the date of the original decree (in suspension due to the appeal) her ex-husband had been transferring his remaining assets from his free holding into his business: the implication was that he had deliberately made his assets difficult to realise and so had deliberately created his own special circumstances. The Inner House did not find that he had acted unreasonably and so they found that it would be unreasonable having regard to his resources to order that all his remaining non-business assets be made over to his ex-wife.

The court decided to modify (to a fairly modest extent) the amount Mr Sweeney had to pay, and they ordered that the amount be payable in instalments: Mr Sweeney saved, and Mrs Sweeney lost, around £100,000 in this latest round of this complex litigation (2005 SLT 1141).

Domestic power-games

Men (and mothers) behaving badly indeed. Families remain a fertile source of domestic power-games which the courts must strive hard to bring to an end.

Update

Section 38 of the Family Law (Scotland) Act 2006 dealt with the choice of law point mentioned in Singh *v* Singh*; the ping-pong litigation in* B *v* B *was on-going 3 years after the case discussed above (2009 SLT 355) and was not finally resolved until December 2010 (*B *v* B *[2010] CSOH 160 when the father abandoned his claim for residence of the child and Lord Tyre had little difficulty in holding that the child's interests demanded that the mother retain residence; more* Sweeney *litigation can be found at 2007 SC*

396. We should never underestimate the desire of couples who have fallen out with each other to obtain a judicial finding that the other one was to blame, nor their willingness to use all means (including their own children) as weapons to further that desire.

Commentary No 27: January 2006

Quiet Revolutions

December 2005 was a watershed month for Scots family law – but there are still areas where the law has not achieved full separation between church and state

December revolutions

On 5 December 2005 the Civil Partnership Act 2004 came into effect and the first civil partnership registrations in Scotland took place on 20 December. The importance of these events cannot be overstated. The 2004 Act is the most significant development in family law for over 100 years. Paradoxically, however, though the Act covers a vast range of issues, including tax and social security, pension and property sharing, damages on death, domestic violence, occupancy rights, housing and tenancy succession, bankruptcy, aliment, immigration, family breakdown and relationships with children, there is nonetheless virtually no new law for practitioners to learn. Anyone familiar with the rules of marriage needs only to remember the simple point that civil partnership is for same-sex couples while marriage is for opposite-sex couples. The 2004 Act does not alter any marriage rule, nor affect that institution in any way but one – it removes the uniquely preferred position of marriage and thus the ability of heterosexual people to say to homosexual people: "we are better than you".

On 15 December 2005 the Scottish Parliament finalised another family law revolution when it completed its consideration of what is now the Family Law (Scotland) Act 2006. I have no doubt that, here and elsewhere, I shall be commenting for some time to come on the detailed provisions of this important piece of legislation, but it is worth mentioning here the fundamental changes being made in relation to cohabitation. For the first time, protection is given to those who have reasonable expectations of sharing in the wealth generated during an informal relationship or who are in fairness deserving of a return for their efforts towards the family. This is clearly a revolution too far for some, but the Act leaves vast areas of discretion to the courts, which are charged with evolving the law to achieve justice within the bald framework set down by the Scottish Parliament.

The religification of Scottish family law

Family law used to be church law. It still is in many countries in the world to the detriment of, especially, their female citizens. But even in the secular modern age it would be wrong to describe Scottish family law as completely separate from religion. Ministers of the Established Church remain automatically celebrants (Marriage (Scotland) Act 1977, s 8(1)(a)(i)), and clerics of other churches and religious bodies are entitled to become celebrants. We recognise and accept religious ceremonies as creating marriages which have civil effects. One would have expected, however, that as time went by the separation of church and state, of family law and religious doctrine, would inexorably grow. But it seems that the reverse has been happening. We see this with a recent statutory development and with a recent decision of the Inner House of the Court of Session.

Where secular meets sacred

The statutory development is contained in the Family Law (Scotland) Act 2006. Sheriffs have been given an unprecedented power to postpone the granting of a divorce if one of the parties is refusing to set the other free. Of course in law it is not for the parties to "set each other free" but for the law to do so. The point, however, is that some religious bodies do not recognise civil (court-granted) divorces and so do not accept that a person who is (lawfully) divorced is free to re-marry. The Roman Catholic Church (I understand) takes this position, but there is nothing the law can do since the position of that body is that no act of man or woman can terminate a marriage before death. Certain sections of the Jewish faith take the similar view that a court-granted divorce does not end a marriage, but differ from the Roman Catholic Church in accepting that the marriage can be terminated before death by the husband granting the wife a "get", or religious divorce. It is the religious rather than the civil divorce that renders the (ex-)wife free to re-marry in the eyes of her faith. She is, of course, whatever her faith says, free to re-marry in the eyes of Scots law even before the granting of the "get".

But it sometimes happens that processes, legal and religious, are used tactically and for illegitimate reasons.

Were the legal system to maintain a complete separation of law and religion, it would deem itself entirely powerless to resolve that issue: it is a personal belief of the ex-spouse that she cannot remarry, not a belief of the law. But our legislators have determined that the Scottish courts should be able to intervene in this sort of scenario and s 15 allows the sheriff to "postpone" the granting of a divorce where the marriage has been proved to have broken down irretrievably, but (i) the applicant for such postponement is prevented from entering a religious marriage by virtue of a requirement of the religion of that marriage, and (ii) the other party is able to remove the religious impediment.

The provision probably promises more than it can deliver. Though the section is not worded in terms of "pursuers" and "defenders", in situations in which there is real dispute it can benefit only defenders. It is the pursuer seeking a legal divorce but refusing to grant a religious divorce that the provision is aimed at. But if it is the defender who is refusing to grant the religious divorce, the threat of postponing the legal divorce plays into and strengthens the defender's hand – at least if his defending is genuine. The defender may continue to refuse to grant the religious divorce and indeed may do so for extraneous reasons (such as to get more in the way of financial provision, or more contact with a child): in these sorts of cases it will not be in the interests of the pursuer to seek a legal divorce and at the same time ask for its postponement. And because religious divorces tend to be gendered (with the power to grant them in the hands of men rather than women), the provision limits its benefits to female defenders – it gives nothing to male defenders or to female pursuers. My prediction is that we will not see these new rules being operated often, if at all.

The meaning of consent

Case law has also recently brought family law and religion closer together. It has long been a rule of Scots law that marriage is based on consent, which must indicate a real intention to take each other as husband and wife. The outward manifestation of that consent (saying "I do" before witnesses and signing the marriage schedule) will normally be proof positive of that intention. But sometimes the outward manifestation does not indicate positive intention – as in the case of the forced marriage, which is no marriage because the consent is not real. But a different situation arises when no one forces parties to give the outward manifestation of consent, and they do so for a reason other than a genuine consent to marry, such as to defraud someone like the immigration authorities.

In *Hakeem* v *Hussain* 2003 SLT 515 Lord Clarke held that a couple who married in a registry office, signing the marriage schedule which was then registered, could not escape the marriage on the argument that, as good religious believers, they did not consider themselves married until a religious ceremony had taken place (which in the event did not take place). This was a good and sensible decision. The Inner House, however, has overturned it. In what is now called *H* v *H* 2005 SLT 1025 an Extra Division has held that while the parties consented to signing the marriage schedule, their religious faith meant that true consent to marriage was consent before God rather than consent before the registrar: as such the marriage was void for lack of consent and their fraudulent and irreligious scheme was reported to the Crown Office.

This is a dangerous decision. Many faiths which are well represented in this country do not consider the signing of the marriage schedule or its registering as making a "marriage" and parties do not see that consent as the "consent" required by the 1977 Act. What would happen if a religious marriage were undertaken a week before the civil registration, and one party died in the interim? Were they married? Not in law, whatever their own beliefs were and even if they had commenced living together as husband and wife. If genuine consent to marriage is more important than the forms in the 1977 Act, then we have revived the common law of irregular marriages which was repealed in 1939.

The root cause of these problems is the increasing unwillingness of Scots law to maintain that crucial separation between religious law and civil law. A much purer form of civil relationship has been created by the Civil Partnership Act 2004 which, I suggest, is the model that should guide future development of legal marriage for those who are denied, because of their sexual orientation, access to the 2004 Act itself.

Update

There have been no reported cases on s 15 of the Family Law (Scotland) Act 2006, but a more supportive article than mine was published in response to what I said above: see Deanna Levine, "Getting a Get in Scotland" March 2006, Journal of the Law Society of Scotland, *p 26 and a more detailed article by the same author: "Divorce Law, the Jewish Client and the Get" 2009 SLT (News) 61.*

Commentary No 28: April 2006

Rushed Law and Wrongful Death

Creative interpretation will be needed to avoid injustice through a late amendment to the Family Law (Scotland) Act on suing for wrongful death

Though sometimes unavoidable, it is never a good idea for new provisions to be added into legislation at late stages of the parliamentary process. This deprives the provision of the benefits of careful scrutiny by the appropriate committee, and by its adviser. Such scrutiny was denied a very late addition to the Family Law (Scotland) Act 2006, introduced as amendment 102 on the last day of the Stage 2 debate (30 November 2005). Though the Scottish Law Commission's proposals, upon which the amendment was based, had been widely consulted on, the precise wording of the amendment had not been (as the two Strathclyde LL.B. graduates on the Justice 1 Committee perceptively noted in the debate). In at least one respect, the words used will require imaginative judicial construction before it achieves its purpose.

Ill-fitting rules

The provision is s 35, which amends the Damages (Scotland) Act 1976 by removing some categories of relative from the list of "immediate family" in Schedule 1 thereto, and adding some other categories. The stated purpose was to give effect to the recommendations of the Scottish Law Commission in their Report on Title to Sue for Non-Patrimonial Loss (Scot Law Com no 187). Title to sue for such loss under the 1976 Act is a matter of no little social significance, because its granting provides legal recognition that the relationship between a deceased and a survivor is worthy of respect and protection. When the 1976 Act was originally passed, only spouses, parents, children and those accepted as children of the family were recognised. In 1982 title to sue was extended to couples who were not married to each other but who lived together as if they were husband and wife – an important recognition that the social relationship was legitimate and worthy of the law's protection, that the emotional distress at losing a (heterosexual) partner was likely to be as severe (and as legitimately felt) as such distress at losing a spouse.

However, it had long been felt that the existing rules were too narrow in some respects while at the same time were too broad in others. In particular, the rule that allowed relatives by affinity to sue on the same basis as relatives by consanguinity was considered to be unduly generous. There was a feeling that a mother's loss is of a different order from that of a mother-in-law. Yet Mrs Monteith was allowed to sue for her son-in-law's death on the same basis as his own mother: *Monteith* v *Cape Insulation* 1998 SC 903. At the same time, the Scottish Law Commission believed that the exclusion of siblings and of grandparents was not justified, and that the limitation of cohabitants to opposite-sex couples (see *Telfer* v *Kellock* 2004 SLT 1290) was out of step with the modern acceptance of the legitimacy of same-sex couples, and of their unanswerable demands for equality.

The closer immediate family

Section 35 addresses all these issues, other than same-sex cohabitation. There had been an attempt to deal with that particular issue in the Civil Partnership Act 2004, though in the event the attempt failed since the amendment to the 1976 Act in para 42 of Schedule 28 to the 2004 Act referred to the wrong subparagraph in Schedule 1 to the 1976 Act. One may doubt whether that would have happened if this central element of devolved law had been dealt with by the devolved legislature. Be that as it may, para 2 of Schedule 2 to the Family Law (Scotland) Act 2006 corrects the error and treats same-sex cohabitants in the same way as opposite-sex cohabitants.

The uncontentious provisions are in s 35(5), which adds four new categories to the list of "relatives" who count as "immediate family" for the purposes of the 1976 Act and who therefore are entitled to sue for non-patrimonial loss. First, siblings. This finally fills a gap identified by the court in *McKendrick* v *Sinclair* 1972 SC (HL) 25. The judicial call in that case for a statutory amendment to bring in siblings was ignored by the Parliament that passed the 1976 Act, but has been heeded here. Secondly, grandparents and grandchildren (but no further in the ascending or descending line). Thirdly, persons who accepted the deceased as a child of their family. This removes an anomaly in the present law: a child accepted by the deceased as a member of his or her family can sue on the death of the deceased, but the accepting adult could not sue on the death of the child. Now the accepting adult can. And fourthly, persons who were brought up in the same household as the deceased and who were accepted as a child of the family in which the deceased was a child: this includes children who are not siblings of the deceased but were brought up as if they were.

The concept of children "accepted as a child of the family" is retained, and indeed extended by the fourth category just mentioned. The Scottish Law Commission had recommended that this was a more appropriate indicator of title to sue than the status-based indicator of affinitive relationship, bearing in mind that there will be a substantial overlap. A step-parent may accept a child as a child of his or her family, or he or she may not, or the child may be an adult by the time the step-relationship is created. Entitlement to sue under the 1976 Act is presently based on the step-relationship itself (a relationship of affinity), but s 35(5) provides that in the future entitlement to sue will be based on the act of acceptance.

Affinity as a bar

So far so good. The problem comes with s 35(3), which is designed to remove affinity as the indicator of entitlement. In its own terms (which were not those suggested by the Scottish Law Commission) it is far too broad. It adds a new s 1(4A) to the 1976 Act in the following terms: "Notwithstanding section 10(2) of, and Schedule 1 to, this Act, no award of damages under subsection (4) above shall be made to a person related by affinity to the deceased." In its literal sense, this provision means that even although a person comes in the list in Schedule 1, as for example being an accepted child, they are knocked out of that list if their relationship with the deceased is one of affinity.

This is not what was intended. The removal of affinity was supposed to be the removal of an indicator of entitlement, but the words used convert affinity into a positive – and absolute – bar. This interpretation must be avoided. If the new s 1(4A) is given its literal meaning, the result would be that cohabitants who accept each other's children as children of the family would have a claim in circumstances in which spouses and civil partners who do so would not – because marriage and civil partnership create relationships of affinity (a new s 1(4B) spells this out in case there was any doubt), but cohabitation does not.

Not only is it highly unlikely to have been the parliament's intention to preference cohabitants over spouses but this literal interpretation of the new s 1(4A) satisfies no legitimate aim. It might well be contrary to Arts 8 and 14 of the ECHR to give cohabitants a claim for damages in circumstances in which spouses have no such claim, when the loss to each is identical. If this is so, then it becomes legitimate, even necessary, to read in words to the provision to remove the discrimination and give effect to what the Parliament can be taken to have intended. I suggest the following words, in square brackets, should be read in: "(4A) Notwithstanding section 10(2) of, and Schedule 1 to, this Act, no award of damages under subsection (4) above shall be made to a person [solely on the basis that he or she is] related by affinity to the deceased." There is no doubt that this changes the sense of the subsection, but nor is there any doubt (in my view) that it better reflects what was always intended.

Modesty? The very idea

I notice, finally, in the February *Journal*'s letters page that a correspondent suggested that I had hidden my own light under a bushel in my January column, by not revealing that I had been Justice 1's adviser during the passage of the 2006 Act. I have been accused of many things over the years, but never before of modesty. Let me redress matters with this assertion: had the amendment now contained in s 35 been laid at an earlier stage, Justice 1 would have been properly advised and the wording would have been altered before enactment. And the fact that it was the law graduates on Justice 1 who expressed discomfort at being asked to enact words they had only just been presented with goes a long way to subvert the claim, also in February's *Journal*, that a law degree no longer makes good lawyers.

Update

I do feel vindicated. A case arose in 2010 which involved the very issue that I identify in the above commentary. In Mykoliw *v* Botterill *2010 SLT 1219 Lord Pentland (referring to what he described as this "illuminating commentary") had little difficulty in rejecting the notion that a literal interpretation ought to be given to s 35(2), for the very reasons I identify here and he held instead that an interpretation that avoided the ludicrous result of giving to cohabiting couples something that was denied to married couples should be adopted. So he read the words "no award of damages ... shall be made to a person related by affinity to the deceased" to mean "no award of damages shall be made to a person whose only relationship to the deceased is one of affinity". Interestingly, though he discussed the compatibility of the new rule with the European Convention, he felt able to come to that result without formally relying on the interpretative obligation in s 3 of the Human Rights Act 1998. The normal canons of construction, in particular the requirement to avoid absurdity or anomaly, allowed him to adopt the interpretation that he did.*

Commentary No 29: July 2006

Clean Break under Attack

Author disagrees with Lord Hope's view that Scots law is too restrictive to achieve a fair settlement in some divorce cases involving high-earning spouse

The statutory contrast

Financial provision on divorce and dissolution is governed in Scotland by the Family Law (Scotland) Act 1985, an Act that has not needed substantial revision since it came into force. It was of course amended in 1999 to reflect pension reforms and then again in 2006 to solve the *Wallis* conundrum. But by and large it has worked well these 20 years, and though there has been a high level of litigation the courts have not had any doctrinal difficulty with the approach encapsulated in the Act.

It is very different in England, where ancillary relief (as it is called there) is governed by Pt II of the Matrimonial Causes Act 1973, as amended by the Matrimonial and Family Proceedings Act 1984. In that jurisdiction the higher courts have often felt the need to restructure the approach to be taken, due to the far less rigid framework set out in the English legislation. Our 1985 Act favours legal certainty, to encourage pre-court settlement; their 1973 Act favours flexibility, trusting judicial discretion to achieve fairness in the individual case. In *Thomas* v *Thomas* [1995] 2 FLR 668 Waite LJ said at 670D: "The discretionary powers conferred on the court by the ... Matrimonial Causes Act 1973 to redistribute the assets are almost limitless". This is alien stuff to us, which is the major reason why decisions from the English courts on financial provision on divorce and dissolution are usually ignored in Scotland.

However, even in Scotland much attention has been given to a recent English House of Lords decision of great importance to the operation of the 1973 Act. This is because the Scottish judge on the Appellate Committee, Lord Hope of Craighead, criticised the way things are done in Scotland and called for our legislation to be amended to become more like the English. His speech was directed not to the cases before him but to the hypothetical question of how these cases would have been decided had they arisen in Scotland. Such a comparative discursus would usually be welcome, especially from such a source and particularly for law teachers. But Lord Hope's comments in *Miller* v *Miller; McFarlane* v *McFarlane* [2006] UKHL 24 are not welcome for they misinterpret Scots law, and his proposed reform would rob our system of its most successful feature.

Career loss and clean break

Both cases involved very wealthy couples, but the marriages were quite different. In *Miller* the marriage was short, lasting less than 3 years. But within that period of time the husband's wealth had increased substantially and he acquired expectations of even more substantial increases in the future. In *McFarlane* the marriage had lasted for 16 years and had produced three children. The wife had given up her career as a solicitor just before the birth of the second child; the husband maintained his career as a chartered accountant and, because the wife was at home, was able to enhance it significantly. Both cases raised what the English judges referred to as the issue of "compensation", that is to say the extent to which one spouse should be compensated by the other for the loss of expectation of a certain standard of living, either through the lost career or through diminished standards caused by the divorce.

Lord Hope could not see how such women could be dealt with fairly under the Scottish system. He calls for added levels of statutory flexibility, to be achieved by increased levels of judicial discretion: he is clearly not persuaded by the benefits of certainty in this area of the law. More than this, however, he seems not at all convinced by the philosophy of the clean break. It is this philosophy that underpins the 1985 Act, and its benefits in terms of social policy are too well known to be rehearsed in this short commentary. Indeed even Lord Nicholls, who gave the lead judgment, accepted that the benefits of the principle were "self-evident" (para 35).

Clean break in the 1985 Act

Rather oddly, Lord Hope sees the clean break philosophy as being encapsulated in s 9(1)(d) and he assumes that the women's claims would be made under that paragraph. This is the s 9 principle that allows for a "three year readjustment" period to be funded by way of periodical allowance. Yet surely a more important location of the clean break principle is the injunction to courts in s 13(2)(b) not to make a periodical allowance at all unless an award of a capital sum or property transfer order would be inappropriate or insufficient. Lord Hope, who never mentions s 13(2)(b), sees the 3-year readjustment period as insufficient to deal with the concept of "compensation aimed at redressing a significant prospective disparity between the parties arising from the way they conducted their marriage" (para 114). He suggests that social changes to marital relationships since 1985 have shifted the balance of fairness, and he concludes that flexibility achieves fairness better than certainty. This leads to his call for reform of the 1985 Act because, in his view, "the flexibility which sheriffs and judges need to adapt the law to what would be regarded as fair today as compared with what was regarded as fair 25 years ago is denied to them".

Dealing particularly with Mrs McFarlane's claim, Lord Hope asserts (para 116) that "It would not be possible to design an award under the Scottish system that provided her with an amount of income for the future that gave fair recognition to her entitlement". This of course assumes what it sets out to prove, which is what Mrs McFarlane was "entitled" to. Making no reference to statutory authority, Lord Hope says that Mrs McFarlane "is entitled to an award that reflects the agreement that she and her husband entered into [that she give up her career to bring up the children], because in their case the capital assets that would be needed for this are not available" (para 116, emphasis added). Not so. She is "entitled" to what the legislation governing her marriage gives her. "Fairness" might suggest something else, but it is not an entitlement.

Even if Scots law requires "fairness" over and above what it provides in terms of the 1985 Act, Lord Hope then indicates an unduly narrow interpretation of s 9, for the major flaw he identifies is that Mr McFarlane would continue to enjoy the benefits of his high earning capacity, while Mrs McFarlane "could not" be compensated for her future economic disparity, due to his lack of capital. "She would be required instead to adjust to a lower standard of living. And she would have to do this over a period of no more than three years." In the next paragraph of his speech (para 117) Lord Hope agrees with Lord Nicholls that the situation of Mrs McFarlane (a higher earner who gives up her career) "is a paradigm case for an income award that will compensate her for the significant future economic disparity . . . arising from the way the parties conducted their marriage. That is impossible under the rules which apply in Scotland".

Cumulative effect

But a fair result is not impossible in Scotland, for the following reasons. First, the cumulative nature of the principles in s 9(1) should never be forgotten. It is a mistake to approach s 9(1)(d) in isolation, and in any case that principle is not designed for the purpose Lord Hope sees it addressing. That principle is of narrow scope and only applies when there is "dependence to a substantial degree", so it would not cover, for example, a woman who compromises but does not give up completely her earning capacity and therefore is not so "dependent". Secondly, the lack of immediately realisable capital on the part of the husband can be dealt with by means of an award of a capital sum to be paid in instalments (permitted under s 12(3)). Thirdly, making the award one of a capital sum (in instalments, if necessary) brings into play the principles in s 9(1)(a), (b) and (c), which can easily achieve all that Lord Hope wants to achieve for Mrs McFarlane.

Section 9(1)(a) contains the flexibility perceived to be inherent in the word "fair". Matrimonial property must be shared "fairly" and, though this is presumed to mean "equal sharing", any claimant is able to argue for a different division on the basis that equality does not achieve fairness. Future earning capacity is a matter that can be taken into account in Scotland in determining a fair division (contrary to what Lord Hope believes): see for example *Cunniff* v *Cunniff* 1999 SLT 992, where the wife received 100% of the matrimonial property instead of 50% explicitly because the husband had high earning potential and she had none. And it is important to note that it was no judicial innovation by the Inner House to permit judges and sheriffs to take into account future earning potential: s 27(1) of the Act defines "resources" available for distribution under s 8 to mean "present and foreseeable resources". So future disparities in wealth caused by differential earning capacities can indeed be taken into account in determining what is a "fair" distribution of matrimonial property (a concept for England, bewilderingly, that the English judges in this case could not agree the content of – do we really want that level of "flexibility", ie uncertainty, in Scotland?).

Continuing economic advantage

Sometimes of course s 9(1)(a) is of limited value because there is little or no matrimonial property, but the 1985 Act has a solution for that because resources may be distributed (in instalments if necessary and by definition at a later date) in order to achieve a "fair" result under s 9(1)(b) also: "fair account should be taken of any economic advantage derived by either party … and of any economic disadvantage suffered by either party in the interests of the other party or of the family". This is an underused provision but is much more flexible than s 9(1)(d), and a more obvious route to deal with the likes of Mrs McFarlane who gave up a career for the sake of her husband and children. This was clearly an economic disadvantage, and a commonly suffered one.

The fact that s 9(1)(b) uses the past tense "suffered" should not be taken to limit the court's consideration to past disadvantages but should, it is submitted, also refer to past acts which create continuing disadvantages, such as an agreement between parties that one would sacrifice their career for the other. Confirmation that this must be so is found in s 9(2), which defines "economic advantage" for the purpose of s 9(1)(b) to include "gains … in earning capacity": capacity by definition refers to the future. If this is so, then the fact that Mrs McFarlane gave up her career some time ago to allow Mr McFarlane to continue with his conferred an "economic advantage" on Mr McFarlane, within the terms of s 9(1)(b), which continues after divorce. There is nothing in s 9(1)(b) to prevent the court taking into account that continuing advantage, and making an award (of a one-off payment, or of capital instalments) to give a fair share of that advantage to the likes of Mrs McFarlane.

So the Scottish legislation can, in my view, achieve exactly what Lord Hope stated it could not do. That leaves his call for amendment without valid basis (other than a reference to *Wallis* v *Wallis*, as if the narrow point in that tedious case was symptomatic of an underlying weakness in the whole Act). But what does he actually want to happen? He suggests (para 121) two amendments to the 1985 Act.

Reasons not to amend

First, s 9(1)(d) should be amended in order to extend the three year period if, in exceptional circumstances, the judge finds that the disadvantage of reduced earning capacity ought to be compensated out of the other's future income because the capital needed to provide this is not available. But this is not needed because other principles in s 9 (bearing in mind the inclusion in s 9(2) of future earning capacity, and the instalment provision in s 12(3)) can achieve precisely the compensation sought. In my view removing the three year limitation to s 9(1)(d) would seriously compromise the clean break principle – as well as being a denial of the reality, accepted by their Lordships in *Miller; McFarlane*, that it is usually impossible for both parties to maintain existing standards of living after divorce.

Lord Hope's second suggestion is to allow a periodical payment to be made under s 9(1)(b) (a principle he never, in fact, discusses). This would not so much compromise as remove completely from our law the idea of a clean break on divorce.

So it is really the clean break principle that is under attack here. Parties would continue to have a financial relationship with each other after divorce or dissolution. Parties would be given no encouragement by the law to readjust to a lower standard of living or to return to independence, and would indeed be discouraged from doing so. Marriage and civil partnership in themselves, whether short, medium or long, would create an enforceable expectation of lifelong sharing. Lord Hope may want all this. I certainly do not.

Update

In conversations with Lord Hope since this commentary appeared, he has made plain to me that his speech was not intended to "attack" (as the title of my Commentary suggests) the clean-break principle, which both he and Lord Nicholls give clear support to. Rather he was focusing on the concept of "fairness" and its different understandings in the two systems. Nor is he at all persuaded of the practicality of the use of capital instalments in cases like Miller *and* McFarlane. *It seems to me, however, that we should not assume that "fairness" has (or even should have) the same meanings in different legal systems, even those as closely connected as Scots law and English law. The Scottish Government, it was reported in the September 2006 issue of the* Journal, *decided not to heed Lord Hope's call to amend the 1985 Act.* Wallis *was, of course, dealt with in s 16 of the Family Law (Scotland) Act 2006.*

Commentary No 30: October 2006

Lesbian Families, Parenthood and Contact

Issues in enforcing contact orders against the recalcitrant behaviour of the residence parent, with reference to the recent case involving a lesbian couple

It is not so much the civil partnership legislation (hugely important though that is), but the increased social visibility and acceptability of same-sex relationships that will lead to the family courts dealing more and more with the problems of family breakdown in the gay and lesbian community. And it may come as a surprise to some that the problems and difficulties that same-sex families have are the same as those faced by the heterosexual community.

An unexceptional case

In July of this year the House of Lords handed down their opinions in *In Re G (Children)* [2006] UKHL 43. But for the gender of the couple, the circumstances were unexceptional. An unmarried couple had been bringing up two children since birth. But they separated when the younger child was one and the older child was three. Contact arrangements were put in place, but after some difficulties the parties (both of whom by now had new partners) went to court and these arrangements were bolstered by court order. The residence parent, in an attempt to marginalise the contact parent from the children's life, and in direct defiance of the court order prohibiting this, then surreptitiously moved to a new town at some distance from the contact parent. The contact parent in response sought a shared residence order, and though this was refused at first instance it was granted by the Court of Appeal. The defying residence parent then appealed to the House of Lords.

The background to the children's births was common enough in lesbian society, and is not unknown otherwise. Having decided that they wanted to have children as a couple, the parties had travelled abroad for the younger to be inseminated with anonymous donor sperm. So even although only one had a legal parental relationship with the children, both could be said to have been involved in the creation of the lives of the children.

There were two questions that had to be explored by the House of Lords: first, the weight to be given to the fact that one party had a biological connection to the children while the other party did not; and secondly, the appropriateness of altering residence arrangements as a response to the deliberate and unlawful acts of the residence parent in seeking to frustrate contact arrangements put in place by court order. The lead speech was given by Baroness Hale (who knows a thing or two about family law).

Importance of biological connection

Thorpe LJ in the Court of Appeal had rejected the proposition of the residence parent that "cogent reasons must exist if a court is to prefer the claims of a person who is not a child's natural parent to one who is". It has long been the law that there is no legal presumption in favour of the natural parents, because welfare is paramount. The House of Lords over three decades ago had held this in *J* v *C* [1970] AC 668, and a more recent application can be seen in the Court of Session decision in *Osborne* v *Matthan* (*No 2*) 1998 SLT 1264. Nevertheless in giving content to the welfare principle, there has long been an understanding that "maintaining the ties of nature" will tend to conduce to rather than detract from the child's welfare. The Court of Appeal was overturned for not having given sufficient regard to this understanding: they had not paid enough attention to the fact of parenthood in assessing welfare. But what do we (or the courts) understand by that ambiguous concept, "parenthood"?

In her recognition that "parenthood" has multiple meanings, Lady Hale's speech is one of the most radical family law opinions to come from the House of Lords in many years. She identifies (paras 33–35) three separate ways in which a person may be or become what she describes as the "natural parent of a child": genetic, gestational, and social and psychological. A woman can be one, or two, or all three; a man can be either one or two of these types of "parent". Both parties in the instant case were "social and psychological parents" to the children at the centre of the dispute, and this is (Lady Hale suggests) as "natural" as genetic parenthood.

That assessment is as revolutionary as it is welcome; but it does introduce an unfortunate degree of ambiguity into her conclusion. At para 38, she resolved this part of the dispute as follows: the residence parent is "both their biological and their psychological parent. In the overall welfare judgment, *that* must count for something" (emphasis added). What is "that"? Is it that being biological parent must count, and being psychological parent must also but separately count, or only that being both must count, or that being both trumps being one? And does being the gestational parent count separately, or at all?

Lord Nicholls, in a short concurring speech, is clearer and more traditional (at para 2): "In reaching its decision the court should always have in mind that in the ordinary way the rearing of a child by his or her biological parent can be expected to be in the child's best interests ... I decry any tendency to diminish the significance of this factor". Lord Scott too (at para 3) declared: "mothers are special", and even although he accepted the children's "other parent" was a good and loving mother too, the specialness he identifies clearly does not come from being social or psychological parent. Biology is a trump card, in other words, though the ace of trumps remains welfare.

In sum, the end result of this part of the case seems to be rather like the approach to the "maternal preference" argument in *Brixey* v *Lynas* 1997 SC (HL) 1 – it is neither a presumption nor a principle that children are best left with their biological parent, but is (as Lord Jauncey put it in *Brixey* in relation to the maternal preference) "recognition of a widely held belief based on practical experience and the workings of nature".

Enforcing contact orders

The other issue, one of enduring political import, was how to enforce a contact order. The residence parent in this case had defied a court order by moving town, deliberately to make it difficult for contact to be maintained by the non-resident parent. Lady Hale accepted that the normal mechanisms for enforcing court orders are simply not appropriate in family disputes of this nature. She pointed out (para 43) that "in this particular case the mother had behaved very badly ... it had been a terrible thing to do to the children" (flitting them in the middle of the night without warning or giving them a chance to say goodbye to their friends). Yet the Court of Appeal's decision that the sole residence order be changed to a joint residence order, because the residence mother had shown she could not be trusted to obey the contact provisions in her residence order, was overturned. The residence parent had been obeying it since the present court action commenced, so there was now no reason to amend it.

Lady Hale did emphasise (para 45) that the residence parent "should now be in no doubt about ... the possible consequences should she not adhere to the [contact] arrangements which we have ordered". I am sure she isn't in any doubt. She defied court orders in the past and the House of Lords has let her get away with it. Why should she have any doubt about their response to her defiance in the future? The judicial hope that a recalcitrant, disappearing, parent will be aware of the consequences of bad behaviour, together with an expectation that it would not be repeated, was expressed in almost identical words by Lord McEwan less than 2 weeks later in *M* v *M* 2007 Fam LR 62 when he granted the recalcitrant parent a residence order.

Continuing grievance

The bottom line is that if the residence arrangements are in the child's interests, they will not be altered by a court in order to enforce contact arrangements (also in the child's interests): in the card game of child law, residence trumps contact. So the case illustrates again what we already knew, that some more imaginative approach is needed to ensure the enforcement of contact orders. The recent (English) Children and Adoption Act 2006 allows penalties for breach, such as community service and a requirement to attend classes to help recalcitrant parents to work through their difficulties. The matter exercised the Scottish Parliament (and particularly the lead committee) during the progress of the Family Law (Scotland) Act 2006, but the only change made to the existing law was to require courts who are considering making contact orders to take account of the likelihood of co-operation between the parties (s 11(7D) of the Children (Scotland) Act 1995, inserted by s 24 of the 2006 Act). This will do nothing to address the real issue, which remains a genuine grievance for all non-residence parents, including fathers and co-parents, gay, lesbian and straight.

Update

Baroness Hale's judgment was identified as the one to read in the later Supreme Court case of Re B (A Child) (Residence Order: Biological Parent) *[2010] 1 All ER 223 and the judgment of Lord Nicholls was said there to have "blunted" the important message that the notion of "parental rights" have no role to play in determining the child's best interests. The mother's partner in cases such as this now has the opportunity to become, in law, the child's parent: Human Fertilisation and Embryology Act 2008, ss 42 and 43: see Commentary No 39 below for a discussion.*

And see Commentary No 41 below for a case of a recalcitrant mother refusing to obtemper a contact order who got her come-uppance.

Commentary No 31: January 2007

Adopting New Solutions

Author welcomes the new Adoption and Children (Scotland) Act but doubts whether, as intended, it has made the law any clearer in two key respects

The Adoption and Children (Scotland) Bill successfully completed its parliamentary progress on 7 December 2006. Press coverage was, disappointingly, limited to the single issue of "gay adoption" but, pleasingly, was on the whole supportive of the parliament's overwhelming endorsement of couple-adoption beyond marriage partners. Joint adoption will now be open to civil partners, as well as cohabiting couples (whatever the gender mix) in enduring family relationships. The Act, of course, does much more. I want to draw readers' attention to only two different issues, both of which underwent substantial amendment as the Act worked its way through the Scottish Parliament.

Grounds for dispensing with parental consent

The rule is not changed that an adoption order needs either the consent of the parents and guardians or, if that consent is not forthcoming, the dispensing by the court of consent. The grounds for dispensation under the existing law are set out in s 16 of the 1978 Act, and the process by which the court decides whether to dispense has been laid down in a series of Court of Session cases. The original intention of the Executive, expressed in para 18 of the policy memorandum which accompanied the Bill as introduced, was to simplify the complexities of the existing grounds. I am not sure that any simplification has been achieved.

Section 31 of the Act sets out five grounds, the existence of one of which will allow the court to consider whether to dispense with parental consent to adoption. The grounds are (a) that the parent or guardian is dead (s 31(3)(a)); (b) that the parent or guardian cannot be found or is incapable of giving consent (s 31(3)(b)); (c) that the parent or guardian has parental responsibilities or parental rights but is unable to discharge them and is likely to continue to be unable to do so (s 31(3)(c) and (4)); (d) that the parent or guardian does not have parental responsibilities or parental rights and is unlikely to obtain them (s 31(3)(c) and (5)); (e) that where neither (c) nor (d) applies the welfare of the child otherwise requires the consent to be dispensed with (s 31(3)(d)).

Grounds (a) and (b) do not really change the law and are uncontentious. Grounds (c) and (d) are the successors to the old grounds of "persistent failure" and "serious ill-treatment", but they are deliberately non-judgmental in the way the old grounds were not and are to be welcomed for that reason. (Though since "parent" is defined in s 31(15) as a parent with parental responsibilities and rights, it is difficult to see when ground (d) can ever apply.)

Two questions in one

Ground (e) is even more problematical, because if an applicant can establish this ground he will always also have satisfied s 14(3), whereby welfare is the court's paramount consideration in determining whether to dispense with parental consent. There were two flaws with this. First, the Court of Session has insisted that the decision of whether to dispense with consent is different from and subsequent to the decision of whether a ground for dispensation exists – and, crucially, that the questions must be tackled in the correct order. The new formulation conflates these two logically separate questions into one. Secondly, the European Court of Human Rights has told us time and again that child protection mechanisms cannot be activated just because a child would be better off with one set of carers than another. Otherwise a child could be removed from satisfactory parents and given to highly satisfactory parents.

An adoption system must be able to accommodate a proposed adoption being frustrated by a parental refusal of consent, even when it is in the welfare of the child to be adopted. Welfare is the paramount consideration but it cannot on its own be the justification for state interference in family life. Courts are going to have to be imaginative in giving "welfare" in s 31(3)(d) more limited scope than it has in s 14(3).

Permanence orders and supervision requirements

Though the new Act is in large part a re-enactment of the 1978 Act, there is one part that is totally new: a new order, the permanence order

(PO), is created. This will replace both freeing orders and parental responsibilities orders and is designed to be more flexible than either, giving the court the power to make an order that is tailored to the particular circumstances and the needs of each individual child who requires to be removed from their birth family on a permanent basis. Adoption might or might not be appropriate for such a child and "the permanency planning" for different children can take that fact and all other relevant matters into account.

The single most important issue, discussed at all three stages of the parliamentary process, was the inter-relationship between the new permanence order and other lawful orders, in particular supervision requirements. This is a matter of great practical importance because children who will be made subject to permanence orders will nearly always be in the children's hearing system already. There were two major fears: (i) that a child might be subject to two separate legal processes at much the same time and in relation to identical problems; and (ii) that it was unclear which order took precedence if the two processes resulted in two, inconsistent, orders.

Suspending the supervision process

The first fear is addressed in s 96. This provides that when an application for a PO is made, a supervision requirement may not be made or varied until the PO application has been dealt with. It is important to note that this does not remove the jurisdiction of the children's hearing either during the process for obtaining a PO or during the subsistence of the order once made. A children's hearing may still be arranged even when a PO application has been made and, in the absence of any rule to the contrary, the hearing may issue warrants to detain the child until a decision can be made by them. The hearing may also continue an existing supervision requirement without variation, perhaps requiring a review under s 70(7) of the 1995 Act once the PO is made (if the supervision requirement survives). And the hearing may make a new supervision requirement after a PO has come into force.

Permanence orders and other orders

The second fear, relating to precedence of orders, is dealt with by a number of provisions, not all of which are contained in the new Act. There can be no clash with s 11 orders made under the 1995 Act because s 88 of the new Act provides that the making of a PO has the effect of revoking any existing s 11 order; and s 103 provides that the court cannot make a new s 11 order (except for an interdict or the appointment of a judicial factor) while a PO is in force. The aim is to ensure that any matter that would otherwise be dealt with by the court in private law proceedings will be dealt with by the permanence court (which has much the same powers and to which there is much the same access).

Similarly, s 89 of the new Act provides that on the making of a PO any existing supervision requirement will be brought to an end, though only if the court is satisfied that making the PO renders compulsory measures of supervision no longer necessary. But there is nothing to prevent a supervision requirement being made subsequently. In that case, s 90 of the new Act provides that a local authority may not do anything in the exercise of the parental responsibilities and parental rights it has in terms of the PO which is incompatible with any supervision requirement. The latter has, in other words, precedence.

Now, this rule in its terms applies only to local authorities and the PO may confer most of the parental responsibilities and parental rights on other persons, such as, typically, long-term foster carers. But these other persons may not act incompatibly with a supervision requirement either, because s 3(4) of the 1995 Act (which only applies to natural persons, according to s 15(4) of that Act, thus the necessity for s 90) gives precedence to supervision requirements. The only exception is when an interim PO is made under s 97. If an interim PO is made over a child currently subject to a supervision requirement, the making of an interim order does not terminate the supervision requirement but the terms of the interim order will prevail over any inconsistent terms of that requirement (s 97(5)).

Still to be tested

Much still needs to be fleshed out in regulations and rules of court. Even after this Act comes into force, we are likely to have a lengthy period of uncertainty before the Court of Session gives us guidance on many other matters. The Act has certainly modernised our adoption system and is better for both children and prospective adopters. It cannot, however, be said to have simplified the law in any way at all.

Update

I explored in more detail than is provided here the grounds for dispensing with parental consent to adoption in "Welfare and the New Grounds for Dispensing with Parental Consent to Adoption" 2008 SLT (News) 213;

the conclusions reached there were rejected by Scotland's most experienced adoption advocate Janys Scott, QC, in "A Reply" 2009 SLT (News) 17. The substance of the argument boils down to whether a now capable, reasonable and rational parent should have the power to prevent an adoption that is in the best interests of the child. Under the old law there would be some circumstances in which the answer to this question was affirmative and in my view the 2007 Act should not be interpreted to require that a negative answer always be given. A father might, for example, wish to prevent the child's step-father, with whom the child lives (together with the mother) from adopting the child, and wish to do so to protect his own (good) relationship with the child. This is not irrational or unreasonable and his right to prevent the adoption (for why else do we ask for parental consent?) should not be interfered with merely because the child might gain some marginal benefit from being adopted. Or the child may have been removed from a drug addicted mother who, contrary to expectations, escapes the addiction and its associated life-style and can now offer the child a decent upbringing. Is the fact that the child would be marginally better off remaining where he or she is a sufficient justification for making an adoption order against the wishes of the mother? If so, then Scott's argument achieves this; if not, my argument would require further and better justification to be shown.

The Adoption and Children (Scotland) Act 2007 came into force on September 28, 2009. The perennially awkward issue of precedence of different orders remains uncertain with the restructuring of the children's hearing system by the Children's Hearings (Scotland) Act 2011.

Commentary No 32: April 2007

Bring Them Home

Child abduction cases continue to occupy the courts as parents fail to appreciate the existence and effect of the Hague Convention

Few international conventions are so much a product of their time as the Hague Convention on International Child Abduction, brought into our domestic law by the Child Abduction and Custody Act 1985. Perceived as a great success because of its widespread adoption, the number of cases it has generated in courts around the world tells another story.

A non-deterrent

The original hope was that the incidence of child abduction would be reduced, by the removal of any potential benefit an abductor might obtain by abduction. But the increase in both family breakdown and ease of international travel has more than countered any deterrent effect. And the truth of the matter is, of course, that deterrence only works for those who know of the deterring factor. Few parents have heard of the Convention, and even if they have, they can't quite believe that a court would make its decision on anything other than the welfare of the child: the hope nearly always is that the abductor will have an opportunity to place his (or, more usually, her) assessment of welfare before the court.

It does not work like that, of course. The revolutionary feature of the Hague Convention is that welfare is to be assessed by the court of the child's habitual residence and that the role of any other court is summarily to return the child to that residence. Legal advisers to abductors recognise this, but some clearly have difficulties in persuading their abducting clients of the realities of life. It would be unfair to describe some recent defences to immediate return as spurious, but making bricks without straw is as difficult in the legal trade as it is in the building trade.

One other feature of the Hague Convention worth mentioning is that most cases are depressingly similar, with the wrongful act being committed by the residence parent who fails to see why the other parent's relationship with her child should inhibit in any way her own lifestyle choices.

A common factual background

In *AL, Petr* [2007] CSOH 55 the mother and father met in Australia and subsequently had a child. The mother returned to her native Scotland with the child, ostensibly on a short-term holiday, but then decided to remain here. The father sought the child's return.

In *T, Petr* 2007 SLT 543 the parties, who were Polish, had two children. They then divorced. The mother came to Scotland to seek work and brought the children with her. The father sought their return.

In *HJAV* v *CAW* [2006] CSOH 115 a Scotswoman entered into a relationship with a Dutchman and bore two children while they lived in the Netherlands. The mother brought the children to Scotland, allowing the father to believe this was merely temporary. The father sought their return.

In *H* v *H* 2006 Fam LR 59 a mother and father from Scotland relocated themselves and their child to New Zealand to explore the possibility of permanently settling there. After 2 years it was agreed that the mother and child would come back to Scotland before a final decision was made, but on returning here the mother decided to keep the child in Scotland and she raised an action in the Scottish court for (sole) residence. The father sought the child's return to New Zealand.

Defence of last resort

Within this common factual background a variety of issues have been put to the court for resolution. In *AL, Petr*, the tedious defence of "grave risk of physical or psychological harm", or that return would place the child in "an intolerable situation" was raised. This test is a high one, far beyond mere consideration of the child's welfare. It is too often used as the last refuge of an abducting parent with no better argument.

In the present case the mother argued that the father adopted an unsuitable lifestyle. He drank too much, smoked cannabis and had convictions for drink driving; he had a negative attitude towards the mother which he might transmit to the child. In addition, the mother was pregnant by her new partner in Scotland and had been advised by her GP that she should not fly until after the birth. Lady Paton had little problem in holding that this litany of unsuitability came nowhere near creating a situation of grave risk of harm, or intolerable situation. She found "a picture of a father whose lifestyle may not be ideal, but who takes care of his son". The issue of the mother's inability to fly due to her pregnancy was dismissed as not relevant – there were various other options to ensure the child's safe and immediate return to the country of his habitual residence.

Protected rights?

T, Petr, also decided by Lady Paton, raised the question of whether the divorced father had any rights of custody at all that were protected by the Hague Convention. This turned on the extent to which Polish law distributed parental power between parents, and the terms of the father's divorce from the mother. The decree of divorce explicitly granted to the father the right of co-decision-making as to choice of school, profession and medical treatment for the child. The mother argued that these were not sufficient to amount to a "right of custody" as understood in the Hague Convention context.

Lady Paton preferred to look to the provisions of general Polish law before examining the decree of divorce. She found that the appropriate code conferred joint "parental authority", but allowed that to be removed or modified in certain circumstances, including divorce. She held that unless the decree of divorce explicitly removed parental authority, it remained vested in both parents except insofar as the decree modified it. She found nothing in the decree of divorce in the present case which removed co-decision-making powers.

Indeed, Lady Paton went further and found that, in certain circumstances, having nothing more than co-decision-making in choosing school, profession and medical treatment might indeed amount to the right to determine the child's place of residence, which is itself a right of custody. She regarded it as "unrealistic to assert that co-decision-making powers relating to choice of school or profession cannot or should not affect the child's place of residence". Otherwise these rights would be diminished into mere rights to be consulted. She accepted the consistent line of authority from the House of Lords that the phrase "rights of custody" should be construed in its widest sense.

And talking of the House of Lords, we should also note their most recent decision on the topic: *In Re D (A Child)* [2007] 1 AC 619 (which again involved the common factual background). The major question in the case concerned whether the father had a right to veto the child's removal from Romania, and if so, whether such a veto and nothing more amounted to "rights of custody" for Hague Convention purposes. I pointed out 10 years ago (1997 SLT (News) 175) that a mere right to prevent a child's removal from the jurisdiction of its habitual residence amounted to a "right of custody" for Hague Convention purposes, and that analysis was accepted by the Inner House in *AJ* v *FJ, Petr* 2005 SC 428. That case in turn was followed by the House of Lords in the present case. In the event, since the father could not establish such a veto under Romanian law he had no rights of custody and the court did not, therefore, order the child to be returned there.

Consent issues

In *HJAV* the dispute concerned whether the mother's actions amounted to a wrongful removal or a wrongful retention and whether the father's actions amounted to acquiescence. Lord Uist held that there had been a wrongful removal since he found she always intended to come to Scotland permanently. On whether the father had acquiesced in that, Lord Uist was careful to point out that the father's continuing to support the children financially even after that removal, and his attempts at reconciliation, provided no evidence of his acquiescence.

Consent was also at issue in *H* v *H*, where Lady Clark found that the father's agreement to the child being brought to Scotland was given in the context of a continuing matrimonial relationship and could not be translated into the situation of marital breakdown.

Law and reality

All of these cases from the past year in the Court of Session have in common that the residence mother is overstepping her authority by removing or retaining the child from the jurisdiction of its habitual residence. The Hague Convention has not achieved a change in mindset as to the power balance between parents in relation to their children. Neither, of course, has the Children (Scotland) Act 1995. Both provisions envisage a sharing of upbringing, but until parents understand and accept the full consequences of this, the legal position will remain far from practical reality and these disputes will continue to be as common, and as unedifying, as they have been since the 1985 Act came into force.

Commentary No 33: July 2007

High Road, Low Road

Some contrasts in the approaches of Scots and English law to property claims by cohabitants, in the light of a recent English House of Lords appeal

Last year, in these pages, I discussed the English financial provision on divorce case of *Miller* v *Miller; McFarlane* v *McFarlane* [2006] 2 AC 618 (Commentary No 29 above), which was made notable in Scotland by Lord Hope expressing the view that Scots law on the matter should be reviewed and brought closer to English law. The major difference in this area between the two jurisdictions is that in England the focus is very much on the uncertain concept of fairness, while in Scotland the benefits of certainty are given more weight.

I want this month to discuss another financial provision case from the House of Lords in which, again, Lord Hope usefully sets out how Scots law would deal with the issue. This time, however, the case involved separating cohabitants. The claims an ex-cohabitant may make to share the wealth generated during the relationship are very much more limited than those of a spouse on divorce or a civil partner on dissolution, even after the coming into force, in Scotland, of the Family Law (Scotland) Act 2006.

Balance of advantage

Imagine the following scenario. A couple, Moneybags and Pauper, get together in 1975, renting accommodation for their joint use. In 1983 Moneybags inherits a sum of money from an uncle and uses it as the deposit for the purchase of a new family home, title to which is taken in her name alone. She is in employment and the mortgage is paid by standing order from her sole bank account. Pauper, who is unemployed, contributes physical labour to the decoration, renovation and extension of the property. By 1993 both parties are in paid employment and Pauper now begins to contribute to the mortgage, though to a lesser extent than Moneybags. In 2007 the couple separate, at which point in time the mortgage has been paid off and the property has a net value of £600,000.

Had they married in 1975, or entered a civil partnership in 2006, a claim under s 9(1)(a) of the Family Law (Scotland) Act 1985 would prima facie entitle Pauper to a half share of the net value, that is to say £300,000. If they remained unmarried or unempartnered (if that is what the word is to be), all that is available to Pauper is a claim under s 28 of the 2006 Act to recover "contributions". Now, this includes more than the direct financial contributions made to the mortgage and, under s 28(3)(a), the court will take account of the extent to which Moneybags "has derived economic advantage from contributions made by" Pauper. But however the enhancement to the house is valued, it is highly unlikely to reach a figure anywhere near one half of the value of the property. So in these days of increasing house prices, it remains financially advantageous for the less well-off of the two to marry or civilly empartner rather than to cohabit, and financially disadvantageous for the other.

A real question

The scenario above is similar to that in the English case of *Stack* v *Dowden* [2007] 2 AC 432. That jurisdiction does not yet have, of course, any equivalent to our Family Law (Scotland) Act 2006 and the only claim possible, therefore, was a common law claim. All the judges in *Stack* agreed that if the title to the property is in the name of one party alone, then it is for the other party to show that they have a share in that ownership; similarly if the property is jointly owned the onus is on the party seeking to show that ownership is shared other than equally. (It was indeed this latter scenario that *Stack* itself was concerned with.)

The real question before the House was how the presumption of either sole or equal ownership could be overturned. They held that what needs to be identified is the parties' shared intention, actual, inferred or imputed from their whole course of conduct in relation to the property, and that if this common intention indicates a departure from sole or equal ownership then that intention will be given effect to as opposed to the terms of the title. In English parlance, a "constructive trust" must be shown which requires beneficial title to be shared differently from legal title.

In *Stack* Ms Dowden was awarded 65% of the value of the house (her share of the "equity"), on the basis that she contributed financially far more to its purchase than, as the legal title indicated, 50%. Baroness Hale, incidentally, gave the interesting warning at para 85 of her speech that while the extra 15% of the house's value amounted to over £111,000, the costs of pursuing that sum all the way to the House of Lords were "quite disproportionate" to that figure.

Same starting point . . .

As in *Miller; McFarlane*, above, the most interesting speech from a Scottish perspective is that of Lord Hope, who explains to us how Scots law would deal with the issue. He suggests that the problem would be resolved in much the same way on both sides of the border. He is correct to point out that the Family Law (Scotland) Act 2006 does not provide the answer. He is also correct (self-evidently so, in a system that does not distinguish between the legal and beneficial interests in heritable property) to state that, as in England, if property is taken in the name of one of a couple, the presumption here is that of sole ownership, and if taken in the name of both, the presumption is of equality of shares. So the starting point is the same in both jurisdictions. And the contentious issue is also the same: how do you overturn the presumption?

In Scotland, cases such as these have of late been dealt with through the law of restitution – obligations law rather than property law. Recent examples referred to in Lord Hope's speech include *Satchwell* v *McIntosh* 2006 SLT (Sh Ct) 117 and *McKenzie* v *Nutter* 2007 SLT (Sh Ct) 17.

In *Satchwell*, title to the property was taken in the name of one of the cohabitants but the other had contributed to the purchase price and to certain refurbishment costs. The non-entitled cohabitant successfully claimed back the monies directly contributed. In *McKenzie*, title was taken in joint names but only one had contributed to the purchase price and to refurbishment. When the other cohabitant insisted on a division and sale she was held to be unjustly enriched and required to pay her share of the proceeds to the other. The injustice lay in the fact that the agreement had been that each would sell their existing properties in order to purchase the joint property: one did and the other did not. (The English courts would probably hold this created a common intention that generated a constructive trust.)

Satchwell is likely, today, to be dealt with under the 2006 Act. But *McKenzie* went rather further in that a full share of the proceeds of sale was recovered: fairness demanded that the value of the property was shared, rather than simply the value of the contribution.

... different routes

While the result in all these cases might well, on their facts, be the same in Scotland and in England, it is important to note that the route to that result is very different – with the consequence that on different facts a different result might emerge. In England, absent a statute, the matter is analysed as one of "common intention constructive trust", with the courts aiming to give effect to what is taken to be the intention of the parties. This is not a search for a "fair" outcome (per Baroness Hale at para 61 and Lord Neuberger at paras 127 and 144). In Scotland, however, where the matter is dealt with as unjustified enrichment, notions of fairness are central to the analysis. So, in England (as we learnt last year in *Miller; McFarlane*), fairness is central to the division of property at the end of marriage or civil partnership, but at best incidental (as we learn here) at the end of a cohabitation; in Scotland fairness is central at the end of a cohabitation but is no more than a moderating influence on certainty at the end of a marriage or civil partnership.

The 2006 Act of course might well change things. If the courts are willing to take a liberal view of s 28 of the 2006 Act, and assess the advantages and disadvantages that underpin claims under that section to the full extent of property values, then the continued need for the common law remedy would evaporate. And an attractive consistency of approach between claims of separating cohabitants would be achieved with those of divorcing/dissolving spouses/civil partners. The claims of the former would remain very much more limited than those of the latter, but the balance between fairness and certainty would be the same. This would bring a welcome harmony to an increasingly fractured Scottish family law.

Commentary No 34: October 2007

Three Proposals

Further important legislative developments in family law have been foreshadowed by three different sets of proposals published during the summer

Family law in the United Kingdom remains dynamic and, it seems, ever-changing. The great modernising statutes of the 1980s and 1990s are already overshadowed by developments like the Civil Partnership Act 2004, the Gender Recognition Act 2004 and the Family Law (Scotland) Act 2006. The pace of change shows no sign of slowing, and three new proposals of far-reaching import made this summer are worth paying some attention to, even before their enactment into law.

The Human Tissue and Embryos Bill

In May, the UK Department of Health published for consultation a draft Human Tissue and Embryos Bill, which is designed substantially to amend and update the 1990 Human Fertilisation and Embryology Act. Two proposals deserve particular notice.

First, the existing s 13(5) of the 1990 Act is to be scrapped. This requires the providers of infertility treatment to take account of the welfare of any child who may be born as a result of the treatment, "including the need of that child for a father". It is difficult to see what practical effect this odd provision ever had, for the Act did not include any rule to the effect that treatment cannot be provided to single women (or female couples). Yet the provision had a clear symbolic message – that the law preferred children to be born to heterosexual couples. Now, few doubt that it is indeed good for any child to have a father-figure in his or her life, but it is likely that equally few people today believe that the absence of such a father-figure is so contrary to a child's welfare that the law should strive to prevent the child's very birth. The removal of s 13(5) is to be welcomed.

The second proposal of note concerns s 28(2) and (3). This is the provision that confers paternity, when a child is born after infertility treatment to a heterosexual couple, on the male member of the couple when he is not genetically the father. When the Civil Partnership Act 2004 was being debated, there was a hope that this provision would be extended to allow same-sex couples (in practice, female couples) to gain equivalent advantage and that, in Scotland, the presumption of paternity in s 5 of the Law Reform (Parent and Child) Scotland Act 1986 would be amended to create an equivalent presumption when a child is born within a civil partnership.

That latter aim always was rather misconceived. The 1986 Act creates a rebuttable presumption not of parenthood but of fatherhood: such a presumption would virtually automatically be rebutted by the very femaleness of those in whose favour it was hoped it would act. However in 2004 the Government undertook to re-examine the issue, and it has now done so. The 1990 Act, it should be noted, is a reserved matter.

What is now proposed is that the 1990 Act be amended and that when a woman becomes pregnant as a result of infertility treatment provided by a licensed clinic, her female partner should be recognised as the child's "second parent", on the same terms as such a woman's male partner would be recognised as the child's father. A consequential amendment to the 1986 Act (not mentioned in the draft Bill) would be required in Scotland.

It is of course no longer inconceivable that a child may have two parents of the same gender. This has been possible in England since same-sex couple adoption became possible a few days after the Civil Partnership Act 2004 came into force, and it will be possible in Scotland on the bringing into force of the Adoption and Children (Scotland) Act 2007. Parenthood, it should never be forgotten, is a legal and social construct, more than a matter of fact.

Cohabitants and financial provision

The Family Law (Scotland) Act 2006 provides for Scotland a set of rules allowing for financial readjustment at the end of a cohabitation, either on separation or death. The English Law Commission (Law Com no 307) has now made recommendations for England and Wales. These are very different from the scheme applying in Scotland, but Scottish solicitors may well be called upon to advise clients in cross-border situations and so will need to become familiar with the English rules, whatever they eventually are.

Under the 2006 Act, only those who satisfy the definition of "cohabitant" can access the new remedies and, I understand, some of the early disputes that have arisen have been on this point. The English recommendation is to be far more precise about which cohabitants are eligible. Eligibility may come in one of two forms: having a child together, or satisfying a "minimum duration requirement". Such a requirement is not uncommon in countries that recognise cohabitation rights, but it was resisted in Scotland, and in my view rightly so. A minimum duration requires both a start and an end, and cohabitations are seldom clear cut at either end: in other words the scope for dispute about eligibility is doubled by such a rule.

The 2006 Act is silent on the effect of any agreement between the parties. The English proposals suggest that there be written into the legislation an "opt-out", so that couples can disapply the statute and make their own financial arrangements. This has superficial attractions – the desire to respect the autonomy of couples who wish to determine for themselves the legal consequences of their personal relationships. But the proposal has at least one serious drawback. It is based on the assumption that two people have a single desire. They might not. Doubtless the opt-out will work only when both sign an agreement, but that is entirely innocuous only where we are convinced of the equal bargaining power of both parties. Whether the legislation will permit the courts to strike down opt-out agreements, and on what basis they might do so, are matters that remain to be seen.

The English Law Commission suggests creating much more distance between the principles for assessing claims applicable on divorce and on separation than exists in the Scottish Act. For separating cohabitants, they suggest that the claimant must show that he or she made "qualifying contributions" to the relationship. This may not, at the end of the day, be substantially different from the Scottish approach to cohabitation, but it is a significant departure from the much looser, fairness-based approach to the issue on divorce in England.

The 2006 Act gives no guidance to Scottish courts as to how to value claims on death. Claims on death of one of a cohabiting couple have been available in England since the Inheritance (Provision for Family and Dependants) Act 1975, and the jurisprudence built up may give some limited guidance to Scottish courts. There already exists a 2-year qualifying period of cohabitation, and the only recommendation of substance contained in the Law Commission's report relating to *mortis causa* claims is to recognise the existence of children as an alternative qualification.

Intestate succession

The Scottish Law Commission has been as busy as its English sister. It has recently produced a discussion paper on reform of the law of intestate succession (Scot Law Com DP 136). This area of succession law, typically perceived as a matter of the law of property and its transmission, is, I have always thought, better seen as an aspect of family law. It is certainly family law developments, particularly the introduction of civil partnership and the creation of cohabitation rights on death, that have led to the Succession (Scotland) Act 1964 becoming ever more out of touch with the realities of family life. So the current proposals, recognising families in their modern form, are greatly to be welcomed.

I intend to comment on these important proposals in rather more detail, but in another place. However, it is as well to note here that there is no suggestion of moving away from the discretionary court-based award to cohabitants that was introduced in the 2006 Act. But important questions on the issue are raised by the SLC, including in particular whether legislation should give rather more guidance to the courts than the 2006 Act does, as to how to assess claims once competently made. One suggestion is to follow the English recommendations mentioned above, whereby it is based on "qualifying contributions". Another important recommendation is that the claim by a surviving cohabitant should be extended to the testate as well as intestate estate of the deceased. This would be a significant extension of the claim created by the 2006 Act.

Watch this space

All of the above proposals are likely to generate heated debate and may well be substantially varied before being enacted. This column is unlikely to run out of issues to comment on for some years to come.

Update

The Human Fertilisation and Embryology Act 2008 came into force at various dates during 2009. Section 13(5) of the 1990 Act, discussed above, was not in the end scrapped completely but was reworded so that instead of treatment providers having to take account of "the need of that child for a father" they must now take into account "the need of that child for supportive parenting". The new rules conferring parenthood on the partner of the mother are extended to same-sex couples, and the consent provisions are tightened. The matter is discussed below at Commentary No 39.

At the time of writing, the English Law Commission's proposals for cohabitants have not been implemented; it is not a matter of priority to a Conservative-led Government.

The Scottish Law Commission followed up their discussion paper with a Report on Succession *(SLC 215) which was published in 2009. My commentary on some of the issues in the Discussion Paper was published in (2008) 12 Edinburgh LR 77.*

Commentary No 35: January 2008

Letter from South Africa

Latest cases show the courts in the UK and South Africa continuing to grapple with issues arising from the Child Abduction Convention

A mere 10 years ago a commentator who wished to write about current legal issues in another country would find it easiest to do so by travelling to that country and accessing a library there. Even then, law reporting could take a year or more, and anyone wishing to be completely up to date had to rely on obtaining quick access to court transcripts.

Today, that all seems so primitive, and so costly. A click of a mouse, a Google search, and a good broadband connection will bring the commentator all the information he or she needs, and more. So there is no urgent need for me to be here, sitting on the Zimbabwe bank of the Zambesi, in order to read Zimbabwe cases, nor for me to spend 6 months in South Africa to discover what are currently the major issues in South African family law. But here I am and, as if to prove the point, one of the cases I want to comment on this month is from the House of Lords (though it does coincidentally have a Zimbabwe connection).

One of my columns last year (Commentary No 32 above) concerned a number of cases decided by the UK courts on the Hague Child Abduction Convention, a simple and straightforward piece of law with a clear set of aims and objectives, but which continues to generate a large amount of reportable litigation. Perhaps this is not surprising, since each opposed case requires court action, and each court action attracts legal aid, but it is more of a surprise that after 20 years, new issues of some legal import continue to arise from depressingly similar fact scenarios. So I return to the issue again this month.

Continuing discretion

A most interesting judgment has recently been handed down by the House of Lords in *Re M and Another (Children) (Abduction: Rights of Custody)* [2008] 1 AC 1288. The lead speech was delivered by Baroness Hale of Richmond, one of the most insightful commentators on this (and other) issues. The scenario presented was relatively typical: two children, aged 13 and 10, had been born and bred in Zimbabwe where, after their parents' separation, they lived with their father. On a visit to their mother, they were secreted out of the country and brought to the UK, where the mother sought (and failed to obtain) asylum.

Though originally the children wanted to go home, after some time their attitude changed and they expressed the wish to remain in England with their mother. Now, the mother had made it difficult for the father to trace the family and so, by the time the father made the Hague Convention application, the children had been in the UK for more than 2 years and, the judge at first instance held, were "settled" in the UK. This meant that there was no obligation under the Convention to order their immediate return: the facts raised an Art 12 defence.

The issue before the House of Lords was whether the court had a discretion under the Convention to order return even when this defence was made out, or whether settlement took the case outwith the Convention entirely. The matter had some practical significance, in that if the Convention did not apply, a wider examination of the facts and circumstances would be required in order to allow the court to make a judgment based solely on the child's welfare, while if the Convention continued to apply, the decision would be made taking account of the principles underpinning the Convention itself.

Baroness Hale warned against making too much of this distinction and, in the end, she held that the court retained a discretion under the Convention. As such, it is appropriate to take account of the aims of the Convention, including comity between contracting states, respect for foreign judicial processes, and deterrence of abduction in the first place (see especially para 42). These are not overriding considerations but merely factors to be taken into account in addition to welfare considerations. In particular, the immediate return of the child (which is the primary objective of the Hague Convention) is no longer a major aim in "settlement" cases, for the very reason that too much time has passed.

Taking off the gloss

Another important aspect of the case concerns how and when the court's discretion can be exercised. Judges in both Scotland and England have expressed the view that even when a defence has been made out, it is only in "exceptional" cases that return should not be ordered. Insofar as this has become an additional test to be satisfied, Baroness Hale disapproved of the approach as an unwarranted gloss on the simple words of the Convention. It is sufficiently exceptional, she said, that more than a year has passed and the child is settled in the new environment.

There is further important guidance for the future in Lady Hale's speech. She urges strongly (as she has done in other, non-abduction, cases) that a child-centric approach needs to be adopted in all Hague Convention cases. Thus the "comparative moral blameworthiness" of the parties is of little significance from the child's perspective. Also, individual children should not be made to suffer by immediate return for the sake of general deterrence of the evil of child abduction worldwide. She also explicitly agreed with the judge at first instance that to return a child to a country with as many problems as Zimbabwe would not in itself be to place the child at grave risk of psychological harm or to place the child in an intolerable position. The standard for that defence to be established is high, as has been held in many earlier cases. The children were not returned.

Two curiosities

South Africa incorporated the Hague Convention into its law in 1996 and the most recent decision of the Supreme Court of Appeal on the issue, handed down in June 2007, is *Central Authority* v *Houwert* [2007] SCA 88 (RSA). Again, the facts are typical. The mother was South African, the father Dutch, and the child habitually resident in and national of the Netherlands. The mother and child travelled to South Africa, on return tickets, and shortly after arrival the mother informed the father that neither she nor the child would be returning to the Netherlands. The father sought return under the Hague Convention.

The primary issue in the case was whether the father had agreed to the child's removal to, or acquiesced in his retention in, South Africa: this is the Art 13(a) defence. The Supreme Court of Appeal pointed out that even if the defence were successful, the court retained the discretion to order return if this were considered appropriate in light of the aims of the Convention itself. But on an examination of the facts in the present case, the court had little hesitation in holding that the defence had not been made out: the mother had given the impression that the trip to South Africa was temporary, and the father had raised Hague Convention proceedings within weeks of being informed that the mother did not intend to return. A mandatory order of return was necessary.

There are two oddities in this case. First, the court at first instance had similarly found no defence under the Convention, but had then ordered the return of the mother rather than of the child. That alone meant the original order needed to be recalled, and a new one issued, ordering the return of the child. Secondly, the Supreme Court of Appeal's order was very much more extensive than a mere order for return: it required substantial expenditure on the part of the father. The court awarded interim custody of the child to the mother and ordered the father to pay maintenance for the mother and child until the Dutch court had made its final determination. The father was also ordered to pay the air fare and other travel costs of the mother and child. Additionally, the father was required to vacate his home to allow the mother and child to live there while the Dutch proceedings were underway, to pay any medical or dental expenses incurred by either mother or child, and to provide the mother with a motor vehicle, paying all associated costs including oil and petrol.

None of this is required by the Hague Convention and the South African court was exercising its own inherent jurisdiction. As such, none of these incidental orders will be enforceable under the aegis of the Convention, though doubtless the father will feel obliged to abide by their terms in order to avoid accusations of bad faith in the custody dispute before the Dutch courts. It is, however, to be hoped that courts in other jurisdictions resist the temptation to go so far beyond the scope of the Hague Convention in the orders they make in addition to the order for the return of the child.

Commentary No 36: April 2008

Conscience and Public Service

The author argues that where public duties are involved, there should be no place for invoking rights of conscience at the expense of those in civil partnerships

Registration officers in England and Wales (the equivalent of our district registrars) were not legally employed by the local authorities that paid them until the coming into force in December 2007 of the Statistics and Registration Service Act 2007, s 69. One consequence of this is that they had no recourse to employment tribunals. An inequity resolved by the 2007 Act doubtless, but it is rather disheartening that one of the first claims by a registrar to an employment tribunal has been made against Islington Council, on the basis of that council's refusal to exempt her from being involved in the registration of civil partnerships. She claims it would be an infringement of her right under Art 9 of the European Convention to freedom of religion and conscience to force her to register the civil partnerships of same-sex couples.

Now, unlike the position in (for example) South Africa, the UK's Civil Partnership Act 2004 contains no provision permitting registrars to refuse to officiate at civil partnership registrations. The government resisted calls from certain groups for the inclusion of a so-called "conscience clause", similar to that which permits health-care professionals to refuse to assist at terminations of pregnancy (Abortion Act 1967, s 4(1)). They were right to do so, for the abortion analogy is not good, for at least three reasons: health care professionals are not carrying out public duties in the way that registrars are; abortion is not an inherent and necessary part of health care, in the way that registration of civil partnership is within the registration system; and refusing to perform abortions does not constitute systemic discrimination against an equality-vulnerable class. Invoking Art 9 is an attempt to introduce by the back door a conscience clause that does not exist on the face of the 2004 Act.

Authorised or obliged?

In Scotland the Registrar General has a duty under s 87 of the Civil Partnership Act 2004 to authorise such number of district registrars as is thought necessary for "the purpose of affording reasonable facilities throughout Scotland for registration as civil partners". This is the same duty as is found in s 17 of the Marriage (Scotland) Act 1977 in relation to civil marriages. Not all district registrars are authorised to officiate at either civil marriages or civil partnerships. Some may conduct both, some either and some neither.

It is for individual local authorities (which employ district registrars and which determine the terms of their employment and their range of duties) to assess the local need for registrars to be involved in each aspect of the registration process. So there is scope in the system for an individual district registrar not to be authorised to conduct civil partnership registrations. The question, which is more likely to arise in smaller local authority areas, is whether a district registrar can be obliged to accept authorisation to register civil partnerships.

Some guidance may be obtained from a recent decision of the employment appeal tribunal in the case of *McClintock* v *Department for Constitutional Affairs* [2008] IRLR 29. Here, a justice of the peace sought to be relieved from dealing with adoption cases which might involve him having to make an adoption order in favour of a same-sex couple, and when his request was refused he felt obliged to resign. His claim for unfair dismissal was rejected by the EAT on the ground that judges could not "cherry pick" which laws to apply and which to refuse to deal with.

That case, however, did not tackle head-on the ECHR point. The jurisprudence from Strasbourg indicates very clearly that Art 9 is infringed only if the exercise of the right of religion and conscience is made very much more difficult by the rule or procedure that is being challenged. Seldom will terms and conditions of employment be enough for that purpose if the employee has a choice of seeking other employment. In *Kjeldsen, Busk Madsen and Pedersen* v *Denmark* (1976) 1 EHRR 711 parents' claims for an infringement of their right to philosophical and religious objection to sex education in state schools were rejected on the ground that they had the option of educating their children at home. In *Ahmad* v *UK* (1981) 4 EHRR 126 a teacher who wanted to absent himself from teaching duties in order to attend prayers at particular times had his Art 9 claim rejected because he had accepted a contract of employment which did not accommodate such absences, he had not brought his religious requirements to the employer's notice when seeking employment, and he was at all times free to seek other employment which would accommodate his religious observances. The applicants' claims in both *Konttinen* v *Finland* (1996) 87-A DR 68 and *Stedman* v *United Kingdom* (1997) 23 EHRR CD 168 were rejected because, having found that their working hours conflicted with their religious convictions, they were free to relinquish their posts.

In the public service

Might a local authority refuse to employ an applicant for a post of district registrar on the basis that the applicant would refuse, if employed, to take part in civil partnership registrations? While I see the argument that people with strong religious or philosophical convictions should not themselves be discriminated against in their employment opportunities, I think this has to be countered by emphasising the public servant nature of the post of district registrar. Once Parliament has decided to put in place a registration system for same-sex couples, it is for public servants to accept the policy decisions that have been made.

The proposition that public servants have a right to religious or philosophical objections to public processes really needs to be resisted, because it is impossible to draw a line other than the one Parliament has already drawn in setting out the duties attached to the post. A registrar may well oppose mixed-race marriages, but cannot expect to have that view accommodated in their performance of their public duties, because society and the law have a stronger interest in ensuring race equality. To allow an opt-out for civil partnership is to treat homophobia differently from racism and to regard it as in some measure legitimate. Clothing the claim in religiosity does not make it any more acceptable.

Genuine requirements

We are, of course, still getting used to sexual orientation being an unlawful ground for discrimination, and often statutory exceptions are made. The Employment Equality (Sexual Orientation) Regulations 2003 prohibit sexual orientation discrimination in employment, though reg 7 contains two troubling exceptions: (1) where "having regard to the nature of the employment or the context in which it is carried out, (a) being of a particular sexual orientation is a genuine and determining occupational requirement, and (b) it is proportionate to apply that requirement"; and (2) where the employment is for the purposes of an organised religion and discrimination is necessary "(i) so as to comply with the doctrines of that religion, or (ii) so as to avoid conflicting with the strongly held religious convictions of a significant number of the religion's followers".

There have been no cases on these exceptions, though both are worryingly broad. It is not difficult to imagine claims that particular employments have heterosexuality as a genuine occupational requirement. After all, most jobs that have gender as a requirement assume heterosexuality. Why else do we insist that only female police officers can strip-search female suspects? And the religious exception allows any church to refuse to employ a gay person in any capacity whatsoever, from clergy to cleaner, if either its leaders' scriptural interpretations or the convictions of a significant number of its members support that.

Rights in balance

Perhaps, however, the political environment is changing. When the Equality Act (Sexual Orientation) Regulations 2007 made sexual orientation discrimination in the provision of goods and services unlawful, the major opposition came from religious bodies who ran adoption and fostering agencies and who wished to be able to continue their practice of discriminating against gay and lesbian people by refusing to provide them with adoption and fostering services. The government, slightly surprisingly, resisted this and instead gave voluntary adoption agencies an exemption, but only until 31 December 2008 (2007 Regulations, reg 15). There are only two voluntary adoption agencies in Scotland, both run by the Roman Catholic Church, and they will need to change their practices (but not their employment policies).

In conclusion, neither the refusal to employ nor the dismissal of anyone unwilling to conduct civil partnership registrations would be legally challengeable. There is no interference in either case with the right to religious freedom because that right must, as with the other rights under the European Convention, be balanced with the rights of others. The right of gay and lesbian people not to suffer discrimination is weightier than the right of others to practise discrimination in the name of religious freedom.

My thanks are due to Mrs Lynn Rodgers of General Registers of Scotland who provided me with factual information. Any opinion expressed thereon is mine alone.

Update

The Registrar mentioned at the start of this Commentary won her case at the Employment Tribunal but that decision was overturned by an Employment Appeal Tribunal: Ladele *v* Islington London Borough Council *[2009] ICR 387. She appealed to the Court of Appeal but lost there too: [2010] 1 WLR 955. The court held that a refusal to conduct a civil partnership by someone prepared to perform marriages amounted to unlawful discrimination under the Equality Act (Sexual Orientation) Regulations 2007 and, on the natural meaning of the Regulations, the prohibition of discrimination on the ground of sexual orientation in the provision of goods, facilities and services took precedence over any right a person would otherwise have by virtue of his or her religious belief to practise discrimination on that basis. The various Equality Acts and Equality Regulations were gathered together in the Equality Act 2010, which came into force in October 2010.* Ladele *was followed in* McFarlane *v* Relate (Avon) Ltd *[2010] IRLR 196, where a relationship counsellor refused to provide services to same-sex couples. The case is notable for its startlingly robust dismissal of religious beliefs as an unacceptable justification for discriminating against gay and lesbian people.*

Commentary No 37: July 2008

Speaking Up for Children

The joint report by the four UK Children's Commissioners to the UN Committee on the Rights of the Child provides a reality check for government and should dispel complacency

Children: UK perspectives

The UN Convention on the Rights of the Child ("UNCRC") came into force in the UK in 1991. Though a wide-ranging human rights instrument, it does not have the direct effect, or enforceability, of (say) the European Convention on Human Rights. Rather, enforcement is sought through a system of governmental reporting and UN responding.

States parties are obliged to submit every 5 years a report to the UN Committee on the Rights of the Child on how they are fulfilling their UNCRC obligations, and that committee has the power to make recommendations in its "Concluding Observations". The committee's concluding observations on the UK's second report were published in 2002, and the next round of reporting and responding is currently in progress. The UK's third and fourth report (combined at the request of an overstretched UN committee) was presented in July 2007.

On 9 June 2008 the UK Children's Commissioners published their own joint report to the United Nations Committee on the Rights of the Child. The Commissioners' joint report will be an invaluable, because independent, assessment. It also gives full recognition to the fact that there are four legal systems within the UK subject to the UNCRC, and it identifies the substantial social and legal differences between the four. This is a most useful counter to the UK Government's frankly bizarre statement in its 2007 report that, while Scotland and Northern Ireland do have separate legal systems, "similar statute and common law principles are applied throughout the UK" (p 6).

It is unsurprising when a government presents an upbeat report on its own progress, but nor is it surprising that an independent body, like the joint Commissioners, paints a far less rosy picture. The Commissioners' report will make uncomfortable reading for government at all levels in the UK, and indeed for everyone who has a concern for our children. The health, for example, of Scotland's children is castigated as "appalling" (p 7). And the increased demonisation of young people by the media across the UK is singled out for special criticism (para 176).

The report is not limited to legal issues, and it covers social, administrative, political and economic matters. Space precludes an examination of these, and even of all the legal matters. But there are two areas, both with clear Scottish dimensions, that deserve particular attention here.

Juvenile justice

This is the field in which Scots law is most obviously different from the law in the rest of the United Kingdom. The Commissioners' report makes plain that Scotland does better than England in the field of juvenile justice, for our children's hearing system clearly focuses on the needs of children in trouble with the law and adopts a welfare approach in responding to that trouble. Instead of concentrating primarily on the troublesome behaviour itself, the Scottish system seeks to address the issues that led to that behaviour.

The result is, as the report confirms, that children under 16 are much less likely to be punished or locked up than in England, and the Commissioners "welcome the Scottish Government's recently announced intention to end the detention in adult prisons of under-16s on remand" (para 33). There is, however, no room for complacency in Scotland, for "after that age, young persons are largely classed as adults for the purpose of criminal justice. Scotland locks up too many people aged 16 and 17" (p 7).

Even more worryingly, the welfare principle is constantly under attack and is, to put it at its lowest, compromised by new initiatives to deal with bad behaviour by young people, such as the antisocial behaviour order (ASBO). There is nothing, of course, in the Antisocial Behaviour etc (Scotland) Act 2004 limiting ASBOs to children, but the report points out that they have been used disproportionately on children (para 177). This reflects, or perhaps is the consequence of, what the report describes as "the consistently negative portrayal of young people in the media [where] 71% of media stories about young people are negative" (para 176).

Again, the position this side of the border is an improvement on the position in the south, in at least two respects: a breach of an ASBO cannot result in a custodial sentence for a child under 16, and details cannot be publicised in the press. The Commissioners' conclusion, which needs to be strongly endorsed, is that "it is vital that the Scottish Government resists importing initiatives that threaten the best interests of the child and that shift the focus from the child's needs and welfare" (para 173).

The conceptual difficulties with fitting ASBOs into the pre-existing Scottish system are well known. Whether ASBOs have made any difference at all in terms of good outcomes for either young people or society as a whole is not, for as the report points out: "There has been no proper evaluation of the effectiveness of ASBOs by the Government" (para 180). This is a defect urgently in need of remedy.

Non-discrimination and equal protection

Article 2 of the UNCRC requires that children be protected from all forms of discrimination, at least in respect of the rights provided for in the Convention. The present UK Government has extended protections from discrimination far beyond any previous government in this country, and it might have been expected that in this area at least there would be little criticism due. Quite the reverse. It is in respect of the UK's record in tackling discrimination against children that some of the harshest, and most justified, criticisms are found in the Commissioners' report. Such discrimination is endemic and institutionalised.

The UK Government had been criticised in 2002 for not sufficiently monitoring the extent to which children are exposed to discrimination. The Commissioners point out that "The UK Government and devolved administrations have made little or no progress" here (para 24), and they highlight in particular continuing concerns for children in gypsy and travelling families, and from ethnic minorities. Also of concern is the position of lesbian, gay, bisexual and transgender young persons: the disgraceful statistics are presented (para 25) that fully half of all teachers do not intervene when they hear homophobic language, and that 30% of lesbian and gay pupils say that adults – teachers and support staff – are responsible for homophobic incidents in their schools. No change from 1973, then.

Disability discrimination is particularly and disappointingly prevalent in educational provision. The report points out (para 129) that only 12% of mathematics textbooks and 8% of science textbooks used for GCSE are available in large print or braille, virtually ensuring that blind or partially sighted pupils cannot achieve their full educational potential. The health service is no better: the Commissioners point to "evidence of institutional discrimination in the NHS against people with a learning disability, leading to neglect and unequal healthcare" (para 84).

Another aspect of discrimination concerns corporal punishment. The rules have of course been amended by s 51 of the Criminal Justice (Scotland) Act 2003, but they still fall short of what is required by the Convention and children remain the only members of society who can be hit; as such they are "denied the equal protection of the law" (para 40). Following the 2003 Act the Scottish Government undertook to inform parents about positive parenting, but the Commissioners consider that the booklet produced, which provides information about the 2003 Act, falls short of the public education campaign recommended by the UN Committee in 2002.

Yet the UK Government continues to fail to get the message. It has announced welcome plans to extend age discrimination legislation to cover goods, facilities and services, but seems to think age discrimination is a problem only for the elderly: the protections they have in mind will apply only to those over the age of 18. However, as the Commissioners point out, shop signs like "no school children" or "only two children at a time" are now common, go largely unnoticed by adults, but impact seriously on children's day-to-day activities. They conclude that "unfair treatment based on prejudices and negative stereotyping should be no more acceptable for children than for any other members of society" (para 31).

Underlying the whole report, indeed, is the Commissioners' identification of a deeply worrying trend across society to see children as a group to be threatening and dangerous: a clear stereotyping that would not be acceptable if based on, for example, race. The Commissioners recommend the monitoring of the situation of children vulnerable to discrimination, and that government at all levels should develop, on the basis of such monitoring, comprehensive strategies containing specific and well-targeted actions aimed at eliminating all forms of discrimination.

Timely reminder

This report is to be welcomed. Government (unlike, perhaps, the media) is not bad-intentioned towards children, but it does sometimes need reminding of its international obligations, and of its failings. A central aspect of the role of the Commissioners, appointed by government, is to do just that.

Commentary No 38: October 2008

Hearing Better

The Government proposals on the children's hearing system are likely to effect improvements, but further measures should be included

It is pleasing, if a little surprising, that governments of various hues, from the Tories of the 1990s, Labour/LibDem in the 2000s and now Nationalist, have consistently shown strong support for Scotland's children's hearing system. On 1 August 2008, the Scottish Government published a consultation document on possible reforms of this system, and Fiona Hyslop, Cabinet Secretary for Education and Lifelong Learning, affirmed the Government's commitment to the principles underpinning the system including, most importantly, the principle that children who have offended and children who have been neglected and abused are equally deserving to be considered as children in need.

The consultation document seeks views on a number of structural changes and policy amendments that will more or less radically alter the way the hearing system is presently operated. The aim is to strengthen and streamline the system without affecting its underlying philosophy. The details are yet to be worked out for most issues and a number of decisions have yet to be made. The consultation period ends on 24 October 2008 and it is expected that a Bill will be published in June 2009.

Structural changes

The major structural change being proposed is the creation of a single national body replacing those bodies that are currently organised at local authority level, including the 32 children's panels, the 30 children's panel advisory committees (CPAC), and the 32 panels of safeguarders and curators *ad litem*. Clearly there is needless duplication here, but there are also structural anomalies. My friend Liz, who trained as a panel member with me in Glasgow, moved to Perth after only one year of service sitting on hearings. She was given the choice of retraining in her new area or leaving the system. This pointless requirement cost the system a valuable member, as well as wasting her earlier training space. A national approach will avoid this waste in the future.

Putting the system on a national basis would also enhance consistency of practice across Scotland. Nevertheless a crucial element in the system, indeed justification for the very existence of children's panels, is local delivery of services. Panel members, in particular, therefore need to retain a local link with the children they are dealing with, for the primary benefit of Scotland's unique hearing system is that decisions are made by lay panels who can legitimately claim both a knowledge of the local community of which the child is a part and an understanding of what, in that community, amounts to acceptable parenting. This representative role should never be forgotten.

The role of local authorities will, if these proposals are accepted, be very substantially reduced, though they will retain the important duty of giving effect to hearings' decisions. This development is to be welcomed, and not only for practical reasons. At the moment, though functionally independent of local authorities, hearings retain many structural links with them, in terms of appointment, training and payment of expenses of panel members and safeguarders. Families who appear before hearings see this structural link between the local authority (whose social workers have – usually – instigated the investigations that led to the hearing being convened) and the hearing itself, and find it understandably difficult to accept that the hearing is not simply a branch of the social services. Thus a perception of lack of independence exists and the current system serves to obscure the (legal) independence of the hearing. Breaking the link is likely to lead to greater confidence in the independence of the system.

Grounds for referral

The consultation paper does not invite any discussion of the existing grounds for referral to the children's hearing. This is unfortunate, because in my view amendments to s 52(2) of the Children (Scotland) Act 1995, which contains the grounds, can usefully be made.

In particular I think the time has come to repeal s 52(2)(g), the "incest and related offences" ground. This was necessary in the original Social Work (Scotland) Act 1968, since at that time incest was not a "scheduled offence", with the result that children who had suffered from the (common law) crime of incest could not be referred as sexual offence victims. This rationale disappeared in 1986 when incest and, by then, related offences were made scheduled offences by the Incest and Related Offences (Scotland) Act 1986. Nevertheless the ground was re-enacted in the Children (Scotland) Act 1995. But this remains pointless since all children who are victims of incest or the related offences can now be referred under s 52(2)(d), and the continued existence of this additional ground is a needless complication. (It is used very infrequently.) Nothing is lost by repeal.

And I wonder whether we need to retain s 52(2)(k), the solvent abuse ground. This was introduced by the Solvent Abuse (Scotland) Act 1983, as a result of a moral panic whipped up by the media concerning "glue sniffing" by children. I doubt whether this remains the social problem today that it once was, and in any case a child who puts him or herself at risk by this practice can be referred on the basis of s 52(2)(a) (beyond parental control) or even s 52(2)(j) ("any drug, whether or not a controlled drug").

A rather more recently introduced ground is contained in s 52(2)(m), that the reporter has been required by the sheriff, under s 12 of the Antisocial Behaviour etc (Scotland) Act 2004, to refer the child's case to a children's hearing. This rule fits very uneasily into the present system. First, it bypasses the crucial element of reporter discretion. Secondly, its wording is entirely circular: the ground for referral is that the reporter has been required to refer. It would be more sensible to allow the reporter to determine for him or herself whether the life circumstances of the child are such that a referral is necessary, and to word the ground in such a way as directs attention to the child's behaviour that took him or her to the sheriff court under the 2004 Act. This would better harmonise the antisocial behaviour legislation with the philosophy of the children's hearing system and the opportunity is there to do so now.

Children having sex

There is another amendment to the grounds for referral to a children's hearing that might usefully be considered, as a result of the recently published Sexual Offences (Scotland) Bill. The Scottish Government rejected (thankfully) the Scottish Law Commission's original recommendation to make sexual activity by children under the age of 16 a ground for referral, though since the Bill makes all such sexual activity a criminal offence any child indulging in such activity can be referred in any case. That in itself is not problematic, but we must always remember that the hearing system is designed to provide care for children in need of support and not to punish children for their behaviour (including their sexual behaviour).

The problem with children being referred to a hearing on the basis of sexual activity (I limit these comments to consensual sexual activity) is that if the ground used is s 52(2)(i) – that the child has committed an offence – then the child may be branded a sex offender, at least for purposes of disclosure under Pt V of the Police Act 1997 (as amended by the Protection of Vulnerable Groups (Scotland) Act 2007), and for purposes of rehabilitation under the Rehabilitation of Offenders Act 1974. This is a disproportionate response to consensual sexual activity: for example if the activity is between two 15-year-olds and a ground under s 52(2)(i) is established, neither of the pair will realistically be able to work with children throughout their lives.

The hearing may well have a role to play in either discouraging underage sexual activity, or putting in place measures designed to minimise the risks involved, but punishment of this nature, even indirect, is not justified. The solution, however, is simple: when the child is under 16 he or she is not only the "perpetrator" of a criminal offence but is also necessarily a "victim", and the branding of the child as a sex offender with its disproportionate consequences can be avoided completely by referring the child under s 52(2)(d) instead of s 52(2)(i). When both participants are under 16 and the sexual activity is entirely consensual, then in my view reporters who consider it appropriate to arrange a children's hearing should be required to use s 52(2)(d) and not s 52(2)(i). This could be done very easily by amending s 52(2)(i) to add the words "except an offence under s 27 [as it presently is] of the Sexual Offences (Scotland) Bill 2008".

The proposals currently being considered are likely to achieve the Government's aim of streamlining the children's hearing system without compromising the principles that make it so valuable. But more could be done, with little cost. The Scottish Government does seem open to persuasion.

Update

A draft Bill was indeed published in June 2009, to be met with howls of anguish from many interested parties. But the Scottish Government proved itself willing to listen and, the Bill finally presented to the Scottish Parliament in February 2010 was less radical than its 2009 draft but still aimed to achieve the primary political objectives. Even that Bill, however, had a fairly rocky road through the Parliamentary process, given the political divide between those who like centralisation and those who like local authority control. The Bill was passed in November 2010. The national body was created and local authority involvement in the running of the system was reduced. The grounds of referral were amended in the ways suggested above, and in other ways too. No change was made to the offence ground, but, for Disclosure purposes, a child will carry a criminal record for life only in relation to a specified list of offences. See Commentary No 45 below and update attached thereto.

Commentary No 39: January 2009

Parenthood Reborn

The law is having increasing difficulty keeping up with medical science, and social change, even in defining who is a parent

It is a truth that has bedevilled the male psyche since the dawn of civilization that women always know who their children are, but men never do. The law has had to respond to this by deeming and presuming and defining "father" in much more complex ways than it defines that far simpler idea, "mother".

These complexities have increased exponentially through technological advances, and changes in our understandings of family life, in the past 30 or 40 years. The Human Fertilisation and Embryology Act 1990 was a remarkably early attempt to regulate processes and families but, through no fault of its own, it has not aged well. The Human Fertilisation and Embryology Act 2008 substantially amends the earlier Act and aims to bring the law into line with the astounding changes in both scientific knowledge and how we construct the concepts of "family" and "parent". Only the latter issue will be considered here.

The basic need: good parenting

The 1990 Act was passed at the height of the Conservative Government's infatuation with "family values" as the basis of all policy; it was barely two years previously that that malign provision, "section 28" (of the Local Government Act 1988) – "Thou shalt not promote homosexuality as a pretended family relationship" – had been passed. While lesbian couples and single women were not explicitly barred from accessing infertility services, licensed clinics were nevertheless required by s 13(5) of the 1990 Act to "take account" of the welfare of any child likely to be born as a result of the treatment, "including the need of that child for a father".

The 2008 Act amends s 13(5) so that the factor to be considered is "the need of that child for supportive parenting". Sensibly, we no longer assume that disadvantage flows from single parenthood, or lesbian mothers, nor that maleness in a parent guarantees children's welfare.

Lesbian couples as mothers

The 2008 Act cannot quite bring itself to allow a child two mothers, but, following the lead of the recent adoption legislation and the Civil Partnership Act 2004, it provides for a child having two parents who may or may not be of the same sex: children will have a "mother" and in addition either a "father" or another "parent".

There is no change to the 1990 rule that if a married woman gives birth after infertility treatment at which sperm from someone other than her husband is used, her husband will nevertheless be treated for all purposes of law as the child's father, unless it is shown that he did not consent to that treatment (2008 Act, s 35, replacing 1990 Act, s 28(1)). But this rule is extended to civil partners. So if a civil partner gives birth after infertility treatment, her partner will be treated for all purposes of law as "a parent of the child", unless it is shown that she did not consent to that treatment (2008 Act, s 42).

The 1990 Act, s 28(2), deemed fatherhood on the unmarried (necessarily male) partner of a woman who becomes pregnant through infertility treatment. The 2008 Act repeats this (ss 36 and 37) and applies an equivalent rule to same-sex couples (ss 43 and 44). So the male partner of the woman who bears a child becomes "the father" and the female partner becomes "a parent".

Additionally, the very nature of the rule is changed. Under the 1990 Act, the (unmarried) male partner of the mother would be treated as the father whenever it was shown that the treatment had been provided to him and the woman "together". The concept of "treatment together" led to an inordinate amount of litigation, for many couples separated during the course of frequently long-term treatment. So this concept has been replaced by the issue of consent. But notice: while a husband or civil partner becomes father or parent by not withholding consent to the treatment, the unmarried or unempartnered partner will become father or parent by giving written consent to being treated as parent.

Section 3 of the Children (Scotland) Act 1995 is consequentially amended to ensure that a person who is a parent by virtue of s 42 of the 2008 Act (ie the civil partner of the mother) shall have automatic parental responsibilities and parental rights in relation to the child. And the unempartnered female partner of a mother will have automatic parental responsibilities and parental rights if she is deemed parent by s 43 and is registered as such – putting her in the same position as the unmarried father.

Adoption

The 2008 Act aims to provide a parenthood regime after infertility treatment that is consistent with the adoption regime, but this is not completely achieved. Under both the English Adoption and Children Act 2002 and the Adoption and Children (Scotland) Act 2007, the law permits a child to have two parents of the same sex, either registered as civil partners or not. But to become joint parents under the 2008 Act, unmarried/unempartnered couples must satisfy a requirement that does not appear in the adoption legislation: ss 37(1)(e) and 44(1)(e) provide that the couple must not be within the "prohibited degrees of relationship" (defined in s 58(2)) in relation to each other.

Now, there is no such requirement in any other legislation governing cohabiting couples. Doubtless it will normally be implied from the conjugality inherent in cohabitation: it is difficult to imagine the court holding a couple who are, say, aunt and nephew, to be "living together as if husband and wife in an enduring family relationship" (Adoption and Children (Scotland) Act 2007, s 29(3)). But the English Act uses a different definition of unmarried/unempartnered couple: "two people living as partners in an enduring family relationship" (Adoption and Children Act 2002, s 144(4)). This could, conceivably, cover the non-conjugal family relationship of aunt and nephew, or niece. For there is more to "family" than conjugality.

Financial provision on dissolution

Section 9(1)(c) of the Family Law (Scotland) Act 1985 is also amended, though confusingly so. Presently, this provides as one of the principles for financial provision on dissolution of a civil partnership that there should be a fair sharing, after dissolution, of any economic burden of caring for any child who has been accepted by both civil partners as a child of the family. The 2008 Act extends this to the economic burden of caring for any child of whom the civil partners are the parents "by virtue of sections 33 and 42" of the 2008 Act.

Had this amendment referred to s 42 alone it would have been understandable: the person deemed "parent" by that section would be obliged to share in the ongoing costs of caring for the child whether or not she had accepted the child as a child of the family. But the amendment applies only to children born to a couple who are parent by virtue of s 42 and mother by virtue of s 33. So it is limited to the situation where one woman conceives using an embryo not her own.

Not covered is the far more common scenario of a civilly empartnered woman conceiving using her own embryo – in other words, through simple artificial insemination. Now, while someone who is not a parent might properly be allowed to escape ongoing costs of caring for a child they have never accepted as their own, it is very different with a woman who is for all purposes of the law a parent – the question of acceptance should not arise and she should no more be allowed to escape these costs than a father who deserts his pregnant wife. But limiting the amendment to partners who are parents through both ss 33 and 42, allows a parent to escape liability if she shows she has not accepted the child as a child of the family. The easy solution would be to hold that the very giving of consent necessary to become parent under s 42 is in itself the act of acceptance. But if that is correct, then the need for this amendment is lost.

And it is to be noted that no amendment is made to the Family Law (Scotland) Act 2006, which governs claims for financial settlement at the separation of cohabitants. Section 28(2)(b) makes competent a financial claim to share upbringing costs when both cohabitants are the parents of the child, whether or not there is "acceptance" of that child. It serves no policy to rely on acceptance for civil partners when both are also parents, and indeed is contrary to the policy behind the 2006 Act that the liabilities of cohabitation should be looser than the liabilities of marriage/civil partnership. The amendment of s 9(1)(c) of the 1985 Act thus contains error.

There is clearly much to be commended in these new provisions, but once again it is shown that defining who a child's parents are is a complex and artificial process. The law is unlikely to remain static in this area.

Commentary No 40: May 2009

Where Fact Makes Law

New Zealand has a more all-embracing approach to cohabitants' rights than is recognised in Scotland, but the court still has to look carefully at the facts of each case

Since the coming into force of the Family Law (Scotland) Act 2006, Scots law has allowed ex-cohabitants to make financial claims against each other when they split up (2006 Act, s 28). Before being able to do so, however, the pursuer has to establish that he or she was indeed a "cohabitant" as defined in s 25. Early indications suggest that this will be a matter that is strenuously disputed in many cases. Other countries have been facing the same problem for rather longer than Scotland, and foreign jurisprudence can be of some assistance.

Having recently spent the (northern) winter months in the balmy, if windy, environs of Wellington, New Zealand, I was interested to discover how the issue is approached by the New Zealand courts. Few countries in the world have gone quite so far as New Zealand in equating the position of cohabitants with those of married/civilly empartnered couples, for the view is taken there that the needs of the parties, and the justice of claims, do not depend on the legal form the relationship takes.

In relation to financial provision on separation (and in most other areas), the claims arising from what are called in New Zealand "*de facto* relationships" are identical to the claims arising from marriage/civil partnership. This of course is not so in Scotland, but the preliminary question in both jurisdictions is the same: does the relationship satisfy the relevant definition?

"*De facto* relationships" defined

Since amendments in 2001, New Zealand's Property (Relationships) Act 1976 has allowed a party to any of three types of relationship – marriage, civil union, or *de facto* relationship – to seek financial readjustment when the relationship breaks down. This basically takes the form of an equal division (subject to certain qualifications) of "relationship property", which is defined rather more broadly than "matrimonial/ partnership property" in Scotland.

The definition of "*de facto* relationship" for the purposes of this Act is found in s 2D: it is a relationship between two persons, both of whom are over 18 and who are not married/civilly empartnered to each other, but who "live together as a couple". (Whenever a party is under 18 it would seem that the couple are only *de facto* a *de facto* couple but not *de iure* a *de facto* couple.)

Section 2D(2) provides that in determining whether two persons live together as a couple, the court must take into account all the circumstances of the relationship, including various specified factors, such as:

- the duration of the relationship;
- the nature and extent of the common residence;
- whether or not the relationship was sexual;
- the degree of financial dependence or interdependence;
- the ownership, use and acquisition of property;
- the degree of mutual commitment to a shared life;
- the care and support of children;
- the performance of household duties;
- and the reputation and public aspects of the relationship.

This list is not exhaustive. It serves a similar function to the far shorter list of factors in s 25(2) of our own 2006 Act. The length of the relationship and the financial arrangements between the parties appear in both lists (though worded differently), and the other element mentioned in s 25(2), "the nature of the relationship", must (if it is not to be tautologous of the very question at issue) allow the Scottish court to take account of any other factor relevant to determining the issue, such as any of the factors listed in the New Zealand legislation.

Colouring in

The New Zealand courts frequently emphasise that none of the listed factors is on its own determinative one way or the other, and all the factors are taken into account to provide an overall "colour". This allows a certain flexibility, which is sometimes used to ensure that justice is done.

In *RPD* v *FNM* [2006] NZFLR 573, a woman had three children by the man she lived with. She earned her living through prostitution, and the man "earned" his by pimping for her. She saved her money; he did not. The judge found that their financial interdependence fell within the context of a business relationship, that their personal relationship was characterised by the man taking a great deal and contributing little in return, that there was a lack of commitment on both sides, and that their relationship was not public but on the contrary was "obscured from public view". When the man claimed a share of the woman's savings, the court refused to hold the parties to be in a *de facto* relationship, but rather that they were in a parasitic business relationship (even although a *de facto* relationship was established at a later period, in respect of which the man could claim little).

Sexual activity between the parties is relevant, but not crucial, and it is clear that in New Zealand the complete absence of any sexual element to the relationship would not preclude the finding that the couple were in a *de facto* relationship. This is unlikely to be so in Scotland, where "living together as if they were husband and wife" may well imply a sexual element at least at the start of the relationship. (Civil partners are – legally speaking – entirely non-sexual and so it might well be argued that "living together as if they were civil partners" does not require any sexual element.) Conversely, in neither Scotland nor New Zealand will the fact that the couple have sexual partners outwith the relationship negate a *de facto* relationship that otherwise exists: *Scragg* v *Scott* [2006] NZFLR 1076.

Property and perception

The use and ownership of property was also discussed in *Scragg*. The couple had a sexual and social relationship but they lived apart – indeed for the most part they lived in different countries. However, they visited each other, often for periods of many months, and when they did so they always lived in the other's house. Also, the man had purchased the woman's house for her. The High Court held that the parties had "lived together as a couple" and therefore were in a *de facto* relationship for the purposes of the 1976 Act.

On the other hand, in *RRB* v *GF* (25 June 2008, New Zealand Family Court) a claim was made by a woman against the man who had bought a house for her and her children, who socialised with her, had sexual relations with her and spent many nights (and holidays) with her and her children, but who kept his own clothes and other personal possessions at his parents' house – and slept there, with a hotly disputed level of frequency. The court held that while the woman's house was used for various "joint activities", it was never a common residence because the man never saw it as his home, and so the couple were not a de facto couple.

Subjective perception by the parties plays an important role in New Zealand, for there is a mental element to the existence or otherwise of *de facto* relationships. This is seen most clearly with another factor specified in the s 2D(2) list: the degree of mutual commitment to a shared life. In *PZ* v *JC* [2006] NZFLR 97 a student aged 41 started out as the lodger of a 78-year-old, but the relationship developed into "an affectionate, mutually supportive and close relationship in certain domestic areas of their life, including, it seems, sexual contact". However, there was no clear indication that the 78-year-old was committing himself to a "couple-relationship" instead of a landlord–lodger relationship, and the claimant failed in her attempt to persuade the court that a *de facto* relationship existed. It will be interesting to see whether a subjective mental element is considered necessary in Scotland.

Conclusions on the facts

In *Scragg* the High Court warned that the variety of forms that personal relationships can take is so great that each case must be dealt with on its own facts and none may be regarded as setting a precedent. It also emphasised that the concept of "living together as a couple in a *de facto* relationship" was chosen by the New Zealand Parliament explicitly to bring in more relationships than would be caught in a formulation such as "living together in a relationship in the nature of marriage", the formula used in Scotland. This suggests that de facto relationships might be found to exist in New Zealand when, on identical facts, a cohabiting relationship would not be found in Scotland. For this reason the cases discussed above need to be read with care before attempting to apply analogous reasoning in claims before the Scottish courts. I hope that they are, nevertheless, of some interest to family practitioners here. In any case, everyone should visit New Zealand.

Update

There have, at the time of writing, been almost a dozen reported decisions on s 28 of the Family Law (Scotland) Act 2006, the provision that allows a claim for financial readjustment to be made when cohabitation comes to an end prior to death. Unsurprisingly, given the amount of discretion the legislation deliberately vests in sheriffs and judges, there have been a variety of approaches adopted in the assessment of these claims. In the Outer House decision of C *v* S *2008 SLT 871 Lord Matthews applied the approach developed in relation to a divorce claim under s 9(1)(b) of the Family Law (Scotland) Act 1985. In* Gow *v* Grant *2010 Fam LR 21 Sheriff Mackie considered that the requirement in the statute to identify disadvantages suffered suggested that the true aim is to provide compensation for losses. In* F *v* D *2009 Fam LR 111 Sheriff Hendry seemed to prefer an approach based on unjustified enrichment since one party had been enriched by the relationship more than the other. Given the difficulties in appealing judgments that are based on the sound exercise of judicial discretion, and the trust that the legislation places in judges at first instance, it may be some time before the Inner House or the Supreme Court has the opportunity to give guidance on the proper approach. It is open to argument that, given the diversity of cohabiting relationships, no further guidance than the words of the statute is appropriate. That does however leave separating cohabitants in a far less certain financial position than separating spouses or civil partners. One might accept that equiperating their rights, as New Zealand has done, is a step too far, but equiperating their expectations of certainty and predictability in the vindication of these rights is, surely, a feasible and legitimate aim.*

Commentary No 41: July 2009

Whose View Prevails?

Some recent developments in family law, in particular the vexed question of the intransigent parent refusing contact

Enforcing contact orders

One of the most intractable problems in modern family law is the practical enforceability of child contact orders. The letter of the law itself is perfectly clear: a contact order under s 11(2)(d) of the Children (Scotland) Act 1995 will be made by a court only after it has concluded that it is in the welfare of the child to make the order. Any person who deliberately seeks to frustrate that order is acting against the court's assessment of welfare and is in contempt of the court that granted the order. In theory, the law's response to such contempt is no different in this context from any other. In practice, however, there is a serious reluctance ever to imprison or fine a parent acting in this way.

The typical example concerns the mother with residence not allowing contact between the child and the father holding a contact order under s 11. Even when the father goes back to court and the mother is threatened with contempt proceedings, she might still resist. In the literature such a mother is usually referred to as the "implacably hostile" parent. Sometimes she does genuinely believe that the court's assessment of the child's welfare is wrong.

There is a perception that the courts, unwilling to impose the sanction of imprisonment, feel themselves effectively powerless in the face of such a parent. A recent case shows, however, that sometimes the court's patience snaps. In *M* v *S* 2009 Fam LR 149 the mother had strenuously resisted for almost 2 years, in the face of numerous court hearings, the implementation of a contact order made by the sheriff. She failed to attend court hearings, made (false) allegations of sexual abuse of the child against the father, feigned illness when warrants for her arrest were issued, and made (spurious) complaints of professional misconduct against the curator who failed to agree with her that contact with the father should be terminated, and against a clerk of court who did not call an ambulance quickly enough in response to one of her episodes of apparent illness. Numerous solicitors whom she had employed had quickly sought leave to withdraw. The sheriff took the view that this pattern of behaviour amounted to a serious contempt of court and he jailed her for 4 months. The case went to the Inner House of the Court of Session, on a petition to the *nobile officium*, which is the only method of appealing against imprisonment for contempt of a civil court.

Clearly sympathising with the sheriff's immense frustration, the Lord Justice-Clerk concluded that he could see no reason whatsoever to recall the sentence. "If we did, we would encourage the petitioner in the view that it is for her to decide which orders of the court she will obey. We would also undermine the authority of the sheriff and deprive the respondent of his rights. In effect, therefore, we would perpetrate an injustice at our own hand" (para 46).

He also concluded that the mother had been in contempt of the Court of Session itself, for she had been released pending the hearing of the petition to the *nobile officium* on giving a written undertaking to that court that she would in the meantime allow contact, and once liberated had declared that she had no intention of doing so. But in order to give the mother time to reflect on the gravity of her offence, sentence for that contempt was deferred for 6 months, with a warning that any penalty might be severe.

So, sometimes, the court will impose the penalty of imprisonment for contempt, even when this means depriving the child of the primary carer. In extreme cases – and this was probably one – the residence parent's behaviour is so perverse as to raise concerns about whether the child should remain in that person's primary care. This happened in an English case, *Re M (Intractable Contact Dispute: Interim Care Order)* [2003] 2 FLR 636 where the mother had lied to the children, telling them that they had been abused by their father and his parents, and the court responded by transferring residence from the mother to the father, with supervision by the local authority.

Both these cases are extreme. There is no doubt that the mothers in both the cases were acting neither reasonably nor rationally: rather their own interests and feelings were clearly dominating their minds, to the exclusion of their children's welfare. But in less extreme cases, the problem is that the mother may well be acting rationally in response to a genuine belief that her assessment of the child's welfare is more accurate than the court's.

All good parents will doubtless do what they believe is best for their children, some even if the state (through the court) believes otherwise. But one can be rational, even reasonable, and yet wrong. If a court has made a decision as to welfare, then any contrary view is, legally speaking, wrong. Once a contact dispute gets to court, the parent's assessment of the child's welfare is never decisive. The real test of the court's willingness to enforce its own contact orders will come in a far less extreme case than *M* v *S*, where the mother is genuine, rational and even reasonable in her belief that contact would harm the child, but the court simply disagrees.

Sexual offences

On 10 June 2009, the Scottish Parliament passed the long-awaited Sexual Offences (Scotland) Act 2009. One of the primary aims of this legislation is to clarify what the law understands by consent within the context of rape and other sexual offences. It also amends the law of sexual offences involving children. At long last the law is made both gender-neutral and sexuality-neutral, and so all the bizarre distinctions currently drawn by the Criminal Law (Consolidation) (Scotland) Act 1995 will simply disappear.

The Parliament rejected the suggestion of the Scottish Law Commission that sexual activity involving parties both of whom are under 16 should be decriminalised. Both will now be guilty (as opposed to only the boy, as at present). Offences will remain scheduled to the Criminal Procedure (Scotland) Act 1995, with the result that whenever a person under 16 is involved in sexual activity, a ground for referral to the children's hearing will exist. But reporters will have the choice of whether to refer the child on the basis of being guilty of, or of being a victim of, a scheduled offence.

The long-term consequences to the child of being found guilty of a sexual offence are severe, and it is to be hoped that in the generality of cases reporters will choose to refer children on the basis of being victims. They will of course be able to prove such a case on the balance of probabilities rather than beyond reasonable doubt. A difficulty with that hope might be the case of *Constanda* v *M* 1997 SLT 1396, where the Court of Session held that the reporter ought not to avoid referring on the basis of a criminal offence, and thereby avoid the higher standard of proof, by using the same facts to found a different ground if the real essence of the case is the child's criminal behaviour. Reporters are likely therefore to be faced with the unenviable task of examining the nature of the sexual activity the child has been involved with and making a decision of whether the child was in essence a criminal or a victim. This is unfortunate since it is unlikely that many cases will fall neatly on one side or the other of this false dichotomy.

Same-sex marriages

Just as 1999 was a year of profound change in the legal recognition of same-sex relationships across the Western world, so too is 2009 shaping up to be another bumper year for reform. Same-sex marriage (as opposed to civil partnership) has been introduced this year in Norway, Sweden, Vermont, Maine, New Hampshire and Iowa, doubling the number of jurisdictions in which same-sex couples can marry. In addition, civil partnership has been introduced in Hungary and is likely to be introduced in Ireland also.

One departure from the trend was in California, where the Supreme Court, only a year after it opened marriage to same-sex couples, accepted the constitutionality of a ballot initiative (a referendum) to remove that right. It did hold that all the marriages that had been created between its original decision and the passing of the ballot initiative would remain valid.

Two public petitions have this year been presented to the Scottish Parliament for the opening of both marriage and civil partnership to couples of any gender mix, and while some MSPs have expressed support, legislation is, I suspect, unlikely to follow soon. Though it does not generate in this country the political vitriol seen in the USA, the issue remains live and will, sooner or later, have to be addressed by our parliamentarians.

Commentary No 42: October 2009

Money and Your Life

Marriage contracts and separation agreements: their uses and benefits; and two recent cases where an agreement was challenged

Marriage contracts: personal choice

At one time it was relatively common for marrying couples (or at least those with significant property) to enter into marriage contracts with each other, or to create ante-nuptial trust settlements in favour of the wife. This was necessary to avoid the draconian common law effects that marriage had on a woman's right to own property. But these effects were gradually removed over a 60-year period between 1861 and 1920, after which time a married woman was permitted not only to own property but also to administer it on her own behalf. Revolutionary stuff, and given explicit recognition in statute by s 24 of the Family Law (Scotland) Act 1985.

Since 1920 the popularity of marriage contracts and marriage trusts has all but evaporated. Writing in 2005 in his book *Family Law Agreements*, the practitioner/author George Jamieson positively advises Scottish solicitors against recommending to their clients that they enter into marriage agreements, for a number of reasons, including the fact that the 1985 Act creates a "fair and sensible system" for property distribution on divorce. He also warns that "it is generally undesirable to discuss the arrangements for the breakdown of a marriage before it has begun or at regular intervals during the marriage: this may damage or destroy the trust between the parties to the contemplated marriage, or become a recurring source of trouble after marriage".

Nevertheless, on the website of at least one Scottish legal firm, it is suggested that the frequency with which clients request advice about entering marriage contracts is increasing once more. There may sometimes be good reason for a married or civilly empartnered couple to regulate their affairs by a personal contract rather than leaving their property relationship to the default rules set out in Scots law.

It is, for example, relatively common for persons marrying for a second or subsequent time to feel aggrieved at their treatment by the courts during their previous divorce: such people frequently wish to keep things under their own control in the future. Or there may be doubt as to which legal system governs the marital/property relationship, which can be removed by a marriage contract choosing as its proper law the system most conducive to the parties' wishes. And for the exceptionally wealthy, whose assets far outstrip reasonable needs, autonomy might be considered more important than equality of relationship. Unlike English law, where pre-nuptial agreements are unenforceable but will be given "due weight" (*Radmacher* v *Granatino* [2009] 2 FLR 1181), Scots law has no problem with the enforceability of such marriage contracts as are entered into.

Separation agreements: preferred route

A special form of marriage contract, and one that is not only common but strongly to be encouraged, is the separation agreement. This is an agreement entered into by parties who have decided that their marriage/ civil partnership ought to be brought to a legal end through divorce/ dissolution, but who wish to divide up their property in a way that is convenient to themselves rather than leaving it to the court to do so according to the law.

The end result in either case might well be virtually the same: an equal sharing of assets acquired during the relationship, compensation for some identified disadvantage suffered for the benefit of the family, an additional sum to recognise childcare obligations. But the real benefits of a separation agreement are (i) the encouragement to the parties to remain on speaking terms, and (ii) the saving of the expense necessarily involved in an adversarial court process. For these reasons most family law practitioners will seek to persuade their clients to enter into a separation agreement before going down the litigation route.

Separation agreements are, of course, enforceable in Scotland in the normal way: they are contracts (or, sometimes, unilateral promises) and parties are free to oust the jurisdiction of the court in order to resolve disputes which, without agreement, the court would be obliged to resolve for them. (This applies, it should be noted, only to the financial aspects of the agreement: other matters of potential dispute, in particular the residence of the children and contact arrangements with the non-resident parent, are often included in separation agreements but the jurisdiction of the court to deal with these matters can never be ousted.) General enforceability of separation agreements saves court time, and public money.

But they do not avoid court cases completely for, as well as the normal common law methods of challenging contracts, a separation agreement may be set aside or varied by the court under s 16 of the 1985 Act if it can be shown to be not fair and reasonable at the time it was made.

The leading case is *Gillon* v *Gillon (No 3)* 1995 SLT 678. Here Lord Weir set out the following principles: "(1) It is necessary to examine the agreement from the point of view of both fairness and reasonableness. (2) Such examination must relate to all the relevant circumstances leading up to and prevailing at the time of the execution of the agreement, including amongst other things the nature and quality of any legal advice given to either party. (3) Evidence that some unfair advantage was taken by one party of the other by reason of circumstances prevailing at the time of negotiations may have a cogent bearing on the determination of the issue. (4) The court should not be unduly ready to overturn agreements validly entered into. (5) The fact that it transpires that an agreement has led to an unequal and possibly a very unequal division of assets does not by itself necessarily give rise to any inference of unfairness and unreasonableness."

Two recent cases

There have been a couple of recent decisions on s 16. In *Clarkson* v *Clarkson* 2008 SLT (Sh Ct) 2, the parties had agreed that on their divorce the wife would take the matrimonial home plus a capital sum, while the husband would retain his business. The husband subsequently sought to resile from the agreement, having discovered that in valuing his business account had not been taken of a VAT liability: that liability effectively reduced the business's value to nil, with the result that the agreement left the wife with virtually all the assets.

Now, to challenge a separation agreement it must be shown that it was not fair and reasonable at the time it was entered into: in other words a change of circumstances after the agreement is reached is not relevant. The wife's defence was that on the information available at the relevant time the agreement was perfectly fair and reasonable and that the subsequent discovery of the true valuation of the business was not a relevant change of circumstances. She also argued that misevaluation on its own does not render an agreement unfair and unreasonable.

The sheriff, rejecting these defences, allowed a proof before answer. There had not been a change of circumstances, since the business always was valued at nil and it remained so: all that had changed was the parties' level of knowledge. Misevaluation might well render an agreement unfair and unreasonable. This must be so, for otherwise the deliberate hiding of assets, or the failure to make full and frank disclosure, would be innocuous.

Another recent decision is *MacDonald* v *MacDonald* 2009 Fam LB 99/5. Here the wife undertook to make no claims against the husband on divorce, and accepted that the matrimonial home would be transferred into the husband's name. The wife signed this agreement against the advice of her solicitor, who doubted whether there had been full disclosure of the husband's assets.

The sheriff found that there had been ample evidence that the wife had been bullied by her husband into signing it, including constantly visiting and telephoning the wife, shouting and swearing at her in order to persuade her to sign. The sheriff concluded that in these circumstances, even if, in themselves, the terms of the agreement were not unreasonable, it would be unfair and unreasonable to hold the wife to them. Nor was it unreasonable, given the bullying, for the wife to have failed to press her husband for more disclosure of his assets. The sheriff's decision was upheld by the Sheriff Principal (Lockhart), except that it was pointed out that the sheriff could only make a finding in principle that the agreement was unfair and unreasonable: its actual setting aside would have to wait until the decree of divorce was pronounced.

Protection (for some)

Separation agreements are socially and legally useful, and parties about to divorce each other ought to be encouraged to enter into them where possible. But s 16 recognises that the bargaining power of parties, particularly in the domestic situation, is seldom the same. Protection is given to the weaker party, and cases like *MacDonald* illustrate just how necessary that protection sometimes is. Cohabitants, of course, are left to fend for themselves.

Update

In October 2010 the Supreme Court heard an appeal in the English case mentioned in this commentary, concerning the enforceability of ante-nuptial marital agreements. In English law such agreements are, generally speaking, not enforceable on the ground that to recognise enforceability would be to allow parties to oust the jurisdiction of the court to make financial provision on divorce (or, in that recondite English phrase, "ancillary relief"). In this respect, English law is virtually alone in the western world. The matter was considered (for some reason) so important that a bench of nine justices was convened. They held that while not enforceable in the way that a contract would be, ante-nuptial agreements were so important that their existence should normally be given decisive weight in determining what financial provision to make: Radmacher v Granatino *[2010] UKSC 42. So the wealthier spouse, who had it seems a fortune of some £100 million and was expecting to inherit much more was able to resist a £5 million claim from the less wealthy spouse because they had agreed before marriage not to make any claims against each other. Of the nine justices, one was a woman and the decision was an 8 to 1 split. The dissenter, Lady Hale, warned that the facts of the present case (the wealthy spouse was a woman) should not be allowed to obscure the normative reality: which is that ante-nuptial agreements usually operate to prevent women claiming from their wealthier ex-husbands.*

At the end of the day, the Supreme Court accepted that in determining the weight to be given to ante-nuptial agreements the circumstances in which the agreement was entered into would be relevant and, as such, the results in most cases are unlikely to be substantially different from the results that would be reached in Scotland. The conceptual difference is that the principles applying in Scotland are laid down in statute while the English approach relies on the judgments of fairness made by individual judges. Radmacher *is on a par, it seems to me, with the English approach to financial provision generally: see Commentary No 29.*

Commentary No 43: January 2010

Hearing and Speaking

Additional provision for legal representation at children's hearings should enable them to fulfil better the purpose for which they were created

Important changes are in the offing for the children's hearing system. Very soon the Scottish Government will be presenting to the Scottish Parliament a Children's Hearings (Scotland) Bill which will restructure the way the system operates, though without, one hopes, departing significantly from the foundational principles upon which the system is based.

Doubtless these changes will be discussed fully in these pages and elsewhere in months and years to come. But there have already been significant changes. Legal representation for children has been available since the coming into force of the Children's Hearings (Legal Representation) (Scotland) Rules 2002, and more recently legal representation of relevant persons has been available since 4 June 2009, when the Children's Hearings (Legal Representation) Amendment Rules 2009 (SSI 2009/211) came into force.

The 2002 Rules were enacted as a result of the Inner House's decision in *S* v *Miller* 2001 SLT 531, that it was contrary to the child's right to a fair hearing, protected by Art 6 of the European Convention on Human Rights, not to have funded legal representation in (very basically) two situations: where sending the child to secure accommodation is under active consideration, and where the child would not, without legal representation, be able effectively to participate at the hearing. The 2009 amendments to these rules were designed to pre-empt another Inner House decision, that of *K* v *Authority Reporter* 2009 SLT 1019, and they permit funded legal representation of relevant persons where this is necessary to ensure that the person being represented has the chance to participate effectively at the hearing.

The court in *K* v *Authority Reporter* accepted that the failure to provide state-funded legal representation of relevant persons amounted to an "in-built systemic flaw in the legal aid scheme as it applied to the children's hearing system" (para 60). The 2002 Rules, now amended, establish what has always been described as an "interim scheme", but that scheme will continue to apply unless and until it is replaced by new rules to be contained in the 2010 Bill.

Effective participation

The key concept in the current scheme is that of "effective participation". The rules do not provide that legal representation of children and parents is available at all hearings. Instead they are designed to address the issue that was before the Court of Session in both the cases mentioned above: when does Art 6 of the European Convention require a party to civil proceedings to be provided with state-funded legal representation? The answer given in both cases was that this was required when the party would not otherwise be able to participate effectively in the proceedings.

"Effective participation" is the ability to contribute to the decision-making process in a way that communicates the main point of view of the participant to the hearing members. This has to be read in light of what is expected by way of participation. It is not expected that a one-year-old child will participate, and so hearings do not routinely appoint legal representatives to children of that age. The decision always needs to be made in the context of the nature of the participation that is required, and the stage in the process.

For example, at a grounds hearing, a relevant person who cannot understand, cannot give agreement, and the matter must be sent to the sheriff for proof. There is no effective participation needed there, and the fact that a legal representative would understand the grounds is neither here nor there: the matter goes to the sheriff if the relevant person cannot understand the grounds, even if that person's legal representative does. So in that type of case there is no need to appoint a legal representative (at least at that stage).

Similarly if the hearing is a simple and straightforward one in which there is no change proposed and limited scope for discussion, "effective participation" can be interpreted at a much lower level than in a complex hearing with much contention.

It would be wrong for hearings to adopt a policy of automatically making an appointment if a specified set of circumstances presents itself, for example in all cases in which the relevant person comes to the hearing under the influence of drugs or drink. Hearings must at the very least assume that the relevant person has capacity to participate effectively, and must make an individualised judgment that this is just not possible in the case before them. It may well be that (except perhaps in the most extreme cases) the panel members will have to attempt to conduct a hearing and give the relevant person the chance to participate before concluding that, in fact, the person is incapable of effective participation. If a person attends the hearing the worse for wear through drink or drugs and is clearly unable effectively to participate, the proper approach will be to continue the hearing to allow the person to sober up, rather than to appoint a legal representative.

Further guidance

In *K* v *Authority Reporter* the Inner House was asked to give some guidance as to when it would be appropriate for hearings to make an appointment of a legal representative. They said this in response:

> "In our opinion guidance on this particular issue is to be found in *Marangos* v *Cyprus* [2008] ECHR 1604 in para 35 of the judgment of the ECtHR: 'The question whether the provision of legal aid is necessary for a fair hearing must be determined on the basis of the particular facts and circumstances of each case and will depend, *inter alia*, upon the importance of what is at stake for the applicant in the proceedings, the complexity of the relevant law and procedure and the applicant's capacity to represent him or herself effectively.' "

> "In our opinion, that broad approach falls to be applied to the particular facts and circumstances of the case in which an individual's Convention rights under article 6(1) are engaged, including the personal characteristics and capabilities of the individual concerned. Those facts and circumstances will include, but are not limited to, the importance and potentially long term consequences of decisions taken at children's hearings, the stress that may be experienced by parties involved in proceedings relating to family life, the complexity of the factual and legal issues involved, the ability of the individual to understand those issues and the contents of any reports or other documents relevant to those issues, and the availability of any representatives prepared to assist the individual during the hearing."

It is also to be noted that a new r 3B was added into the 2002 Rules by the 2009 amendments, and it provides that "A person's ability to effectively participate in a children's hearing may be affected, in particular, by" a number of factors, including "(a) the complexity of the case, including the points of law in issue; (b) the nature of the issues involved; (c) the ability of the individual ... to consider and challenge any document or information before the hearing; (d) the ability of the individual ... to present their views in an effective manner".

It is ability to challenge any document or statement made at the hearing that is crucial to effective participation. Too often in the past statements which should have been challenged have been accepted by the hearing simply because no one was able to challenge them.

Role of the legal representative

The regulations do not specify the role that the legal representative is to play. It is to be remembered that there are other participants, who may well be able to assist in the child's or relevant person's participation. The legal representative is different: he or she will act *on behalf of his or her client* and is not to be seen as playing the same role as the safeguarder, or other representative of the child. In other words, the legal representative will take instructions from the client, and act upon them: the legal representative has no role in assessing the welfare of the child (or at least no more of a role than they would have in a normal residence or contact dispute before the sheriff).

The interim scheme is likely to be with us for some years to come. It is not expected that legal representatives will appear at hearings as a matter of course, but it is generally beneficial to everyone when they do appear. Lawyers are trained to act as procedural watchdogs, and to articulate the points of view of those whom they represent. So long as children's hearings continue to operate discursively in the search for a solution that best meets the child's needs, it will remain of crucial importance that each participant's point of view is expressed effectively and taken into account. Not only will this consist with article 6 of the European Convention, but it will consist with the very philosophy by which the children's hearing system has always operated.

Update

Just a month after this piece was published the Children's Hearings (Scotland) Bill 2010 was presented to the Scottish Parliament and as predicted it made significant changes to the way in which Scots law fulfils its obligations to provide a system that is compatible with the European Convention on Human Rights, and in particular Art 6 thereof. The concept of "legal representative", that is to say a person appointed by the hearing, identified and paid for by the local authority, and answerable to the child and relevant person, will disappear. Both children and relevant persons will be able to choose their own solicitors, if they wish to do so. The crucial difference is that payment of such a solicitor will come from the Scottish Legal Aid Board. In emergency cases the child will be automatically entitled to legally funded representation and in other circumstances will be so entitled subject to the satisfaction of the normal tests. The relevant person will also be entitled to legal aid, though never automatically. Assistance by way of representation, that is to say legal advice and assistance, will be extended to children's hearings cases for both child and relevant person. The Bill was passed in November 2010 and received Royal Assent in January 2011; it is expected that these provisions will come into force at some point in 2012.

Commentary No 44: April 2010

Giving and Taking Away

The Children's Hearings Bill intends to make it easier for a person to establish "relevant person" status, but has the effect of initially cutting out some who currently qualify

To be a "relevant person" within the children's hearing system is to hold a number of important rights and responsibilities in respect of a child who is referred to a children's hearing. These include the right and obligation to attend the hearing, and the rights to challenge grounds of referral, to call for a review of any supervision requirement, to appeal against any decision and, since June 2009, to be accompanied to the hearing by paid legal representation (see my January 2010 column in these pages).

Currently, s 93(2) of the 1995 Act defines a "relevant person" as: (i) a parent enjoying parental responsibilities or parental rights under Pt I of the 1995 Act; (ii) any (other) person who has parental responsibilities or parental rights under any Part of the Act; and (iii) any person who ordinarily has charge of or control over the child (other than by reason of employment). In practice it lies with the reporter to decide in the first instance whether any individual does or does not come within this definition (though a business meeting may sometimes assist the reporter in making that decision).

The first two categories leave little room for doubt because they are legally determined; category (iii), on the other hand, requires some assessment of the factual situation and the making of a judgment of whether or not a person "ordinarily" has "charge of or control over" the child. For some time the Scottish Children's Reporter Administration resisted including long-term foster carers within category (iii), but in *S* v *N* 2002 SLT 589 the Court of Session held that the words of the statute imported a factual test and so had to be given their ordinary and natural meaning. There were clearly circumstances in which a long-term foster carer could be said ordinarily to have charge of and control over the child.

Status in fact

More recently the question of whether a person can seek by court action to be recognised as a relevant person has proved surprisingly troublesome. There had been a conflict of sheriff court authority on whether an individual could seek, by means of an order under s 11 of the 1995 Act, to be conferred what has come to be called "relevant person status". In *Principal Reporter, Petitioner* 2006 SLT 1090 Lady Paton in the Outer House, entirely correctly, pointed out that such conferral would not be within the terms of s 11 and so would be incompetent as a claim on its own. That decision was subsequently affirmed by the Inner House in *Principal Reporter* v *K* 2010 SLT 308. A person may seek parental responsibilities and parental rights under s 11 and, if any of them are granted, will become by this means a relevant person, but he or she cannot seek a court order directly conferring "relevant person status", with rights and responsibilities within the children's hearing process but with no consequences beyond.

This position is, in the main, unproblematical. "Relevant person status" is enjoyed by all persons who either have one or more of the parental responsibilities or parental rights or ordinarily have charge of or control over the child. The exclusion of the father who has no parental responsibilities and parental rights (an ever-decreasing phenomenon since the Family Law (Scotland) Act 2006) is justified if he does not have charge of or control over the child; the test is wide enough to include the likes of grandparents and long-term foster carers who are in fact playing a significant role in the upbringing of the child.

The only difficulty is that the reporter has, in practice, the power to determine who ordinarily has charge of or control over the child, and the only way to challenge the reporter's assessment of that fact is to wait until the hearing has made its decision and appeal the decision on the basis of procedural irregularity (failure to involve someone with a statutory right to be involved: see for example *S* v *N*). This is one of the difficulties that the Children's Hearings (Scotland) Bill 2010 seeks to address.

No longer relevant

The Bill retains the concept of "relevant person" as the key to full participation in a children's hearing, but it makes a number of very significant changes both to the definition and to how "relevant person status" might be acquired.

Section 185(1) of the Bill has a rather more limited definition of "relevant person" than is found in the 1995 Act. The definition is limited to those who currently have "parental responsibilities or parental rights" and will no longer include those who do not have such responsibilities or rights but who nevertheless have charge of or control over the child. Nor, because of a new provision in s 185(2), will the definition include, as the current law does (see *S* v *Children's Reporter* 2008 Fam LR 84), any person whose only parental responsibility or right is that of contact. Another limitation (though this smacks of accident rather than design) is the omission of a child's testamentary guardian from the definition of "relevant person", for non-parents will be relevant persons under the Bill only if they can trace their parental responsibilities and parental rights to an order under s 11(2)(b), and testamentary guardians of course obtain parental responsibilities and parental rights under s 7. Nor am I entirely convinced that adoptive parents will come within the definition, since they trace their parental responsibilities and parental rights to the adoption legislation and not the 1995 Act.

This more restrictive definition is balanced to some extent by a new process under which restructured "business meetings" (which will be renamed "pre-hearing panels") will be able to deem an individual a relevant person, notwithstanding that he or she does not come within the definition, if they consider that the individual has (or has recently had) "a significant involvement in the upbringing of the child" (s 80). The effect of this is to move the power to assess the relevance of an individual to a child's life from the reporter to the children's hearing. But it also shifts the initiative from the official to the individual, with the result that foster carers, grandparents, unmarried fathers, and anyone else who wishes to be treated as a relevant person will now be required themselves to instigate a process to allow them to show that they satisfy the new test of "significant involvement", where previously it was part of the reporter's function to address that question whether asked to do so or not.

A clear improvement from the current system is that there will be a direct appeal to the sheriff from the decision on "relevant person status" (s 155), instead of the indirect mechanism described above.

Mechanisms and effects

There are some problems with the new rules in the Bill. Sometimes the hearing system has to operate quickly and before any pre-hearing meeting can be held. And the process will use the definition of "relevant person" in s 185 until such time as a pre-hearing panel confers "relevant person status" on someone who does not fall within the s 185 definition. This will effectively exclude grandparents, foster carers and unmarried fathers from the emergency and interim processes within the system.

So for example when a child protection order is granted by a sheriff, notification must be given to the "relevant persons" (2010 Bill, s 41); likewise any relevant person may seek to have that order varied or terminated (s 46). Anyone who does not come within the s 185 definition will not have these rights, but nor will they have the time to request a pre-hearing panel to give them these rights. The effect is to exclude from some early stages of the system those individuals who would, under the 1995 Act, be included and who may well be included in later stages. The same problem arises in the legal aid provisions. The Legal Aid (Scotland) Act 1986 is to be amended to allow legal aid for representation at pre-hearing panels, but only for children and relevant persons – not people who are requesting pre-hearing panels to give them relevant person status (and who would be relevant persons under the current law).

It seems then that the efforts to provide a more formal mechanism for a person who has no parental responsibilities or parental rights to achieve "relevant person status" will have the effect of excluding from certain parts of the overall process those who, by dint of being in fact relevant to the child's life, would at present be centrally involved in all aspects of the process. Whether the removal of these rights is a price worth paying for the achievement of procedural certainty is a matter of political judgment. Ultimately, of course, the court may be called upon to determine the compatibility of whatever judgment the Scottish Parliament makes with the European Convention on Human Rights, and in particular the obligation to ensure family participation in legal processes of this nature.

Update

The basic structure described above – a new and more limited definition of relevant person, and a process by which those excluded from that definition can be brought within the definition – was accepted by the Scottish Parliament though amendments to the definition did address some of the problems identified above. The Children's Hearings (Scotland) Bill passed Stage Three on the floor of the Parliament on 24 November 2010 and is expected to be brought into force at some point in 2012. Perhaps, after all, the statutory definition of relevant person did need to be revised, for 2010 saw a flurry of cases on the issue. Not only was there Principal Reporter *v* K, *as discussed above, but a few months later the Inner House held in* Authority Reporter *v* S *2010 SLT 765 that unmarried fathers of children over whom they did not have full parental responsibilities and parental rights but in respect of whom they held contact orders were not, in terms of the Children (Scotland) Act 1995, "relevant persons" but that ECHR considerations required that they should be. The Court refused to grant a declaration of incompatibility in respect of the definition section of the 1995 Act and instead read in words to the definition so that it included not only parents with parental responsibilities and parental rights but also parents with contact orders. The Children's Hearings (Scotland) Act will once more exclude such fathers, but at the same time give them a mechanism by which they can apply to the hearing to be granted "relevant person status".*

In the meantime, and very interestingly, Principal Reporter *v* K *was appealed from the Inner House to the Supreme Court, the first time that the highest court in the United Kingdom has decided a Scottish children's hearing case. See 2011 SLT 271. That court held that the definition of relevant person would be contrary to Art 8 of the European Convention if it excluded fathers who had established family life with their children, but it avoided making a declaration of incompatibility by reading into the definition persons with family life in terms of Art 8. The Supreme Court also emphasised that fundamental principles of fairness, such as the right to be heard, had to be protected by the hearing system. It is difficult to see how this decision can be given effect to in the new Act without amendment.*

The section numbers given in this commentary have, of course, changed as the Bill became the Act. "Relevant person" is defined in s 200 of the Children's Hearings (Scotland) Act 2011; relevant person status can be sought by those who are not relevant persons within the definition under s 79; appeals from that decision are taken under s 160.

Commentary No 45: July 2010

Criminalising Children

Current, and proposed, legislation gives rise to anomalies regarding children and criminal records, but the Children's Hearings Bill could be used to provide a solution

The Scottish age of criminal responsibility is amongst the lowest in the developed world. In practice, of course, the majority of children who commit criminal offences are not prosecuted in the criminal courts but are instead referred to the children's hearing: we believe (rightly) that a welfarist rather than a punitive response is the most appropriate way to address a child's offending behaviour.

The Criminal Justice and Licensing (Scotland) Bill 2010, which passed Stage 2 in May 2010, will raise the age at which a child can be prosecuted to 12, but it retains the presumption that a child under the age of eight cannot commit a criminal offence.

So a child who commits an offence between the ages of 8 and 12 cannot be prosecuted, but might still be referred to a children's hearing. This sounds unobjectionable. However the children's hearing system is not purely welfarist and punitive consequences do follow, if a child is referred on the basis of having committed an offence.

Criminal records

The main punitive consequence is that the child acquires a criminal record: the Rehabilitation of Offenders Act 1974 and the Police Act 1997, which established Disclosure Scotland, apply. Section 3 of the 1974 Act provides that where a child has been referred to a hearing on the ground of having committed an offence, "the acceptance, or establishment (or deemed establishment), of that ground shall be treated for the purposes of this Act ... as a conviction, and any disposal of the case thereafter by a children's hearing shall be treated for those purposes as a sentence".

Section 5 of the 1974 Act "rehabilitates" the child (that is to say treats the child as not having committed an offence) after one year from the "conviction", or at the end of the period of the "sentence", whichever is longer. The record is, for most purposes, expunged.

The problem lies in the exceptions to rehabilitation, for criminal records are not expunged for the purposes of disclosure certificates issued by Disclosure Scotland. Anyone applying for positions involving caring for, training, supervising or being in sole charge of persons under the age of 18, or vulnerable adults (for example a teacher, nursery worker or foster carer), is obliged to reveal, through an enhanced disclosure certificate, their "criminal" record – with details of all "convictions" including those "spent" under the 1974 Act. Depending upon the nature of the offence that brought the child to a children's hearing, this might reduce or remove entirely the person's chances of employment in any position involving children or vulnerable adults.

Options for change

The Children's Hearings (Scotland) Bill 2010, which completed its Stage 1 consideration in June, currently makes no change to this position, though many consultees expressed disquiet. In giving evidence to the Education, Lifelong Learning and Culture Committee of the Parliament, the Minister for Children undertook to look at the matter again, to ensure that the criminal record consequences of appearing before the children's hearing were not applied disproportionately (see Official Report, 5 May 2010, col 3537).

What amendments might be made to the Bill at Stage 2 (which is due shortly)? Here are my own suggestions for the Minister.

First, the age of criminal responsibility could be raised to the age of 16, avoiding the problem entirely. Given the Parliament's very recent consideration of the matter, this option is unlikely to find favour. In any event, it would prevent criminal record consequences even for those very few children who, by remaining a risk to others in adulthood, probably do require to be obliged to disclose their past behaviour.

Secondly, the age of criminal responsibility (as well as of prosecution) could be raised to 12. This would restore the natural link between responsibility and prosecution, without preventing badly behaved children under 12 being brought to a children's hearing (on grounds other than the commission of an offence). It would, however, still involve potential criminal record consequences for children 12 years of age or more, and so does not address the problem for the older child with whom it is, perhaps, more likely to be an issue.

Thirdly, given that the crux of the problem lies with the Rehabilitation of Offenders Act 1974, the simplest solution would be to repeal s 3 of that Act. Children could continue to be referred to the children's hearing on the basis of having committed a criminal offence, but the hearing's outcome *and its consequences* would be entirely welfarist and there would be no "criminal record" requiring to be disclosed. If the child's behaviour were so serious that lifelong criminal consequences were justified, that child could be prosecuted (if over 12) in the criminal courts. To avoid the risk that prosecutors would seek to prosecute more children than at present, the Lord Advocate's guidance on prosecution of children would need to focus on protection of others from a child who is likely to remain a risk as an adult.

Fourthly, we might remove the most pernicious feature of the current system – that the 1974 Act applies to grounds that are *accepted*, often without legal advice as to the consequences, as well as grounds established after evidence – and replace it with a rule that rehabilitation and disclosure apply only where the offence has been established, beyond reasonable doubt, in a court of law. Though superficially attractive, this may well be the least satisfactory of all the options, for it would create an unacceptable incentive to children to accept allegations against them by offering them the reward of avoiding any criminal record. This would be more pernicious than the current system, for in order to ensure that the child has complete freedom to decide whether to accept or to deny the grounds, the legal consequences must be the same in either case.

Fifthly, if we accept that some children are likely to remain a risk to others even when they become adults, our focus should be on identifying these children and limiting the criminal record consequences to them alone. Not only would an appropriate test need to be determined, but it would also require to be decided who should make the judgment that the child posed a risk.

If that judgment properly lies with the children's hearing, then an amendment to the Children's Hearings Bill could give them the power to declare, as a disposal, that the child should be subject to the terms of the 1974 Act. If the judgment is more appropriately left to the sheriff, an amendment could require all cases in which the child is referred to a hearing on the basis of having committed a criminal offence to be sent to the sheriff for proof, with the sheriff being given the power to make an order that the 1974 Act is to apply. (This would likely encourage reporters to avoid the offence ground where possible, so minimising the number of cases in which the issue would arise.)

In my view, however, the judgment best rests with the reporter. The offence ground should therefore be amended to read something like "the child has committed an offence and it is likely that the child will remain a risk to others in the future".

The reporter would then have to determine whether both the offence and the risk exist, and can be proved to exist if denied. If the offence exists but the risk does not, for example, in cases of an isolated assault in the school playground, shoplifting, or act of petty vandalism, or incidence of consensual, unpressured and non-exploitative sexual activity, the reporter could still refer the child to a hearing, but on the basis of one of the other grounds, such as being outwith the control of the relevant person, or behaving in a way that has serious adverse effects on the child or another person (grounds 65(2)(m) and (n) in the 2010 Bill). This is my preferred option.

Continuing threat?

It needs to be remembered that there are only very few children whose offences are such that they are likely to continue to pose a threat to others into adulthood. The requirements of disclosure are designed to warn of threats; yet our fear of badly behaved children has led the present system to assume that society needs protection from, and warning about, any child (over 8) who commits any offence for whatever reason and in whatever circumstance. Scotland would be better served by encouraging children to become full members of society, with uninhibited employment prospects, even when, as children, their behaviour had been reprehensible. The system could, if the proposal above were accepted, identify real risks much earlier. The passage of the Children's Hearings (Scotland) Bill gives us an ideal opportunity to do so and it is to be hoped that the opportunity is taken.

Update

The Minister for Children, Adam Ingram, MSP, did indeed look again at the position and he came to substantially the same conclusion as the Education Committee: requiring children who have been referred to a children's hearing on the ground of having committed an offence to continue to disclose such referral for many years into adulthood was a wholly disproportionate requirement. He (and, it has to be said, the Parliament as a whole) was not inclined to decriminalise children completely. Instead he wished the legislation to identify situations in which there was a real and genuine risk that the child would remain, in adulthood, a continuing danger to the public, which the Disclosure Scotland system should properly protect the public from. On 27 October 2010 the Education Committee debated two amendments to the Bill, one from the Minister and one from Ken Macintosh MSP, both designed to achieve this same aim. But they were very different, in terms of how the risk was identified. Ken Macintosh's amendment adopted an individualised approach, whereby each child brought to a hearing for having committed an offence would have their case looked at by the hearing which would also have the task of assessing whether the child was likely to constitute an ongoing risk such as to make disclosure appropriate even long into the future. The Minister's amendment focused on the offence instead of the offender and proposed the drawing up of a (fairly limited) list of offences which would be subject to disclosure and the Rehabilitation of Offenders Act 1974. Referrals to hearings would no longer be regarded as "convictions" for the purposes of the 1974 Act but the acceptance, establishment or deemed establishment of one of the list offences would continue to require disclosure. The useful parliamentary debate revolved around who was the appropriate body to identify the risk. At the end of the day the Minister's amendment was accepted. At the time of writing the "list" has not been drawn up but it is hoped that it is a very short one. In principle, this is not the correct approach: often the technical nature of the offence depends more on what can be proved as opposed to what actually happened (as is seen, for example, with the difference – crucial on other areas – between murder and culpable homicide). However, pragmatically, this may well be the better approach. Asking anybody to identify whether a 15 year old will continue to be a danger to the public in 20 years' time is asking the impossible. Disclosure of a very serious offence allows the body who has sought disclosure to make the assessment, at that time, of whether the individual remains a risk. In any case, the new rules are very much better than the old and are to be warmly welcomed for that reason alone. The appropriate amendments to the Rehabilitation of Offenders Act were made and are contained in s 187 of the Children's Hearings (Scotland) Act 2011.

Commentary No 46: October 2010

Two by Two, by Two

Argument that full marriage rights could be extended to same-sex couples, for there are no technical legal difficulties in the way of achieving this in Scotland

The trouble with gay and lesbian people is that they are never satisfied. Give them a crumb and they want a slice of bread. Give them a slice of bread and they want a full meal. Give them a full meal and they want to eat it at your table. Let them sit at your table and they want the same thing as you are having. In family law terms, the Civil Partnership Act 2004 is (more or less) the full meal, so why should the LGBT community want the same menu as non-LGBT people? The simple answer, equality of choice and opportunity, and of respect, makes the opening of marriage to same-sex couples difficult to resist, at least in a secular society with a rationalist legal system. But how easy would it be to achieve, technically, in Scots law?

Marriage for same-sex couples

Most countries in Western Europe have adopted a civil partnership regime. The most recent to do so is the Republic of Ireland with the passing in July 2010 of the (clumsily titled) Civil Partnership and Certain Rights and Obligations of Cohabitants Act 2010. Some countries have gone further and have opened marriage itself to same-sex couples. These include the Netherlands (2001), Belgium (2003), Spain (2005), Canada (2005), South Africa (2006), Norway (2008), Sweden (2009), Portugal (2010), Iceland (2010), Argentina (2010), and at least five of the United States of America.

At home, the issue might well gain political currency in these days of coalition Government. It is not currently Conservative Party policy to hug a homosexual, but the Liberal Democrats, perhaps in an attempt to show that they remain distinct from their partners, may well push the issue. The Scottish Liberal Democrats at their spring 2010 conference adopted the policy that both marriage and civil partnership should be open to all couples, whatever their gender mix, and in September 2010 the same policy was adopted by the UK party conference. The new UK Labour leader, Ed Miliband, supports equal marriage rights irrespective of gender mix (as, indeed, did all his rivals for the leadership). The matter is on the political agenda both in Scotland and UK-wide.

The European Court speaks

In *Schalk and Kopf* v *Austria*, 24 June 2010, the European Court of Human Rights rejected a claim that the failure by a state to allow a same-sex couple to marry amounted to a violation of the Art 12 right to marry. But the decision was more progressive than that formal holding suggests.

First, the court finally gave long-overdue recognition that gay men and lesbians could rely on the "family life" aspect of Art 8 as well as "private life", to which they had previously been restricted. Public relationships are now as protected as private activities. Secondly, the court held that Art 12 taken with Art 14 requires states that do allow same-sex marriage to treat same-sex married couples in the same way as opposite-sex married couples – unless there are strong justifications for distinguishing the two. And thirdly, the court explicitly contemplated the time when a European consensus would emerge on the issue of same-sex marriage – at which point the court might well require states that limit marriage to opposite-sex couples to remove that limitation.

Cases are pending alleging a violation of Arts 8 and 14 from countries which have no institutional means at all for same-sex couples to be recognised, or (like France) where the recognition is very much more limited than the recognition, through marriage, of opposite-sex couples. At the European Court of Justice, the Advocate General opined on 15 July 2010 that throughout the European Union, same-sex couples should have means of accessing all the employment benefits available to married couples: *Roemer* v *City of Hamburg* (C-147/08).

How can it be done in Scotland?

Countries that have already opened marriage to same-sex couples did not find it particularly difficult to do so in technical terms, and it is unlikely to be any more problematic here. Various amendments would be required to the Marriage (Scotland) Act 1977, most obviously the repeal of s 5(4)(e), under which the fact that the parties are of the same sex constitutes an impediment to marriage. However, in order to avoid the argument that the removal of the statutory impediment does not in itself remove the underlying common-law impediment, there would probably need to be some positive statement for the avoidance of doubt. This could be achieved by adding into the interpretation section words like the following: "'Marriage' includes a marriage or purported marriage between two persons of the same sex." Using "includes" instead of "means" maintains the common-law definition of marriage and simply extends Scots law's understanding of the concept.

The 1977 Act governs how to get married, but most of the actual consequences of marriage are contained in other statutes, which would also need amending. It would be possible to follow the time-consuming approach adopted with the Civil Partnership Act, which was to amend (or replicate) every single one of the statutory provisions that referred to marriage to make them gender neutral, but far easier would be to utilise a statutory deeming provision along the lines of: "The legal consequences of a marriage involving a couple who are of different sexes, whether these consequences are provided under statute or in any other way, apply, with such changes as may be required by the context, to a marriage involving a couple who are of the same sex and the terms 'marriage', 'spouse', 'husband', 'wife' and cognate expressions shall be interpreted accordingly."

Divorce for adultery

Adultery was deliberately withheld as a ground for dissolution in the Civil Partnership Act. The present definition is penile penetration of the vagina and Parliament baulked at the thought of wording a homosexual equivalent. The official line was that a civil partner whose spouse had had (homo)sexual relations outwith civil partnership could utilise the "unreasonable behaviour" ground, though, of course, that argument applies equally to married couples and suggests that adultery is irrelevant today. (That argument was rejected as recently as 2006 by the Scottish Parliament, which rejected the opportunity in the Family Law (Scotland) Act 2006 to abolish adultery at the same time as it abolished desertion as a ground for both divorce of marriage and dissolution of civil partnership.) This means that if marriage were extended to same-sex couples, the political choice would have to be made whether adultery as a ground for divorce should continue to be limited to opposite-sex couples.

In (my) order of preference, the choices would be the following. First, abolish adultery for all married couples (retaining, of course, unreasonable behaviour). Secondly, exempt same-sex couples from the benefits/disadvantages of adultery even if they are married, for the same reasons as they are exempted when in civil partnership. Thirdly, extend adultery so that it is broader than its existing specifically heterosexual meaning (rather in the same way that the heterosexualised definition of rape was extended in the Sexual Offences (Scotland) Act 2009). Fourthly, make no change to the law of adultery at all, retaining heterosexual activity as a ground for immediate divorce for everyone.

Reserved matters

Many of the most important consequences of marriage, including taxation, social security and immigration are, of course, reserved to the United Kingdom. If Scotland goes alone on the issue, the Equality Network has made the sensible suggestion that all marriages in Scotland involving same-sex couples be treated for UK reserved matters as if they were civil partnerships – just as Canadian, Dutch, Swedish etc marriages are presently treated throughout the United Kingdom as civil partnerships. Separating state and federal consequences of marriage has not proved an insuperable difficulty for those states in the United States that have opened marriage to same-sex couples.

Religious officiants

No conscience exemption is appropriate for registrars who, by dint of their public office, are required to register civil partnerships (*Ladele* v *Islington Borough Council* [2010] 1 WLR 955), and for the same reason no exemption would be appropriate to allow them to refuse to be involved in conducting civil marriages. Nevertheless, some churches will fear being required to offer marriage services to same-sex couples.

One means of addressing their concerns would be to limit marriage for same-sex couples to civil ceremonies only, emphasising the essentially secular nature of the institution. This would be unsatisfactory since the secularity of civil partnership did not reconcile opposing religions to its acceptability, and in any case, many same-sex couples are believers and want to walk down an aisle together. To prevent churches that are willing to conduct such marriage ceremonies just because other churches are unwilling is to impose the doctrines of one brand of faith on adherents of another.

In fact, in Scotland, there is no need for a conscience clause since there is no requirement on religious officiants to conduct any ceremony that is contrary to their faith and it would, therefore, be within the discretion of individual ministers or churches as to whether to marry a couple who are of the same sex. In other words, if any religious organisation or individual does not wish to be involved in the creation of marriages between same-sex couples, they need not be so. Their refusal to recognise such a marriage would have as much effect in law as the refusal of some churches to recognise the validity of a marriage involving a divorced person.

A matter of time

Same-sex marriage will come to Scotland and the only question is when. Its introduction will not signal the end of the world, but may well symbolise the final victory in law of the secular over the sacred. It seems to me that a tolerant and respectful society could only benefit from that.

Update

Of course the complexities of marriage having reserved consequences work both ways. If England moved on this matter before Scotland then its Parliament would certainly include issues reserved from the Scottish Parliament, leading to an awkward disjunction between the jurisdictions of the UK. On 17 February 2011 the (UK) Government Equalities Office announced a consultation on "how legislation can develop" to address a desire "to move towards equal civil marriage and partnerships" in England and Wales. Whether the procedure that led to a single Civil Partnership Act can be followed for marriage is ultimately a political question, but it is one that the new Scottish Government will have to address early in its period of office. On 6 June 2011 the Scottish Government announced in a Written Answer that it would consult on the issue "as soon as practicable" (S4W – 110)

Commentary No 47: January 2011

The Welfare Imperative

Developments in Europe that could force a fundamental rethink of the application of the Hague Convention on International Child Abduction

The basic premise of the Hague Child Abduction Convention is that the welfare judgment required when parents disagree about where the child is to live is properly made by the court of the child's habitual residence (the "court of origin"). So if the child is wrongfully taken to another country, the court there (the "requested court") must return the child to its habitual residence "forthwith".

The traditional approach has been to minimise the opportunities for the requested court to assess whether return would be in the welfare of the child, because that assessment is time consuming, and to keep the parameters of the specified exceptions to retention within very narrow bounds, for otherwise the Convention's principles risk being entirely subverted. This approach is justified by the major purpose of the Convention, which is to remove any incentive an abducting parent would have in seeking a jurisdiction that is more likely than the child's home jurisdiction to find in that parent's favour.

Speed is of the essence, which is why it is simply not appropriate for the requested courts to spend much time in the sort of minute examination of the welfare of the child that so often bedevils the process in the domestic context. (In the recent decision of *NJDB* v *JEG* [2010] CSIH 83, a domestic contact dispute, determining what was in the welfare of the child took 52 days of evidence spread over nine months: though the Inner House was clearly shocked at this timescale, weeks of evidence are all too common in such disputes.) The traditional approach is followed by courts around the world, including courts in Scotland.

Abduction: the reality

Yet even supporters of the Hague Convention recognise its limitations. It was drafted in the belief that the majority of abductions would be by non-resident parents (normally fathers) seeking to subvert decisions already made by courts, moving the child to an alien country where a second bite of the cherry would hopefully get a better result. The very language of "abduction" conjures images of men snatching children from their legitimate carers, bundling them into the backs of vans and heading for the airport. In reality, abductions are more often than not perpetrated by the resident parent who has, and is exercising, full "custody" rights: that parent "abducts" only in the technical sense of acting in some way that denies the non-resident parent of his "rights of custody" – which in practice need be no more than a right to prevent removal from the jurisdiction. And frequently the country to which the child is abducted is not an alien land, but the mother's original home country, with which the child is often already familiar.

The other major failing that has to be recognised with the Hague Convention is that, insofar as it aimed to reduce the number of abductions by removing the incentive, it has failed abjectly in that aim. The number of international child abductions (as defined by the Hague Convention) continues to rise across the numerous countries that have ratified the Convention, raising serious doubts as to whether the predominant parental motivation is indeed to seek a second bite at a welfare-flavoured cherry: if it is not, then their actions are not addressed by the aims of the Convention.

Welfare focus

Perhaps in response to a recognition of these limitations to the effectiveness of the Hague Convention, the law seems to be turning more and more away from immediate return as an imperative and towards the comfort zone of welfare. In, for example, the exercise of judicial discretion in deciding whether to return a child when one of the defences has been made out (there being no discretion when none of the defences is established), the House of Lords held that the court was entitled to take account of wider considerations of the child's rights and welfare: *Re M (Children) (Abduction)* [2008] 1 AC 1288 at paras 43 and 44. Direction from Europe goes much further in the same direction.

Brussels II-*bis*

Article 11 of the revised Brussels II Regulation (Council Regulation (EC) 2201/2003) modifies the application of the Hague Convention in cases of abductions from and to member states of the European Union. Tightening up the already tight "grave risk" defence in article 13(b) of the Hague Convention, the requested court cannot refuse to return the child even when that defence has been made out, where it is established that adequate arrangements have been made to secure the protection of the child on his or her return.

More importantly for our purposes, if the requested court refuses to return the child, the applicant parent may require the court of origin to examine the question of "custody" of the child (using, of course, a welfare perspective) and, if that court makes an order in favour of the parent from whom the child has been abducted, the requested court must abide by this order. Effectively, the court of origin is given the power to override the requested state's refusal.

Strasbourg speaks

Even more significant is the decision of the Grand Chamber of the European Court of Human Rights in *Neulinger & Shuruk* v *Switzerland*, 6 July 2010. The question before the Grand Chamber was whether the Swiss court's approach to the Hague Convention was compatible with the article 8 right to family life. A Swiss woman living in Israel had a child with her Israeli husband. But the father then joined an extremist religious sect and wished his wife to submit to its doctrines and to bring up the child within its severely limiting strictures. The father's increasingly erratic behaviour resulted in the Israeli court awarding custody to the mother and limiting the father's rights to supervised contact twice a week. Unable to bear the father's interference any longer, the mother took the child to Switzerland, breaching the father's right to prevent the child's removal from the jurisdiction.

The issue before the Swiss court was whether there was a grave risk of harm in sending the child back to Israel, and the court took the view that, the Israeli courts and social services having proved themselves perfectly able to protect the mother and child from the overbearing influence of the father and his extremist views, there was no grave risk of harm. This decision follows the approach of many jurisdictions across the world where this defence is interpreted narrowly.

The European Court of Human Rights nevertheless held that the order to return amounted to an interference with both the mother's and child's right to family life. Though that Court's jurisdiction is limited to determining the compatibility of state laws and actions with the ECHR, and not in the determination of the proper interpretation of state law, it nevertheless concluded that in the present case the "grave risk" defence to return of the child contained in article 13(b) of the Hague Convention had "manifestly not been met in the present case" (para 130).

The problem was that the Swiss courts had not paid enough attention to the welfare of the child. The Court pointed out (para 135) that there is currently a broad consensus, traced in part to article 3 of the UN Convention on the Rights of the Child, that in all decisions concerning children their best interests must be paramount. This was inherent in article 8 of the ECHR, and it followed that article 13(2) of the Hague Convention had to be interpreted in conformity with article 3 of the UN Convention, in order to be ECHR compatible. The result was that article 8 prevented children from being returned "automatically or mechanically": the Hague Convention was not to be interpreted to require return without an assessment of the individual child's welfare (para 138).

Though domestic courts had a certain margin of appreciation, it was the role of the European Court to ensure that domestic courts conducted in every case "an in-depth examination of the entire family situation and of a whole series of factors, in particular of a factual, emotional, psychological, material and medical nature", making a balanced and reasonable assessment of each person's interests "with a constant concern for determining what the best solution would be for the abducted child in the context of an application for his return to his country of origin" (para 139). The Swiss courts had not carried out this type of individualised welfare assessment and had thus acted incompatibly with article 8 of the European Convention.

Start again

This case represents a truly seismic shift in judicial attitudes to the Hague Convention. The presumption, or at least starting point, that the best solution for the abducted child is its return to its habitual residence is jettisoned in favour of a neutral stance, requiring an in-depth examination from the point of view of the child's welfare whether it should be sent back or not. How UK judges will apply this approach remains to be seen.

Update

The higher English courts were quick to stamp out any idea that Neulinger *requires any change in how Hague Convention cases are dealt with. In Re E (Children) [2011] UKSC 27 the Supreme Court pointed out that it was not the Swiss court's order for return that was held to be inconsistent with Art 8: rather, now, 3 years later, any attempt to implement the order would be so inconsistent. The Strasbourg court had created its own reality by failing to utilise its expedited procedure to deal with the matter quickly, making it inevitable that the child would be permitted to remain in Switzerland. The Strasbourg court had no business in telling member states how to interpret their laws, for its jurisdiction is limited to declaring whether particular interpretations are or are not consistent with the European Convention on Human Rights.*

Commentary No 48: April 2011

Autism and the Good Society

The educational needs of autistic children, and recent case law on the duties of an education authority in meeting those needs

It is a mark of a decent society that its laws and policies aim to provide all of its children with the opportunity to develop their talents to the highest degree possible. State provision of education is the central tool by which society furthers this aim. Good education is expensive, but its value to society as a whole far exceeds the enhancement of earning power enjoyed by those who are educated best.

The good society knows this, even if the Big Society does not. Scotland fulfils its obligations in this regard by imposing a duty on local authorities to secure adequate and efficient provision of school education (Education (Scotland) Act 1980, s 1), and to bear the costs. Now, some children are more expensive to educate than others, because they have support needs additional to those of the "normal" child. To rely on parents to meet additional educational costs would deny many children with additional needs the opportunities available to other children.

These additional costs therefore also fall to society as a whole, via the local authority: Education (Additional Support for Learning) (Scotland) Act 2004, s 4. This is so even although the Supreme Court has held that the failure of a local authority to identify and provide suitable additional educational facilities for an autistic child is not necessarily an infringement of the child's ECHR right to education, entitling the child to damages: *A* v *Essex County Council* [2011] 1 AC 280.

However, even when suitable facilities are identified and are available, contentious litigation may follow if the parents and the local authority cannot agree that the child truly needs these facilities, or where the parents wish a more expensive provision to be made available for their child than the local authority considers appropriate. This is illustrated in two recent cases with similar factual backgrounds.

Placing requests and resources

City of Edinburgh Council v *MDN* [2011] CSIH 13 arose from a placing request made by parents who wished their child to be placed at a particular residential school which they believed would better meet his needs than his current day school. The child suffered from autism spectrum disorder, with pronounced learning difficulties and highly challenging behaviour both at home and at school. The local authority had refused the placing request, preferring the much cheaper option of keeping the child at his existing day school.

The authority founded on the fact that while Sch 2, para 2 to the 2004 Act obliges local authorities to give effect to placing requests and, where necessary, to meet the fees and other necessary costs of the child's attendance at the requested school, para 3 disapplies that duty where it is not reasonable, having regard both to the respective suitability and the costs of the placement, to place the child in the requested school. In the present case, the local authority decided that it was not reasonable, taking account of the costs, to place the child in the residential school. The Additional Support Needs Tribunal for Scotland overturned that decision, and the authority appealed to the Court of Session.

The costs of the residential school that the parents preferred were around five times the costs of the day school preferred by the local authority, but it had better facilities for managing the child's behaviour, and a range of activities more suited to his interests. The tribunal concluded that the local authority had failed to show that it was "not reasonable, having regard both to the respective suitability and the costs of the placement, to place the child in the specified school". The local authority appealed on the basis that this seriously underplayed the cost factor and that the tribunal had assumed that suitability of provision always trumps cost, but the Inner House found that the tribunal had clearly discussed the cost implications and appropriately balanced them with their assessment that the support needs of the child were appreciably more likely to be met at the residential than at the day school. So there was no error in the tribunal's approach.

Another ground of appeal was the allegation that the tribunal had failed to address what educational needs the child actually had that were to be met at the residential school. This ground too was rejected. The Education (Additional Support for Learning) (Scotland) Act 2009 had amended the 2004 Act to extend the definition of additional support to include non-educational support, and in the present case various non-educational provisions had been identified that the residential school could provide for the child. The court acknowledged the important point that education, particularly for children with additional support needs, requires to be looked at holistically, taking account of the structures and support mechanisms in the child's life, for these have a profound influence on whether and to what extent educational or developmental benefit actually accrues to the child.

Educational provision and looked-after children

Another autistic child was at the centre of the English case of *RO* v *East Riding of Yorkshire Council and Secretary of State for Education* [2011] EWCA Civ 196. After a long and bitter dispute, involving various complex court proceedings under the (English) Education Act 1996 and the Children Act 1989, the parents had been successful in having their child placed in a residential school which, though expensive, would best meet their child's severe special educational needs ("SEN", in the English terminology).

The respite care that the local authority had been providing while the child was at home was withdrawn as being no longer necessary, and the local authority argued that this meant the child was no longer, in terms of the 1989 Act, a looked-after child.

The significance of this was that the child would not be able to access the aftercare provisions in the Act on his attaining the age of 18. The parents sought to have his "LAC status" restored, for that purpose alone. This depended on the child being accommodated under s 20 of the Children Act 1989, but the local authority argued that the statutory authority under which they were providing him with accommodation was the Education Act 1996, and provision under that Act did not give the child "LAC status".

This is not the first time that English local authorities have attempted to avoid their child care obligations by arguing that the child was being accommodated other than under s 20 of the 1989 Act (see *R(G)* v *Southwark LBC* [2009] 1 WLR 1299, where Baroness Hale said that councils could not "sidestep" their duties under the Children Act by labelling an issue as a housing problem rather than a child law problem). Following this in the present case, the Court of Appeal accepted that the two regimes (SEN and LAC) lie side by side and that neither takes precedence over the other; but it further held that since the child's social and educational needs had driven the placement, it could not be said that the SEN placement supplanted rather than supported the LAC regime.

The gateway to LAC status is being accommodated and its purpose is to ensure the child's welfare is preserved and promoted. It was impossible to see the placement at the residential school in purely educational terms since its residential nature was a response to the parents' inability to cope with the child in social terms. So the child remained a looked-after child who, in the fullness of time, would be able to access the aftercare provisions to help him into adult life: that "is as it should and was meant to be", said Rix LJ at para 126.

The Scottish approach

How would this play out in Scotland? Section 17(6) of the Children (Scotland) Act 1995 includes within the definition of "looked-after child", any child who is being provided with accommodation under s 25 of that Act (the equivalent of s 20 of the 1989 Act). The local authority is obliged by s 25 to provide accommodation to a child when (a) no one has parental responsibility for the child, (b) the child has been abandoned or lost, or (c) the person who has been caring for the child is prevented from providing suitable accommodation. It is not immediately obvious that a child being accommodated in a residential school because of additional support needs comes within (c), but the policy of the English cases, to prevent local authorities being able to sidestep their responsibilities by classifying the case as one thing rather than another, is sound and ought to be followed here.

Parents may be said to be "prevented" from accommodating a child if they cannot ensure appropriate education without a residential placement away from home. So the child in *City of Edinburgh* is a looked-after child. This is as it should be, for it ensures equal opportunities are provided to all children as they move into adulthood, and it advances the good society.

Commentary No 49: July 2011

Families in Fear

Kenneth Norrie considers in this, the last of his regular columns for the Journal of the Law Society of Scotland, *the various Acts recently passed by the Scottish Parliament to strengthen protection against abusive domestic relationships – which, he notes, do not display a consistent approach to the scope of protection.*

An active Parliament

The Scottish Parliament has been noticeably active recently in passing legislation dealing with the problems created when families go off the rails. The first piece of legislation to receive Royal Assent in 2011 was the Children's Hearings (Scotland) Act 2011; some aspects of this are discussed below. In addition, there are two other Acts passed in 2011 worthy of our attention.

Domestic abuse

The Domestic Abuse (Scotland) Act 2011 tackles one of family life's most insidious problems, which can range in seriousness from minor assaults with little lasting impact to murder. Invariably, all family members and not just the primary victim are affected by violence within the family. It is all too often a learnt behaviour that easily transmits down the generations, with boys learning that violence is a means of achieving their wishes, and girls learning that victimhood is part of a woman's lot. The extent of female abuse of men, and of abuse within same-sex relationships, remains difficult to assess accurately, but reporting incidence is clearly rising and as a problem it is as damaging to the families involved as male abuse of women.

It has long been recognised that the criminal law is an insufficient weapon in the fight against domestic abuse, not least because it is necessarily reactive rather than protective. The civil law attempts to provide some prospective protection, but there are well-recognised limitations to its effectiveness. Matrimonial and domestic interdicts provide some protection, but only if the case comes within the Matrimonial Homes (Family Protection) (Scotland) Act 1981, the Civil Partnership Act 2004, or the Family Law (Scotland) Act 2006. Interdicts have long been available at common law and, since the Protection from Abuse (Scotland) Act 2001, powers of arrest may be attached to them. In addition, non-harassment orders are available under the Protection from Harassment Act 1997 and can (at present) be taken out against anyone who pursues a course of conduct that amounts to harassment as defined in the Act.

The Domestic Abuse (Scotland) Act 2011 aims to improve the position in two main ways. First, it amends the 1997 Act by removing the requirement that there be a course of conduct before a non-harassment order may be obtained. This extends quite significantly the protections available under the Act, for the victim no longer needs to wait to be harassed a series of times before seeking protection. Secondly, the 2011 Act makes it a criminal offence to breach an interdict with a power of arrest.

Both these provisions apply not in every case, but only in cases involving "domestic abuse", and the most interesting feature of the Act is the definition it gives of "domestic abuse". By s 3(2), a domestic abuse interdict is one granted for the protection of the applicant against his or her spouse or civil partner, cohabitant or person with whom he or she is in an "intimate personal relationship".

This is significantly narrower than the definition of "domestic abuse" proposed in the original Bill that became the Act, for there domestic abuse meant any abuse by a "partner in an established relationship of any length". This definition led to much debate as the Bill was progressing through its parliamentary stages, and while the original version was probably unduly wide, the limited version that was eventually enacted does not capture all forms of behaviour that might otherwise be commonly understood to amount to "domestic abuse".

In particular it is limited to partner abuse (or ex-partner abuse), and so excludes all intergenerational abuse or abuse between family members who are not partners. A man who beats up his daughter, or stepson, or niece, or father, has not been involved in "domestic abuse" for the purposes of the Domestic Abuse (Scotland) Act 2011. This in my view is unfortunate. Not only ought the same legal responses to be available to a victim who is assaulted by his father as by his wife, but it leads to a dissonance (as we will see) between the definition of "domestic abuse" under this legislation and that under other legislation.

Forced marriages

A quite different problem in family life, but which is as destructive of the trust and security amongst family members as family violence, is the issue of forced marriages. It happens with distressing frequency that young people, especially young women, have their lives arranged for them by their parents, including the choice of their prospective spouse.

It may be accepted that some parents who force their own children into marriages not of the child's choosing are acting in what they genuinely believe to be their child's best interests, but far more often the parental motivation is their own misplaced pride and notions of "honour": it is an act of fundamental selfishness, and of violence. In any case, the practice is entirely unacceptable in the modern world, because it deprives young and vulnerable individuals of one of the most essential aspects of a free and fulfilled life: the personal choice of an intimate partner with whom one's life is to be led.

Of course, whenever a person has been forced against his or her true will to give alleged consent to marriage, that marriage is void (Marriage (Scotland) Act 1977, s 20A), and the remedy is for the person to seek a declarator of nullity of marriage. But, like the criminal law in domestic abuse cases, this is a retrospective remedy that is not able (except in a very weak deterrent sense) to provide protection from the harm in the first place. The Scottish Parliament has now attempted to ameliorate this situation by providing a protective remedy in the Forced Marriage etc (Protection and Jurisdiction) (Scotland) Act 2011.

The main purpose of this Act is to create a new order, the forced marriage protection order (FMPO), which may be sought and obtained from the Court of Session or the sheriff court by any person who fears being forced into a marriage against their will. "Force" in this context is wider than the use of coercion, and includes knowingly taking advantage of a person's incapacity to consent or to understand the nature of marriage (s 1(6)). Breach of the order will amount to a criminal offence. A FMPO may be sought by the individual concerned, or by the local authority, or the Lord Advocate (s 3); in addition the court may make the order on its own initiative in civil proceedings in which the person to be protected is a party (s 4(1)), and in criminal proceedings may refer the matter to the Lord Advocate to consider whether to apply for an order (s 4(2) and (3)). The order may contain such prohibitions, restrictions or requirements as the court thinks appropriate to prevent the marriage from occurring or to protect the person in a forced marriage (s 2(1)).

Forcing your child into a gay or lesbian relationship

An interesting feature of the Act is that it does not cover forced civil partnerships, though the Scottish ministers may by order apply the provisions relating to FMPOs to civil partnerships also. Clearly the social circumstances that lead to parents forcing their own children into marriages against their will are highly unlikely to be replicated in relation to civil partnerships, but Scottish ministers may be expected to act in the unlikely event of the issue becoming problematical.

Violence, marriage and children's hearings

The Children's Hearings (Scotland) Act 2011 addresses, in its own way, both of the problems discussed above. Domestic abuse and forced marriage become for the first time grounds upon which a child can be referred to a children's hearing. But this Act, passed some months before the other two, is not neatly tied in with the other legislation, leaving the law distinctly disjointed.

In particular, the limited definition of "domestic abuse" in the Domestic Abuse (Scotland) Act 2011, discussed above, is unlikely to be considered appropriate for the new ground of referral. The purpose of referring a child to a children's hearing is to ensure his or her protection from harm, and there can be no doubt that a child will be as harmed by witnessing his or her sibling being beaten by a parent as by witnessing a parent beating the other parent. This suggests that a much broader interpretation of "domestic abuse" will be appropriate under the Children's Hearings (Scotland) Act than it is given under the Domestic Abuse (Scotland) Act.

And though the forced marriage legislation does not yet extend to civil partnership, the Children's Hearings (Scotland) Act has included being forced into a civil partnership as a ground upon which a child may be referred to a children's hearing. One would not expect to see many children referred to a hearing due to the risk of being forced into a civil partnership, but in any case it would have been tidier for both Acts to deal with the issue in the same way.

Index